COMMENTARY

ON THE

FOUR GOSPELS

COLLECTED OUT OF THE

WORKS OF THE FATHERS

BY

S. THOMAS AQUINAS

Edited by
Paul A. Böer, Sr.

VOL. II

ST. MARK

VERITATIS SPLENDOR PUBLICATIONS
et cognoscetis veritatem et veritas liberabit vos (Jn 8:32)

Catena Aurea: Commentary on the Gospel of St. Mark

Originally published by:

**OXFORD
JOHN HENRY PARKER;
J.G.F. AND J. RIVINGTON, LONDON
MDCCCXLII**

The contents of the *Catena Aurea* by St. Thomas Aquinas is in the public domain. However, this version is copyrighted.

Copyright 2012. Veritatis Splendor Publications.
ALL RIGHTS RESERVED.

AD MAJOREM DEI GLORIAM

Collected Out of the Works of the Fathers

CONTENTS

PREFACE 5
PREFACE TO THE GOSPEL ACCORDING TO ST. MARK .. 7
Mark 1 11
Mark 2 55
Mark 3 78
Mark 4 102
Mark 5 130
Mark 6 153
Mark 7 188
Mark 8 210
Mark 9 237
Mark 10 277
Mark 11 314
Mark 12 339
Mark 13 365
Mark 14 392
Mark 15 443
Mark 16 477

Catena Aurea: Commentary on the Gospel of St. Mark

Collected Out of the Works of the Fathers

PREFACE.

THE Remarks prefixed to the first volume of this Translation of the Aurea Catena, apply in their substance to the following portion of it, which contains the Commentary on S. Mark. Wherever the variations from the original writers were such as to destroy the sense of the passage, the true reading has been followed, and has been placed in the margin. In other cases the text has been translated, as it is found in S. Thomas.

Many of the passages ascribed to S. Chrysostom are not found in the works of that Father. Most of these occur also in a Greek Catena on S. Mark, published by Possinus, from a MS. in the Library of the Archbishop of Tolouse, and still more of them in the Edition which has been recently printed by the Oxford University Press, from a MS. in the Bodleian. A Latin Version of this Catena or Commentary had previously been published by Peltanus, and is found in the Bibliotheca Patrum; and contains far the greater number of the same passages marked as S. Chrysostom's in the Catena Aurea. It is commonly ascribed to Victor of Antioch; though by some, with little probability, to S. Cyril of Alexandria. A Commentary on a portion of S. Mark published by Wastel, who gives the authorship of it and of the Opus Imperfectum in Matthaeum to John of Jerusalem, also contains a number of the same passages which S. Thomas ascribes to S. Chrysostom.

Some of the extracts marked " Cyril" are found in a Commentary of S. Cyril of Alexandria on S. Luke, lately published by Mai.

The passages ascribed to S. Jerome, are taken from a Commentary found among his works, but universally pronounced to be spurious. It has been ascribed to Pelagius, but with more probability to Philippus Presbyter, a friend and

Catena Aurea: Commentary on the Gospel of St. Mark

disciple of S. Jerome. It is entirely mystical, and is in many places hopelessly obscure.

For the translation of the Volume now presented to the reader, the Editors have to make their acknowledgments to JOHN DOBREE DALGAIRNS, M. A. of Exeter College.

J. H. N.

Collected Out of the Works of the Fathers

PREFACE TO THE GOSPEL ACCORDING TO ST. MARK

Isaiah xlix. 5,6.

My God shall be my strength. And he said, It is a light thing that thou shouldest be my servant to raise up the tribes of Jacob, and to restore the preserved of Israel: I will also give thee a light to the Gentiles, that thou mayest be my salvation unto the end of the earth.

The prophet Isaiah foretells in a clear prophecy the calling of the Gentiles, and the cause of their salvation, saying, *My God shall be my strength. And he said, &c.*

JEROME: In which words it is shewn that Christ is called a servant, because He is formed from the womb. For, before these words it is said: *Thus saith the Lord, that formed me from the womb to be his servant.* It had indeed been the will of the Father, that the wicked tillers of the vineyard should receive the son whom He had sent; wherefore Christ says of them to His disciples, *Go not into the way of the Gentiles, but go rather to the lost sheep of the house of Israel.* Because then Israel was not brought back to God for that reason the Son of God speaks to the unbelieving Jews, saying, *My God shall be my strength*, who also has consoled me on the casting away of my people. And he hath said to me, *It is a small thing that thou shouldest be my servant to raise up the tribes of Jacob*, which have fallen by their own wickedness, *and to restore the preserved*, or remnant *of Israel*. For instead of them, *I have given thee for a light to all the Gentiles*, that thou shouldest illuminate the whole world, and shouldest cause *my salvation*, by which all men are saved, to reach to *the ends of the world.*

GLOSS: From the words then, which have been quoted, we can infer two things; first, the divine virtue which was in Christ, by which He was able to lighten the Gentiles; for is is said, *My God shall be my strength.* God therefore *was in Christ, reconciling the world to himself,* as the Apostle says to the Corinthians; whence also *the Gospel,* by which believers are saved, *is the power of God unto salvation, to every one who beieveth,* as the same Apostle says to the Romans. The second thing, is the enlightening of the Gentiles, and the salvation of the world, fulfilled by Christ according to the will of the Father; for it is said, *I will also give thee for a light to the Gentiles.* Wherefore the Lord after His resurrection, that He might fulfill the will of the Father, sent His disciples to preach, saying, *Go ye, and teach all nations;* some He sent to the Jews, some received the ministry of preaching to the Gentiles. But because it was right that the Gospel should not only be preached for those who then lived, but also be written for those who were to come, the same distinction is observed in the writers of the Gospel. For Matthew wrote the Gospel to the Jews in Hebrew, and Mark was the first to write a Gospel amongst the Gentiles.

EUSEB.: For when the glorious light of the word of God had arisen over the city of Rome, the doctrine of truth and light, which Peter was then preaching to them, so shone upon the minds of all, by their patience in listening, that they heard him daily without ever being weary. Whence also they were not content with hearing only, but they earnestly beg of Mark his disciple, to commit to writing those things which he preached by word of mouth, that they might have a perpetual memorial of them, and might continue both at home and abroad in meditations of this sort upon the word. And they did not leave off their importunities, till they obtained what they had requested. This then was the cause of the writing of the Gospel of Mark. But Peter, when by the Holy Ghost he discovered the pious theft which had been put upon him, was filled with joy, for he saw by this, their faith and devotion; and he gave his sanction to what was done, and handed down the writing to the Churches, to be read for ever.

PSEUDO-JEROME: He begins at once with the announcement of the more perfect age of Christ; nor does he spend his labour on the birth of Christ as a little child, for he speaks of his perfection as the Son of God.

CHRYS.: But he makes a compendious and brief beginning, in which he has imitated his master Peter, who was a lover of brevity.

AUG.: Matthew, who had undertaken to relate what concerned the kingly person of Christ, had Mark assigned to him for a companion and an abbreviator, who was to attend upon his steps. For it belongs to kings not to be withour a train of attendants. Since again the priest used to enter alone into the Holy of Holies, Luke, whose design had regard to the priesthood of Christ, had no companion to follow his steps, and in a manner to abbreviate his narration.

BEDE: It is also to be observed, that the holy Evangelists have each fixed upon a different commencement for their narration, and each a different ending. For Matthew, setting out from the

Catena Aurea: Commentary on the Gospel of St. Mark

beginning of the preaching of the Gospel, has carried on the thread of his narrative up to the time of our Lord's resurrection. Mark, beginning with the first preaching of the Gospel, goes on to the ascension of the Lord, and the preaching of His disciples to all nations throughout the world. But Luke, commencing with the birth of the Forerunner, has ended with our Lord's ascension. John, taking his beginning from the eternity of the Word of God, reaches in his Gospel up to the time of the Lord's resurrection.

AMBROSE: Because then Mark began with expressing the divine power, he is rightly represented under the figure of a lion.

REMIG.: Markis signified by the lion; for as a lion sends forth his dreadful voice in the wilderness, so Mark begins with the voice in the wilderness, saying, *The voice of one crying in the wilderness.*

AUG.: Although the figure might also be otherwise interpreted. For Mark did not wish to relate either his kingly race, as Matthew did, who for this is figured by a lion, or his priestly kindred, or consecration, as Luke, figured by a calf; yet he is shewn to have had for his subject the things which the man Christ did, and therefore appears to be signified by the figure of a man, in the four animals.

THEOPHYLACT: Or, the eagle points out the Gospel according to Mark, for it begins with the prophecy of John; for prophecy views with acuteness things which are afar, as an eagle.

Collected Out of the Works of the Fathers

COMMENTARY

ON THE GOSPEL ACCORDING TO

ST. MARK

Mark 1

1. The beginning of the Gospel of Jesus Christ, the Son of God.

JEROME; Mark the Evangelist, who served the priest-hood in Israel, according to the flesh a Levite, having been converted to the Lord, wrote his Gospel in Italy, showing in it how even his family benefited Christ. For, commencing his Gospel with the voice of the prophetic cry, he shows the order of the election of Levi, declaring that John the son of Zachariah was sent forth by the voice of an angel, and saying, The beginning of the Gospel of Jesus Christ, the Son of God.

PSEUDO-JEROME; The Greek word 'Evangelium' means good tidings, in Latin it is explained, 'bona annunciatio,' or, the good news ; these terms properly belong to the kingdom of God and to the remission of sins; for the Gospel is that, by which conies the redemption of the faithful and the beatitude of the saints. But the four Gospels are one, and one Gospel is four. In Hebrew, His name is Jesus, in Greek, Soter in Latin, Salvator; but men say Christus in Greek, Messias in Hebrew, Unctus in Latin, that is, King and Priest.

BEDE; The beginning of this Gospel should be compared with that of Matthew, in which it is said, The book of the generation of Jesus Christ, the Son of David, the Son of Abraham. But here he is called the Son of God. Now from both we must understand one Lord Jesus Christ, Son of God, and of man. And fitly the first Evangelist names Him Son of man, the second, Son of God, that from less things our sense may by degrees mount up to greater, and by faith and the sacraments of the human nature assumed, rise to the acknowledgment of His divine eternity. Fitly also did He, who was about to describe His human generation, begin with a son of man, namely, David or Abraham. Fitly again, he who was beginning his book with the first preaching of the Gospel, chose rather to call Jesus Christ, the Son of God; for it belonged to the human nature to take upon him the reality of our flesh, of the race of the patriarchs, and it was the work of Divine power to preach the Gospel to the world.

HILARY; He has testified, that Christ was the Son of God, not in name only, but by His own proper nature. We are the sons of God, but He is not a son as we are; for He is the very and proper Son, by origin, not by adoption; in truth, not in name; by birth, not by creation.

2. As it is written in the Prophets, Behold, I send my messenger before your face, which shall prepare your way before you.

3. The voice of one crying in the wilderness, Prepare you the way of the Lord, make his paths straight.

BEDE; Being about to write his Gospel, Mark rightly puts first the testimonies of the Prophets, that he might notify to all, that what he should write was to be received without scruple of doubt, in that he showed that these things were beforehand foretold by the Prophets. At once, by one and the same beginning

Collected Out of the Works of the Fathers

of his Gospel, he prepared the Jews, who had received the Law and the Prophets, for receiving the grace of the Gospel, and those sacraments, which their own prophecies had foretold; and he also calls upon the Gentiles, who came to the Lord by publishing of the Gospel, to receive and venerate the authority of the Law and the Prophets; whence he says, As it is written in the prophet Isaiah, Behold, &c.

JEROME; But this is not written in Isaiah, but in Malachi, the last of the twelve prophets.

PSEUD-CHRYS. But it may be said that it is a mistake of the writer. Otherwise it may be said, that he has compressed into one, two prophecies delivered in different places by two prophets; for in the prophet Isaiah it is written after the story of Hezekiah, The voice of one crying in the wilderness; but in Malachi, Behold, I send mine angel. The Evangelist therefore, taking parts of two prophecies, has put them down as spoken by Isaiah, and refers then here to one passage, without mentioning, however, by whom it is said, Behold, I send mine angel.

PSEUDO-AUG. For knowing that all things are to be referred to their author, he has brought these sayings back to Isaiah, who was the first to intimate the sense. Lastly, after the words of Malachi, he immediately subjoins, The voice of one crying in the wilderness, in order to connect the words of each prophet, belonging as they do to one meaning, under the person of the elder prophet.

BEDE; Or otherwise, we must understand, that, although these words are not found in Isaiah, still the sense of them is found in

Catena Aurea: Commentary on the Gospel of St. Mark

many other places, and most clearly in this which he has subjoined, The voice of one crying in the wilderness. For that which Mlalachi has called, the angel to be sent before the face of the Lord, to prepare His way, is the same thing as Isaiah has said is to be heard, the voice of one crying in the wilderness, saying, Prepare you the way of the Lord. But in each sentence alike, the way of the Lord to be prepared is proclaimed. It may be, too, that Isaiah occurred to the mind of Mark, in writing his Gospel, instead of Malachi, as often happens; which he would, however, without doubt correct, at least when reminded by other persons, who might read his work whilst he was yet in the flesh; unless he thought, that, since his memory was then ruled by the Holy Spirit, it was not without a purpose, that the name of one prophet had occurred to him instead of another. For thus whatever things the Holy Spirit spoke by the prophets, are implied each to have belonged to all, and all to each.

JEROME; By Malachi, therefore, the voice of the Holy Spirit resounds to the Father concerning the Son, who is the countenance of the Father by which He has been known.

BEDE; But John is called an angel not by community of nature, according to the heresy of Origen, but by the dignity of his office; for angel in Greek is in Latin, nuntius, (messenger,) by which name that man is rightly called, who was sent by God, that be might bear witness of the light, and announce to the world the Lord, coming in the flesh; since it is evident that all who are priests may by their office of preaching the Gospel be called angels, as time prophet Malachi says, The lips of the priest keep knowledge, and they seek the law at his mouth, because he is the Angel of the Lord of hosts.

Collected Out of the Works of the Fathers

THEOPHYL; The Forerunner of Christ, therefore, is called an angel, on account of His angelic life and lofty reverence. Again, where he says, Before your face, it is as if he said, Your messenger is near thee: whence is shown the intimate connection of the Forerunner with Christ; for those walk next to kings, who are their greatest friends. There follows, Who will prepare your way before you. For by baptism he prepared the minds of the Jews to receive Christ.

PSEUDO-JEROME; Or, the way of the Lord, by which he comes into men, is penitence, by which God comes down to us, and we mount up to Him. And for this reason the beginning of John's preaching was, Repent you.

BEDE; But as John might be called an angel because he went before the face of the Lord by his preaching, so he might also be rightly called a Voice, because, by his sound, he preceded the Word of the Lord. Wherefore there follows, The voice of one crying, &c. For it is an acknowledged thing that the Only-Begotten Son is called the Word of the Father, and even we, from having uttered words ourselves, know that the voice sounds first, in order that that word may afterwards be heard.

PSEUDO-JEROME; But it is called the voice of one crying, for we are wont to use a cry to deaf persons, and to those afar off, or when we are indignant, all which things we know applied to time Jews; for salvation is far from the wicked, and they stopped their ears like deaf adders, and deserved to hear indignation, and wrath, and tribulation from Christ.

Catena Aurea: Commentary on the Gospel of St. Mark

PSEUD-CHRYS. But the prophecy, by saying, In the wilderness, plainly shows that the divine teaching was not in Jerusalem, but in the wilderness, which was fulfilled to the letter by John the Baptist in the wilderness of Jordan, preaching the healthful appearing of the Word of God. The worth of prophecy also shows that besides the wilderness, which was pointed out by Moses, where he made paths, there was another wilderness, in which it proclaimed that the salvation of Christ was present.

PSEUDO-JEROME; Or else the voice and the cry is in the desert, because they were deserted by the Spirit of God as a house empty, and swept out; deserted also by prophet, priest, and king.

BEDE; What he cried is revealed, in that which is subjoined, Prepare you the way of the Lord and make his paths straight. For whoever preaches a right faith and good works, what else does he but prepare the way for the Lord's coming to the hearts of His hearers, that the power of grace might penetrate these hearts, and the light of truth shine in them? And the paths he makes straight, 'when he forms pure thoughts in the soul by the word of preaching.

PSEUDO-JEROME; Or else, Prepare you the way of the Lord, that is, act out repentance and preach it; make his paths straight, that walking in the royal road we may love our neighbors as ourselves, and ourselves as our neighbors. For he who loves himself, and loves not his neighbor, turns aside to the right; for many act well, and do not correct their neighbor well, as Eli. He, on the other hand, who, hating himself loves his neighbor, turns aside to the left; for many, for instance, rebuke well, but act not well themselves, as did the Scribes and Pharisees. Paths are mentioned after the way because moral commands are laid open after penitence.

THEOPHYL; Or, time way is the New Testament, and the paths are the Old, because it is a trodden path. For it was necessary to be prepared for the way, that is, for time New Testament; but it was right that the paths of the Old Testament should be straightened.

4. John did baptize in the wilderness, and preach the baptism of repentance for the remission of sins.

5. And there went out to him all the land of Judea, and they of Jerusalem, and were all baptized of him in the river of Jordan, confessing their sins.

6. And John was clothed with camel's hair, and with a girdle of a skin about his loins; and he did eat locusts and wild honey;

7. And preached, saying, There comes one mightier than I after me, the latchet of whose shoes I am not worthy to stoop down and unloose.

8. I indeed have baptized you with water: but he shall baptize you with the Holy Ghost.

PSEUDO-JEROME. According to the above-mentioned prophecy of Isaiah, the way of the Lord is prepared by John, through faith, baptism, and penitence; the paths are made straight by the rough marks of the hair-cloth garment, the girdle of skin, the feeding on locust and wild honey, and the most lowly voice; whence it is said, John was in the wilderness. For John and Jesus seek what is lost in the wilderness; where the devil conquered, there be is conquered; where man fell, there he rises up. But the name John means the grace of God, and the narrative begins with grace. For it goes on to say, baptizing. For by baptism grace is given, seeing that by baptism sins are freely remitted. But what is brought to perfection by the bridegroom, is introduced by the friend of the bridegroom. Thus catechumens, (which word means persons instructed,) begin by the ministry of the priest, receive time chrism from the bishop. And to show this, it is subjoined, And preaching the baptism of repentance, &c.

BEDE; It is evident that John not only preached, but also gave to some the baptism of repentance; but he could not give baptism for the remission of sins. For remission of sins is only given to its by time baptism of Christ. It is therefore only said, Preaching the baptism of repentance for the remission of sins; for he preached a baptism which could remit sins, since he could not give it. Wherefore as he was the forerunner of the incarnate Word of the Father, by the word of his preaching, so by his baptism, which could not remit sins, he preceded that baptism, of penitence, by which sins are remitted.

THEOPHYL; The baptism of John had not remissions of sins, but only brought men to penitence. He preached therefore the baptism of repentance, that is, he preached that to which the baptism of penitence led, namely, remission of sins, that they who in penitence received Christ, might receive Him to the remission of their sins.

Collected Out of the Works of the Fathers

PSEUDO-JEROME; Now by John as by the bride groom's friend, the bride is brought to Christ as by a servant Rebecca was brought for Isaac; wherefore there follows, And there went out to him all, &c. For confession and beauty are in his presence, that is, the presence of the bridegroom. And the bride leaping down from the camel signifies the Church, who humbles herself on seeing her husband Isaac, that is, Christ. But the interpretation of Jordan, where sins are washed away, is 'an alien descent. For we heretofore aliens to God by pride, and by the sign of Baptism made lowly, and thus exalted on high.

BEDE; An example of confessing their sins and of promising to lead a new life, is held out to those who desire to be baptized, by those words which follow, confessing their sins.

CHRYS. Because indeed John preached repentance, he wore the marks of repentance in his garments and in his food, wherefore there follows, And John was clothed in camel's hair.

BEDE; It says, clothed in a garment of hair not in woolen clothes; the former is the mark of an austere garb, the latter of effeminate luxury. But the girdle of skins, with which he was girt, like Elias is a mark of mortification. And this meat, locusts and wild honey, is suited to a dweller in the wilderness, so that his object of eating was not the deliciousness of meats, but the satisfying of the necessity of human flesh.

PSEUDO-JEROME; The dress of John, his food, and employment, signifies the austere life of preachers, and that future nations are to be joined to the grace of God, which is John, both in their minds and in externals. For by camel's hair, is meant the rich among the nations; and by the girdle of skin, the poor, dead to the world; and by wondering locusts, the wise men of this world; who leaving the dry stalks to the Jews, draw off with their legs the mystic grain, and in the warmth of their faith leap up towards heaven; and the faithful, being inspired by the wild honey, are full-fed from the untilled wood.

THEOPH. Or else; The garment of camel's hair was significative of grief, for John pointed out, that he who repented should mourn. For sackcloth signifies grief; but the girdle of skins shows the dead state of the Jewish people. The food also of John not only denotes abstinence, but also shows forth the intellectual food, which the people then were eating, without understanding any thing lofty, but continually raising themselves on high, and again sinking to the earth. For such is the nature of locusts, leaping on high and again falling. In the same way the people ate honey, which had come from bees, that is, from the prophets; it was not however domestic, but wild, for the Jews had the Scriptures, which are as honey, but did not rightly understand them.

GREGORY; Or, by the kind itself of his food he pointed out the Lord, of whom he was the forerunner; for in that our Lord took to Himself the sweetness of the barren Gentiles, he ate wild honey. In that he in his own person partly converted the Jews, he received locusts for His food, which suddenly leaping up, at once fall to the ground. For the Jews leaped up when they promised to fulfill the precepts of the Lord; but they fell to the ground, when by their evil works they affirmed that they had not heard them. They made therefore a leap upwards in words, and fell down by their actions.

Collected Out of the Works of the Fathers

BEDE; The dress and food of John may also express of what kind was his inward walk. For he used a dress more austere than was usual, because he did not encourage the life of sinners by flattery, but chide them by the vigor of his rough rebuke; he had a girdle of skin round his loins, for he was one, who crucified his flesh with the affections and lusts. He used to eat locusts and wild honey, because his preaching had some sweetness for the multitude, whilst the people debated whether he was the Christ himself or not; but this soon came to an end, when his hearers understood that he was not the Christ, but the forerunner and prophet of Christ.

For in honey there is sweetness, in locusts swiftness of flight; whence there follows, And he preached, saying, there comes one mightier than I after me.

GLOSS. He said this to do away with the opinion of the crowd, which throughout that he was the Christ; but he announces that Christ is mightier than he, who was to remit sins, which he himself could not do.

PSEUDO-JEROME; Who again is mightier than the grace, by which sins are washed away which John signifies? He who seven times and seventy times seven remits sun. Grace indeed comes first, but remits sins once only by baptism, but mercy reaches to the wretched from Adam up to Christ through seventy-seven generations, and up to one hundred and forty-four thousand.

PSEUD-CHRYS. But lest he should be thought to say this by way of comparing himself to Christ, he subjoins, Of whom I am

Catena Aurea: Commentary on the Gospel of St. Mark

not worthy, &c. It is not however the same thing to loose the shoe-latchet, which Mark here says, and to carry his shoes, which Matthew says. And indeed the Evangelists following the order of the narrative, and not able to err in any thing, say that John spoke each of these sayings in a different sense. But commentators on this passage have expounded each in a different way. For he means by the latchet, the tie of the shoe. He says this therefore to extol time excellence of the power of Christ, and the greatness of His divinity; as if he said, Not even in the station of his servant aunt am I worthy to be reckoned. For it is a great thing to contemplate, as it were stooping down, those things which belong to the body of Christ, and to see from below tine image of things above, and to untie each of those mysteries, about the incarnation of Christ, which cannot be unraveled.

PSEUDO-JEROME; The shoe is in the extremity of the body; for in the end the Incarnate Savior is coming for justice, violence it is said by the prophet, Over Edom will I cast out my shoe.

GREGORY; Shoes also are made from the skins of dead animals. The Lord, therefore, coming incarnate, appeared as it were with shoes on His feet, for he assumed in His divinity the dead skins of our corruption. Or else; it was a custom among the ancients, that if a man refused to take as his wife the woman whom he ought to take, he who offered himself as her husband by right of kindred took off that man's shoe. Rightly then does he proclaim himself unworthy to loose his shoe-latchet, as if he said openly, I cannot make bare the feet of the Redeemer, for I usurp not the name of the Bridegroom, a thing which is above my deserts.

THEOPH. Some persons also understand it thus; all who came to John, and were baptized, through penitence were loosed from the bands of their sins by believing in Christ. John then in this way loosed the shoe-latchet of all the others, that is, the bands of sin. But Christ's shoe-hatchet he was not able to unloose, because be found no sin in Him.

BEDE; Thus then John proclaims the Lord not yet as God, or the Son of God, but only as a man mightier than himself. For his ignorant hearers were not yet capable of receiving the hidden things of so great a Sacrament, that the eternal Son of God, having taken upon Him the nature of man, bad been lately born into the world of a virgin; but gradually by the acknowledgment of His glorified lowliness, they were to be introduced to the belief of His Divine Eternity. To these words, however, he subjoins, as if covertly declaring that he was the true God, I baptize you with water, but he shall baptize you with the Holy Ghost. For who can doubt, that none other but God can give the grace of the Holy Ghost.

JEROME; For what is the difference between water and the Holy Ghost, who was borne over the face of the waters? Water is the ministry of man; but the Spirit is ministered by God.

BEDE; Now we are baptized by the Lord in the Holy Ghost, not only when in the day of our baptism, we are washed in the fount of life, to the remission of our sins, but also daily by the grace of the same Spirit we are inflamed, to do those things which please God.

9. And it came to pass in those days, that Jesus came from

Catena Aurea: Commentary on the Gospel of St. Mark

Nazareth of Galilee, and was baptized of John in Jordan.

10. And straightway coming up out of the water, he saw the heavens opened, and the Spirit like a dove descending upon him:

11. And there came a voice from heaven, saying, You are my beloved Son, in whom I am well pleased.

PSEUDO-JEROME; Mark the Evangelist, like a hart, longing after the fountains of water, leaps forward over places, smooth and steep; and, as a bee laden with honey, he sips the tops of the flowers. Wherefore he has shown us in his narrative Jesus coming from Nazareth, saying, And it came to pass in those days, &c.

PSEUD-CHRYS. Forasmuch as he was ordaining a new baptism, He came to the baptism of John, which, in respect of His own baptism, was incomplete, but different from the Jewish baptism, as being between both. He did this that He might show, by the nature of His baptism, that He was not baptized for the remission of sins, nor as wanting the reception of the Holy Ghost: for the baptism of John was destitute of both these. But He was baptized that He might be made known to all, that they might believe on Him and fulfill all righteousness, which is keeping of the commandments: for it had been commanded to men that they should submit to the prophet's baptism.

BEDE; He was baptized, that by being baptized Himself He might show His approval of John's baptism, and that by sanctifying the waters of Jordan through time descent of the dove, He might show the coming of time Holy Ghost in the laver of believers; whence there follows, And straight away coming up out of the water, he saw the heavens opened, and the Holy Spirit like a dove descending and resting upon him But the heavens are opened, not by the closing of the elements, but the eyes of the spirit to which Ezekiel in the beginning of his book relates that they are opened, or this His seeing the heavens opened after baptism was done for our sakes, to whom the door of the kingdom of heaven is opened by the laver of regeneration.

PSEUD-CHRYS. Or else, that from heaven sanctification might be given to men, and earthly things he joined to heavenly. But the Holy Spirit is said to have descended upon Him, not as if He then first came to Him, for He never had left Him; but that He might show forth the Christ, Who was preached by John, and point Him to all as it were by the finger of faith.

BEDE; This is event also, in which the Holy Ghost was seen to come down upon baptism, was a sign of spiritual grace to be given to us in baptism.

PSEUDO-JEROME; But this is the anointing of Christ according to the flesh, namely, the Holy Ghost, of which anointing it is said, God, even your God, has anointed you with the oil of gladness above your fellows.

BEDE; Well indeed in the shape of a dove did the Holy Ghost come down, for it is an animal of great simplicity, and far removed from the malice of gall, that in a figure He might show us that He looks out for simple hearts, and deigns not to dwell in the minds of the wicked.

Catena Aurea: Commentary on the Gospel of St. Mark

PSEUDO-JEROME; Again, the Holy Ghost came down in the shape of a dove, because in the Canticles it is sung of the Church: My bride, my love, my beloved, my dove. Bride in the Patriarchs, love in the Prophets, near of kin in Joseph and Mary, beloved in John the Baptist, dove in Christ and His Apostles: to whom it is said, Be you wise as serpents, and harmless as doves.

BEDE; Now the Dove sat on the head of Jesus, lest any one should think that the voice of the Father was addressed to John and not to Christ. And well did he add, abiding on Him; for this is peculiar to Christ, that the Holy Ghost once filling Him should never leave Him. For sometimes to His faithful disciples the grace of the Spirit is conferred for signs of virtue, and for the working of miracles, sometimes it is taken away; though for the working of piety and righteousness, for the preservation of love to God and to one's neighbor, the grace of the Spirit is never absent. But the voice of the Father showed, that he himself, who came to John to be baptized with the others, was the very Son of God, willing to baptize with the Holy Spirit, whence there follows, And there came a voice from heaven, You are my beloved Son, in you I am well pleased. Not that this informed the Son Himself of a thing of which he was ignorant, but it shows to us what we ought to believe.

AUG. Wherefore Matthew relates what the voice said, This is my beloved Son; for he wished to show that the words, This is My Son, were in fact said, that thus the persons who heard it might know that he, and not another, was the Son of God. But, if you ask, which of these two sounded forth in that voice, take which you will, only remember, that the Evangelists, though not relating the same form of speaking, relate the same meaning.

And that God delighted Himself in His Son, we are reminded in these words, In you I am well pleased.

BEDE; The same voice has taught us, that we also, by the water of cleansing, and by the Spirit of sanctification, may he made the sons of God. The mystery of the Trinity also is shown forth in the baptism; the Son is baptized, the Spirit comes down in the shape of a dove, the voice of the Father bearing witness to the Son is heard.

PSEUDO-JEROME; Morally also it may be interpreted; we also, drawn aside from the fleeting world by the smell and purity of flowers, run with the young maidens after the bridegroom, and are washed in the sacrament of baptism, from the two fountains of the love of God, and of our neighbor, by the grace of remission, and mounting up by hope gaze upon heavenly mysteries with the eyes of a clean heart. Then we receive in a contrite and lowly spirit, with simplicity of heart, the Holy Spirit, who comes down to the meek, and abides in us, by a never-failing charity. And the voice of the Lord from heaven is directed to us the beloved of God; Blessed are the peacemakers, for they shall be called the sons of God; and then the Father, with the Son and the Holy Spirit, is well-pleased with us, when we are made one spirit with God.

12. And immediately the spirit drives him into the wilderness.

13. And he was there in the wilderness forty days, tempted of Satan; and was with the wild beasts; and the angels ministered to him.

Catena Aurea: Commentary on the Gospel of St. Mark

CHRYS. Because all that Christ did and suffered was for our teaching, He began after His baptism to dwell in the wilderness, and fought against the devil, that every baptized person might patiently sustain greater temptations after His baptism, nor be troubled, as if this which happened to Him was contrary to His expectation, but might bear up against all things, and come off conqueror. For although Goth allows that we should be tempted for many other reasons, yet for this cause also He allows it, that we may know, that man when tempted is placed in a station of greater honor. For the Devil approaches not save where he has beheld one set in a place of greater honor; and therefore it is said, And immediately the Spirit drove him into the wilderness. And the reason why he does not simply say, that He went into the wilderness, but was driven, is, that you may understand that it was done according to the word of Divine Providence. By which also he shows, that no man should thrust himself into temptation, but that those who from some other state are as it were driven into temptation, remain conquerors.

BEDE; And that no one might doubt, by what spirit he said that Christ was driven into the wilderness, Luke has on purpose premised, that Jesus being full of the Spirit returned from Jordan, and then has added, and was led by the Spirit in to the wilderness; lest the evil spirit should he thought to have any power over Him, who, being full of the Holy Spirit, departed whither He was willing to go, and did what He was willing to do.

CHRYS. But the Spirit drove Him into the wilderness, because He designed to provoke the devil to tempt Him, and thus gave Him an opportunity not only by hunger, but also by the place. For then most of all does the devil thrust himself in, when he sees men remaining solitary.

BEDE; But He retires into the desert that He may teach us that, leaving the allurements of the world, and the company of the wicked, we should in all things obey the Divine commands. He is left alone and tempted by the devil, that He might teach us, that all that will live godly in Christ Jesus shall suffer persecution; whence it follows, And he was in the wilderness forty days and forty nights, and was tempted by Satan. But He was tempted forty days and forty nights, that He might show us, that as long as we live here and serve God, whether prosperity smile upon us, which is meant by the day, or adversity smite us, which agrees with the figure of night, at all times our adversary is at hand, who ceases not to trouble our way by temptations. For the forty days and forty nights imply the whole time of this world, for the globe in which we are serving God is divided into four quarters. Again, there are Ten Commandments, by observing which we fight against our enemy, but four times ten are forty.

There follows, and he was with the wild beasts.

PSEUDO-CHRYS. But He says this to show of what nature was the wilderness, for it was impassable by man and full of wild beasts. It goes on; and angels ministered to him. For after temptation, and a victory against the devil, He worked the salvation of man. And thus the Apostle says, Angels are sent to minister for them who shall be heirs of salvation. We must also observe, that to those who conquer in temptation angels stand near and minister.

Catena Aurea: Commentary on the Gospel of St. Mark

BEDE; Consider also that Christ dwells among the wild beasts as man, but, as God, uses the ministry of Angels. Thus, when in the solitude of a holy life we hear with unpolluted mind the bestial manners of men, we merit to have the ministry of Angels, by whom, when freed from the body, we shall be transferred to everlasting happiness.

PSEUDO-JEROME; Or, then the beasts dwell with us in peace, as in the ark clean animals with the unclean, when the flesh lusts not against the spirit. After this, ministering Angels are sent to us, that they may give answers and comforts to hearts that watch.

14. Now after that John was put in prison, Jesus came into Galilee, preaching the Gospel of the kingdom of God,

15. And saying, The time is fulfilled, and the kingdom of God is at hand: repent you, and believe the Gospel.

PSEUDO-CHRYS. The Evangelist Mark follows Matthew in his order, and therefore after having said that Angels minister, he subjoins, But after that John was put into prison, Jesus came, &c. After the temptation and the ministry of Angels, He goes back into Galilee, teaching us not to resist the violence of evil men.

THEOPHYL. And to show us that in persecutions we ought to retire, and not to await them; but when we fall into them, we must sustain them.

PSEUD-CHRYS. He retired also that He might keep Himself for teaching and for healing, before He suffered, and after fulfilling all these things, might become obedient unto death.

Collected Out of the Works of the Fathers

BEDE; John being put in prison, fitly does the Lord begin to preach: wherefore there follows, Preaching the Gospel, &c. For when the Law Ceases, the Gospel arises in its steps.

PSEUDO-JEROME; When the shadow ceases, the truth comes on; first, John in prison, the Law in Judea; then, Jesus in Galilee, Paul among the Gentiles preaching the Gospel of the kingdom. For to an earthly kingdom succeeds poverty, to the poverty of Christians is given an everlasting kingdom; but earthly honor is like the foam of water, or smoke, or sleep.

BEDE; Let no one, however, suppose that the putting of John in prison took place immediately after the forty days' temptation and the fast of the Lord; for whoever reads the Gospel of John will find, that the Lord taught many things before the putting of John in prison, and also did many miracles; for you have in his Gospel, This beginning of miracles did Jesus; and afterwards, for John was not yet cast into prison. Now it is said, that when John read the books of Matthew, Mark, and Luke, he approved indeed the text of the history, and affirmed that they had spoken truth, but said that they had composed the history of only one year after John was cast into prison, in which year also he suffered. Passing over then the year of which the transactions had been published by the three others, he related the events of the former period, before John was cast into prison. When therefore Mark had said that Jesus came into Galilee, preaching the Gospel of the kingdom, he subjoins, saying, Since the time is fulfilled, &c.

PSEUD-CHRYS. Since then the time was fulfilled, when the fullness of time was come, and God sent His Son, it was fitting that the race of man should obtain the last dispensation of God. And therefore he says, for the kingdom of heaven is at hand. But the kingdom of God is essentially the same as the kingdom of heaven, though they differ in idea. For by the kingdom of God is to be understood that in which God reigns; and this in truth is in the region of the living, where, seeing God face to face, they will abide in the good things now promised to them; whether by this region one chooses to understand Love, or some other confirmation of those who put on the likeness of things above, which are signified by the heavens. For it is clear enough that the kingdom of God is confined neither by place nor by time.

THEOPHYL. Or else, the Lord means that the time of the Law is completed; as if He said, Up to this time the Law was at work; from this time the kingdom of God will work, that is, a conversation according to the Gospel, which is with reason likened to the kingdom of heaven. For when you see a man clothed in flesh living according to the Gospel, do you not say that he has the kingdom of heaven, which is not meat and drink, but righteousness and peace and joy in the Holy Ghost?

The next word is, Repent.

PSEUDO-JEROME; For he must repent, who would keep close to eternal good, that is, to the kingdom of God. For he who would have the kernel, breaks the shell; the sweetness of the apple makes up for the bitterness of its root; the hope of gain makes the dangers of the sea pleasant; the hope of health takes away from the painfulness of medicine. They are able worthily to proclaim the preaching of Christ who have deserved to attain to the reward of forgiveness; and therefore after he has said,

Repent, He subjoins, and believe the Gospel. For unless you have believed, you shall not understand.

BEDE; Repent, therefore, and believe; that is, renounce dead works; for of what use is believing without good works? The merit of good works does not, however, bring to faith, but faith begins, that good works may follow.

16. Now as he walked by the Sea of Galilee, he saw Simon and Andrew his brother casting a net into the sea: for they were fishers.

17. And Jesus said unto them, Come you after me, and I will make you to become fishers of men.

18. And straightway they forsook their nets, and followed him.

19. And when he had gone a little farther thence, he saw James the son of Zebedee, and John his brother, who also were in the ship mending their nets.

20. And straightway he called them: and they left their father Zebedee in the ship with the hired servants, and went after him.

GLOSS. The Evangelist, having mentioned the preaching of Christ to the multitude, goes on to the calling of the disciples, whom he made ministers of his preaching, whence it follows, And passing along the sea of Galilee, &c.

THEOPHYL. As the Evangelist John relates, Peter and Andrew were disciples of the Forerunner, but seeing that John had borne witness to Jesus, they joined themselves to him; afterwards, grieving that John had been cast into prison, they returned to their trade. Wherefore there follows, casting nets into the sea, for they were fishers. Look then upon them, living on their own labors, not on the fruits of iniquity; for such men were worthy to become the first disciples of Christ; whence it is subjoined, And Jesus said unto them, Come you after me. Now He calls them for the second time; for this is the second calling in respect of that, of which we read in John. But it is shown to what they were called, when it is added, I will make you become fishers of men.

REMIG. For by the net of holy preaching they drew fish, that is, men, from the depths of the sea, that is, of infidelity, to the light of faith. Wonderful indeed is this fishing! for fishes when they are caught, soon after die; when men are caught by the word of preaching, they rather are made alive.

BEDE; Now fisher's and unlettered men are sent to preach, that the faith of believers might be thought to lie in the power of God, not in eloquence or in learning. It goes on to say, and immediately they left their nets, and followed him.

THEOPHYL. For we must not allow any time to lapse, but at once follow the Lord. After these again, He catches James and John, because they also, though poor, supported the old age of their father. Wherefore there follows, And when he had gone a little farther thence, he saw James the son of Zebedee, &c.

But they left their father, because he would have hindered them in following Christ. Do you, also, when you are hindered by your parents, leave them, and come to God. It is shown by this that

Zebedee was not a believer; but the mother of the Apostles believed, for she followed Christ, when Zebedee was dead.

BEDE; It may be asked, how he could call two fishers from each of the boats, first, Peter and Andrew, then having gone a little further, the two others, sons of Zebedee, when Luke says that James and John were called to help Peter and Andrew, and that it was to Peter only that Christ said, Fear not, from this time you shall catch men; he also says, that at the same time, when they had brought their ships to land, they followed him. We must therefore understand that that transaction which Luke intimates happened first, and afterwards that they as their custom was, had returned to their fishing. So that what Mark here relates happened afterwards; for in this case they followed the Lord, without drawing their boats ashore, (which they would have done had they meant to return,) and followed Him, as one calling them, and ordering them to follow.

PSEUDO-JEROME; Further, we are mystically carried away to heaven, like Elias, by this chariot, drawn by these fishers, as by four horses. On these four corner-stones the first Church is built, in these as in the four Hebrew letters, we acknowledge the tetragrammaton, the name of the Lord, we who are commanded after their example, to hear the voice of the Lord and to forget the people of wickedness, and the house of our fathers' conversation, which is folly before God, and the spider's net in the meshes of which we, like gnats, were all but fallen, and were confined by things vain as the air, which hangs on nothing; loathing also the ship of our former walk. For Adam, our forefather according to the flesh, is clothed with the skins of dead beasts; but now, having put off the old man, with his deeds,

Catena Aurea: Commentary on the Gospel of St. Mark

following the new man we are clothed with those skins of Solomon, with which the bride rejoices that she has been made beautiful. Again, Simon, means obedient; Andrew, manly; James, supplanter; John, grace; by which four names, we are knit together into God's host; by obedience, that we may listen; by manliness, that we do battle; by overthrowing, that we may persevere; by grace, that we may he preserved. Which four virtues are called cardinal; for by prudence, we obey; by justice, we bear ourselves manfully; by temperance, we tread the serpent underfoot; by fortitude, we earn the grace of God.

THEOPHYL. We must know also, that action is first called, then contemplation; for Peter is the type of the active life, for he was more ardent than the others, just as the active life is the more bustling; but John is the type of the contemplative life, for he speaks more fully of divine things.

21. And they went into Capernaum; and straight-way on the sabbath day he entered into the synagogue, and taught.

22. And they were astonished at his doctrine: for he taught them as one that had authority, and not as the Scribes.

PSEUDO-JEROME; Mark, arranging the sayings of the Gospel as they were in his own mind, not in themselves, quits the order of the history, and follows the order of the mysteries. Wherefore he relates the first miracle on the sabbath day, saying, And they go in to Capernaum.

THEOPHYL. Quitting Nazareth. Now on the sabbath day, when the Scribes were gathered together, be entered into a synagogue, and taught. Wherefore there follows, And straightway on the sabbath day, having entered into the synagogue, he taught them. For this end the Law commanded them to give themselves up to rest on the sabbath day, that they might meet together to attend to sacred reading.

Again, Christ taught them by rebuke, not by flattery as did the Pharisees; wherefore it says, And they were astonished at his doctrine; for he taught them as one having power, and not as the Scribes. He taught them also in power, transforming men to good, and he threatened punishment to those who did not believe on Him.

BEDE; The Scribes themselves taught the people what was written in Moses and the Prophets: but Jesus as the God and Lord of Moses himself, by the freedom of His own will, either added those things which appeared wanting in the Law, or altered things as He preached to the people; as we read in Matthew, It was said to them of old time, but I say to you.

23. And there was in their synagogue a man with an unclean spirit; and he cried out,

24. Saying, Let us alone; what have we to do with thee, thou Jesus of Nazareth? art you come to destroy us? I know who you are, the Holy One of God.

25. And Jesus rebuked him, saying, Hold your peace, and come out of him.

26. And when the unclean spirit had torn him, and cried with a

loud voice, he came out of him.

27. And they were all amazed, inasmuch that they questioned among themselves, saying, What thing is this? what new doctrine is this? for with authority commands he even the unclean spirits, and they do obey him.

28. And immediately his fame spread abroad throughout all the region round about Galilee.

BEDE; Since by the envy of the devil death first entered into the world, it was right that the medicine of healing should first work against the author of death; and therefore it is said, And there was in their synagogue a man, &c.

PSEUD-CHRYS. The word Spirit is applied to an Angel, the air, the soul, and even the Holy Ghost. Lest therefore by the sameness of the name we should fall into error, he adds, unclean. And he is called unclean on account of his impiousness and far removal from God, and because he employs himself in all unclean and wicked works.

AUG. Moreover, how great is the power which the lowliness of God, appearing in the form of a servant, has over the pride of devils, the devils themselves know so well, that they express it to the same Lord clothed in the weakness of flesh. For there follows, And he cried out, saying, What have we to do with you, Jesus of Nazareth, &c. For it is evident in these words that there was in them knowledge, but there was not charity; and the reason was, that they fear their punishment from Him, and loved not the righteousness in Him.

BEDE; For the devils, seeing the Lord on the earth, thought that they were immediately to be judged.

PSEUD-CHRYS. Or else the devil so speaks, as if he said, 'by taking away uncleanness, and giving to the souls of men divine knowledge, You allow us no place in men.'

THEOPHYL; For to come out of man the devil considers as his own perdition; for devils are ruthless, thinking that they suffer some evil, so long as they are not troubling men. There follows, I know that you are the Holy One of God.

PSEUD-CHRYS. As if he said, Methinks that You are come; for he had not a firm and certain knowledge of the coming of God. But he calls Him holy not as one of many, for every prophet was also holy, but he proclaims that He was the One holy; by time article in Greek he shows Him to be the One, but by his fear he shows Him to he Lord of all.

AUG. For He was known to them in that degree in which He wished to be known; and He wished as much as was fitting. He was not known to them as to the Holy Angels, who enjoy Him by partaking of His eternity according as He is the Word of God; but as he was to be made known in terror, to those beings from whose tyrannical power He was about to free the predestinate. He was known therefore to the devils, not in that He is eternal Life, but by some temporal effects of His Power, which might be more clear to the angelic senses of even bad spirits than to the weakness of men.

Catena Aurea: Commentary on the Gospel of St. Mark

PSEUD-CHRYS. Further, the Truth did not wish to have the witness of unclean spirits; wherefore there follows, And Jesus threatened him, saying, &c. Whence a healthful precept is given to us; let us not believe devils, however they may proclaim the truth. It goes on, And the unclean spirit tearing him, &c. For, because the man spoke as one in his senses and uttered his words with discretion, lest it should be thought that he put together his words not from the devil but out of his own heart, He permitted the man to be torn by the devil, that He might show that it was the devil who spoke.

THEOPHYL. That they might know, when they saw it, from how great an evil the man was freed, and on account of the miracle might believe.

BEDE; But it may appear to be a discrepancy, that he should have gone out of him, tearing him, or, as some copies have it, vexing him, when, according to Luke, he did not hurt him. But Luke himself says, When he had cast him in to the midst, he came out from him, without hurting him. Wherefore it is inferred that Mark meant by vexing or tearing him, what Luke expresses, in the words, When he had cast him into the midst; so that what he goes on to say, And did not hurl him, may be understood to mean, that the tossing of his limbs and vexing, did not weakening him, as devils are wont to come out even with the cutting off and tearing away of limbs.

But seeing the power of the miracle, they wonder at the newness of our Lord's doctrine, and are roused to search into what they had heard by what they had seen. Wherefore there follows, And they all wondered &c. For miracles were done that they might more firmly believe the Gospel of the kingdom of God, which was being preached, since those who were promising heavenly joys to men on earth, were showing forth heavenly things and divine works even on earth. For before (as the Evangelist says) He was teaching them as one who had power, and now, as the crowd witnesses, with power He commands the evil spirits, and they obey Him.

It goes on, And immediately His fame spread abroad, &c.

GLOSS. For those things which men wonder at they soon divulge, for out of the abundance of the heart the mouth speaks .

PSEUDO-JEROME; Moreover, Capernaum is mystically interpreted the town of consolation, and the sabbath as rest. The man with an evil spirit is healed by rest and consolation, that the place and time may agree with his healing. This maim with an unclean spirit is the human race, in which uncleanness reigned from Adam to Moses; for they sinned without law, and perished without law. And he, knowing the Holy One of God, is ordered to hold his peace, for they knowing God did not glorify him as God, but rather served the creature than the Creator. The spirit tearing the man came out of him. When salvation is near, temptation is at hand also. Pharaoh, when about to let Israel go, pursues Israel; the devil, when despised, rises up to create scandals.

29. And forthwith, when they were come out of the synagogue, they entered into the house of Simon and Andrew, with James and John.

30. But Simon's wife's mother lay sick of a fever, and immediately they tell him of her.

31. And he came and took her by the hand, and lifted her up; and immediately the fever left her, and she ministered to them.

BEDE; First, it was right that the serpent's tongue should be shut up, that it might not spread any more venom; then that the woman, who was first seduced, should he healed from the fever of carnal concupiscence. Wherefore it is said, And forthwith, when they were come out of the synagogue, &c.

THEOPHYL. He retired then as the custom was on the sabbath-day about evening to eat in His disciples' house. But she who ought to have ministered was prevented by a fever. Wherefore it goes on, But Simon's wife's mother was lying sick with a fever.

PSEUD-CHRYS. But the disciples, knowing that they were to receive a benefit by that means, without waiting for the evening prayed that Peter's mother should be healed. Wherefore there follows, who immediately tell him of her.

BEDE; But in the Gospel of Luke it is written, that they besought him for her. For the Savior sometimes after being asked, sometimes of His own accord, heals the sick, showing that he always assents to the prayers of the faithful, when they pray also against had passions, and sometimes gives them to understand things which they do not understand at all, or else, when they pray unto Him dutifully, forgives their want of understanding; as the Psalmist begs of God, Cleanse me, O Lord, from my secret faults.

Wherefore He heals her at their request; for there follow, And he came and took her by the hand, and lifted her up.

THEOPHYL. By this it is signified, that God will heal a sick man, if he ministers to the Saints, through love to Christ.

BEDE; But in that He gives most profusely His gifts of healing and doctrine on the sabbath day, He teaches, that He is not under the Law, but above the Law, and does not choose the Jewish sabbath, but the true sabbath, and our rest is pleasing to the Lord, if, in order to attend to the health of our souls, we abstain from slavish work, that is, from all unlawful things. It goes on, and immediately the fever left her, &c. The health which is conferred at the command of the Lord, returns at once entire, accompanied with such strength, that she is able to minister to those, of whose help she had before stood in need. Again, if we suppose that the man delivered from the devil means, in the moral way of interpretation, the soul purged from unclean thoughts, fitly does the woman cured of a fever by the command of God mean the flesh, restrained from the heat of its concupiscence by die precepts of continence.

PSEUDO-JEROME; For the fever means intemperance, from which, we the sons of the synagogue, by the hand of discipline, and by the lifting up of our desires, are healed, and minister to the will of Him who heals us.

THEOPHYL. But he has a fever who is angry, and in the unruliness of his anger stretches forth his hands to do hurt; but if reason restrains his hands, he will arise, and so serve reason.

32. And at even, when the sun did set, they brought unto him all that were diseased, and them that were possessed with devils.

33. And all the city was gathered together at the door.

34. And he healed many that were sick of divers diseases, and cast out many devils; and suffered not the devils to speak, because they knew him.

THEOPHYL. Because the multitude thought that it was not lawful to heal on the sabbath day, they waited for the evening, to bring those who were to be healed to Jesus. Wherefore it is said, And at even, when the sun had set. There follows, and he healed many that were vexed with divers diseases.

PSEUD-CHRYS. Now in that he says many, all are to be understood according to the Scripture mode of expression.

THEOPHYL. Or he says many, because there were some faithless persons, who could not at all be cured on account of their unfaithfulness. Therefore He healed many of those who were brought, that is, all who had faith. It goes on, and cast out many devils.

PSEUDO-AUG. For the devils knew that He was the Christ, who had been promised by the Law: for they saw in Him all the signs, which had been foretold by the Prophets; but they were ignorant of His divinity, as also were their princes, for if they had known it, they would not have crucified the Lord of glory.

Collected Out of the Works of the Fathers

BEDE; For, Him whom the devil had known as a man, wearied by His forty days' fast, without being able by tempting Him to prove whether He was the Son of God, he now by the power of His miracles understood or rather suspected to be the Son of God. The reason therefore why he persuaded the Jews to crucify Him, was not because he did not think that He was the Son of God, but because he did not foresee that he himself was to be condemned by Christ's death.

THEOPHYL. Furthermore, the reason that He forbade the devils to speak, was to teach us not to believe them, even if they say true. For if once they find persons to believe them, they mingle truth with falsehood.

PSEUDO-CHRYS. And Luke does not contradict this, when he says, that devils came out of many, crying out, and saying, You are Christ the Son of God: for he subjoins, And he rebuking them, suffered them not to speak; for Mark, who passes over many things for the sake of brevity, speaks about what happened subsequently to the above-mentioned words.

BEDE; Again, in a mystical sense, the setting of the sun signifies the passion of Him, who said, As long as I am in the world, I am the light of the world. And when the sun was going down, more demoniacs and sick persons were healed than before: because He who living in the flesh for a time taught a few Jews, has transmitted the gifts of faith and health to all the Gentiles throughout the world.

PSEUDO-JEROME; But the door of the kingdom, morally, is repentance and faith, which works health for various diseases;

for divers are the vices, with which the city of this world is sick.

35. And in the morning, rising up a great while before day, he went out, and departed into a solitary place, and there prayed.

36. And Simon and they that were with him followed after him.

37. And when they had found him, they said unto him, All men seek for thee.

38. And he said unto them, Let us go into the next towns, that I may preach there also: for therefore came I forth.

39. And he preached in their synagogues throughout all Galilee, and cast out devils.

THEOPHYL. After that the Lord had cured the sick, He retired apart. Wherefore it is said, And rising very early in the morning, he went out and departed into a desert place. By which He taught us not to do any thing for the sake of appearance, but if we do any good, not to publish it openly. He goes on, and there prayed.

PSEUD-CHRYS. Not that He required prayer; for it was He who Himself received the prayers of men; but He did this by way of an economy, and became to us the model of good works.

THEOPHYL. For He shows to us that we ought to attribute to God whatever we do well, and to say to Him, Every good gift comes down from above, from Thee. He continues: And Simon followed him, and they that were with him.

PSEUD-CHRYS. Luke however says, that crowds came to Christ, and spoke what Mark here relates that the Apostles said, adding, And when they came to him, they said to him, All seek you. But they do not contradict each other; for Christ received after the Apostles the multitude, breathlessly anxious to embrace His feet. He received them willingly, but chose to dismiss them, that the rest also might be partakers of His doctrine, as He was not to remain long in the world.

And therefore there follows: And he said, Let us go into the neighboring villages and towns, that there also I may preach.

THEOPHYL. For He passes on to them as being more in need, since it was not right to shut up doctrine in one place, but to throw out his rays every where. It goes on: For therefore am I come.

PSEUD-CHRYS. In which word, He manifests the mystery of His emptying himself, that is, of His incarnation, and the sovereignty of His divine nature, in that He here asserts, that He came willingly into the world. Luke however says, To this end was I sent, proclaiming the Dispensation, and the good pleasure of God the Father concerning the incarnation of the Son.

There follows: And he continued preaching in their synagogues, in all Galilee.

AUG. But by this preaching, which, he says, He continued in all Galilee, is also meant the sermon of the Lord delivered on the mount, which Matthew mentions, and Mark has entirely passed over, without giving any thing like it, save that he has repeated

Catena Aurea: Commentary on the Gospel of St. Mark

some sentences not in continuous order, but in scattered places, spoken by the Lord at other times.

THEOPHYL. He also mingled action with teaching, for whilst employed in preaching, He afterwards put to flight devils. For there follows: And casting out devils. For unless Christ showed forth miracles, His teaching would not be believed; so do thou also, after teaching, work, that your word be not fruitless in thyself.

BEDE; Again mystically if by the setting of the sun, the death of the Savior is intended, why should not His resurrection be intended by the returning dawn? For by its clear light, He went far into the wilderness of the Gentiles, and there continued praying in the person of His faithful disciples, for He aroused their hearts by the grace of the Holy Spirit to the virtue of prayer.

40. And there came a leper to him, beseeching him, and kneeling down to him, and saying unto him, If you will, you can make me clean.

41. And Jesus, moved with compassion, put forth his hand, and touched him, and said to him, I will; be you clean.

42. And as soon as he had spoken, immediately the leprosy departed from him, and he was cleansed.

43. And he straitly charged him, and forthwith sent him away;

44. And said to him, See you say nothing to any man: but go your way, show yourself to the Priest, and offer for your

cleansing those things which Moses commanded, for a testimony to them.

45. But he went out, and began to publish it much, and to blaze abroad the matter, inasmuch that Jesus could no more openly enter into the city, but was without in desert places: and they came to him from every quarter.

BEDE; After that the serpent-tongue of the devils was shut up, and the woman, who was first seduced, cured of a fever, in the third place, the man, who listened to the evil counsels of the woman, is cleansed from his leprosy, that the order of restoration in the Lord might be the same as was the order of the fall in our first parents; whence it goes on: And there came a leper to him, beseeching him.

AUG. Mark puts together circumstances, from which one may infer that he is the same as that one whom Matthew relates to have been cleansed, when the Lord came down from the mount, after the sermon.

BEDE, And because the Lord said that He came not to destroy the Law but to fulfill, he who was excluded by the Law, inferring that he was cleansed by the power of the Lord, showed that that grace, which could wash away the stain of the leper, was not from the Law, but over the Law. And truly, as in the Lord authoritative power, so in him the constancy of faith is shown; for there follows, Lord, if you will, you can make me clean. He falls on his face, which is at once a gesture of lowliness and of shame, to show that every man should blush for the stains of his life. But his shame did not stifle confession; he showed his wound, and begged for medicine, and the confession is full of devotion and of faith, for he refers the power to the will of the Lord.

THEOPHYL. For he said not, If you will, pray unto God, but, If you will, as thinking Him very God.

BEDE; Moreover, he Bede doubted of the will of the Lord, not as disbelieving His compassion, but, as conscious of his own filth, he did not presume. He goes on; But Jesus, moved with compassion, put forth his hand, and touched him, and said to him, I will, be you clean. It is not, as many of the Latins think, to be taken to mean and read, He wish to cleanse thee, but that Christ should say separately, I will, and then command, be you clean.

CHRYS. Further, the reason why He touches the leper, and did not confer health upon him by word alone, was, that it is said by Moses in the Law, that he who touches a leper, shall be unclean till the evening; that is, that He might show, that this uncleanness is a natural one, that the Law was not laid down for Him, but on account of mere men. Furthermore, He shows that He Himself is the Lord of the Law; and the reason why He touched the leper, though the touch was not necessary to the working of the cure, was to show that He gives health, not as a servant, but as the Lord.

BEDE; Another reason why He touched him, was to prove that He could not be defiled, who freed others from pollution. At the same time it is remarkable, that He healed in the way in which he had been begged to heal. If you will, says the leper, you can make me clean. I will, He answered, behold, you have My will, be clean; now you have at once the effect of My compassion.

CHRYS. Moreover, by this, not only did He not take away the opinion of Him entertained by the leper, but He confirmed it; for He puts to flight the disease by a word, and what the leper had said in word, He filled up in deed; wherefore there follows, And when he had spoken, immediately, &c.

BEDE; For there is no interval between the work of God and the command, because the work is in the command, for He commanded, and they were created. There follows: And he strictly charged him, and forthwith, &c. See you tell no man.

CHRYS. As if He said, It is not yet time that My works should be preached, I require not your preaching. By which He teaches us not to seek worldly honor as a reward for our works. It goes on: But go your way, show yourself to the chief of the priests. Our Savior sent him to the priest for the trial of his cure, and that he might not he cast out of the temple, but still be numbered with the people in prayer. He sends him also, that be might fulfill all the parts of the Law, in order to stop the evil-speaking tongue of the Jews. He Himself indeed completed the work, leaving them to try it.

BEDE; This He did in order that the priest might understand that the leper was not healed by the Law, but by the grace of God above the Law. There follows: And offer for your cleansing what Moses, &c.

THEOPHYL. He ordered him to offer the gift which they who

were healed were accustomed to offer, as if for a testimony, that lie was not against the Law, lint rather confirmed the Law, inasmuch as lie Himself worked out the precepts of the Law.

BEDE; If any one wonders, how the Lord seems to approve of the Jewish sacrifice, which the Church rejects, let him remember, that He had not yet offered His own holocausts in His passion. And it was not right that significative sacrifices should he taken away, before that which they signified was confirmed by the witness of the Apostles in their preaching, and by the faith of the believing people.

THEOPHYL. But the leper, although the Lord forbade him, disclosed the benefit, wherefore it goes on: But he having gone out, began to publish and to blaze abroad the tale; for the person benefited ought to be grateful, and to return thanks, even though his benefactor requires it not.

BEDE; Now it may well be asked, why our Lord ordered His action to be concealed, and yet it could not be kept hid for an hour? But it is to be observed, that the reason why, in doing a miracle, He ordered it to be kept secret, and yet for all that it was noised abroad, was, that His elect, following the example of His teaching, should wish indeed that in the great things which they do, they should remain concealed, but should nevertheless unwillingly be brought to light for the good of others. Not then that He wished any thing to be done, which He was not able to bring about, but, by the authority of His teaching, He gave an example of what His members ought to wish for, and of what should happen to them even against their will.

Collected Out of the Works of the Fathers

BEDE; Further, this perfect cure of one man brought large multitudes to the Lord; wherefore it is added, So that he could not any more openly enter into the city, but could only be without in desert places.

CHRYS. For the leper every where proclaimed his wonderful cure, so that all ran to see and to believe on the Healer; thus the Lord could not preach the Gospel, but walked in desert places; wherefore there follows, And they came together to him from all Places.

PSEUDO-JEROME; Mystically, our leprosy is the sin of the first man, which began from the head, when he desired the kingdoms of the world. For covetousness is the root of all evil; wherefore Gehazi, engaged in an avaritious pursuit, is covered with leprosy.

BEDE; But when the hand of the Savior, that is, the Incarnate Word of God, is stretched out, and touches human nature, it is cleansed from the various parts of the old error.

PSEUDO-JEROME; This leprosy is cleansed on offering an oblation to the true Priest after the order of Melchisedec; for He tells us, Give alms of such things as you have, and, behold, all things are clean to you. But in that Jesus could not openly enter into the city, it is meant to be conveyed, that Jesus is not manifested to those, who are enslaved to the love of praise in the broad highway, and to their own wills, but to those who with Peter go into the desert, which the Lord chose for prayer, and for refreshing His people; that is, those who quit the pleasures of the world, and all that they possess, that they may say, The Lord is my portion. But the glory of the Lord is manifested to those, who meet together on all sides, that is, through smooth ways and steep, whom nothing can separate from the love of Christ.

BEDE; Even after working a miracle in that city, the Lord retires into the desert, to show that He loves best a quiet life, and one far removed from the cares of the world, and that it is on account of this desire, He applied Himself to the healing of the body.

Mark 2

1. And again he entered into Capernaum after some days; and it was noised that he was in the house.

2. And straightway many were gathered together, inasmuch that there was no room to receive them, no, not so much as about the door: and he preached the word to them.

3. And they came unto him, bringing one sick of the palsy, which was borne of four.

4. And when they could not come nigh unto him for the press, they uncovered the roof where he was: and when they had broken it up, they let down the bed wherein the sick of the palsy lay.

5. When Jesus saw their faith, he said unto the sick of the palsy, Son, your sins be forgiven you.

6. But there were certain of the Scribes sitting there, and reasoning in their hearts,

7. Why does this man thus speak blasphemies? who can forgive sins but God only?

8. And immediately when Jesus perceived in his spirit that they so reasoned within themselves, he said unto them, Why reason you these things in your hearts?

Catena Aurea: Commentary on the Gospel of St. Mark

9. Whether is it easier to say to the sick of the palsy, Your sins be forgiven you; or to say, Arise, and take up your bed, and walk?

10. But that you may know that the Son of man has power on earth to forgive sins, (he says to the sick of the palsy,)

11. I say to you, Arise, and take up your bed, and go your way into your house.

12. And immediately he arose, took up the bed, and went forth before them all; inasmuch that they were all amazed, and glorified God, saying, We never saw it on this fashion.

BEDE; Because the compassion of God deserts not even carnal persons, He accords to them the grace of His presence, by which even they may be made spiritual. After the desert, the Lord returns into the city; wherefore it is said, And again he entered into Capernaum, &c.

AUG. But in Matthew writes this miracle as if it were done in the city of the Lord, whilst Mark places it in Capernaum, which would he more difficult of solution, if Matthew had also named Nazareth. But seeing that Galilee itself might be called the city of the Lord, who can doubt but that the Lord did these things in His own city, since He did them in Capernaum, a city of Galilee; particularly as Capernaum was of such importance in Galilee as to be called its metropolis? Or else, Matthew passed by the things which were done after He came into His own city, until He came to Capernaum, and so adds on the story of the paralytic healed, subjoining, And, behold, they presented to him a man sick of the palsy, after he had said that He came into His own city.

PSEUD-CHRYS. Or else, Matthew called Capernaum His city because He went there frequently, and there did many miracles. It goes on: And it was noised that he was in the house, &c. For the desire of hearing Him was stronger than the toil of approaching Him.

After this, they introduce the paralytic, of whom Matthew and Luke speak; wherefore there follows: And they came unto him bearing one sick of the palsy, who was carried by four.

Finding the door blocked up by the crowd, they could not by any means enter that way. Those who carried him, however, hoping that he could merit the grace of being healed, raising the bed with their burden, and uncovering the roof, lay him with his bed before the face of the Savior. And thus is that which is added: And when they could not lay him before him, &c.

There follows: But when Jesus saw their faith, he said to the sick of the palsy, Son, your sins be forgiven you. He did not mean the faith of the sick man, but of his bearers; for it sometimes happens, that a man is healed by the faith of another.

BEDE; It may indeed be seen, how much each person's own faith weighs with God, when that of another had such influence that the whole man at once rose up, healed body and soul, and by one man's merit, another should have his sins forgiven him.

THEOPHYL. He saw the faith of the sick man himself, since he would not have allowed himself to be carried, unless he lad had faith to be healed.

BEDE; Moreover, the Lord being about to cure the man of the palsy, first loosed the chains of his sins, in order to show that he was condemned to the loosening of his joints, because of the bonds of his sins, and could not be healed to the recovery of his limbs, unless these were first loosened. But Christ's wonderful humility calls this man, despised, weak, with all the joints of his limbs unstrung, a son, when the priests did not deign to touch him. Or at least, He therefore calls him a son, because his sins are forgiven him. It goes on: But there were certain of the scribes sitting there, and reasoning in their hearts, Why does this man speak blasphemies?

CYRIL; Now they accuse Him of blasphemy, anticipating the sentence of His death: for there was a command in the Law, that whosoever blasphemed should be put to death. And this charge they laid upon Him, because He claimed for Himself the divine power of remitting sins: wherefore it is added, Who can forgive sin, save God only? For the Judge of all alone has power to forgive sin.

BEDE; Who remits sin by those also to whom he has assigned the power of remitting, and therefore Christ is proved to be very God, for He is able to remit sins as God. The Jews then are in error, who although they hold the Christ both to be God, and to be able to remit sins, do not however believe that Jesus is the Christ. But the Arians err much more madly, who although overwhelmed with the words of the Evangelist, so that they cannot deny that Jesus is the Christ, and can remit sin, nevertheless fear not to deny that He is God.

But He Himself, desiring to shame the traitors both by His knowledge of things hidden and by the virtue of His works, manifests Himself to be God. For there follows: And immediately when Jesus perceived in his spirit that they so reasoned, he said to them, Why reason you these things in your hearts? In which He shows Himself to be God, since He can know the hidden things of the heart; and in a manner though silent He speaks thus, With the same power and majesty, by which I look upon your thoughts, I can forgive the sins of men.

THEOPHYL. But though their thoughts were laid bare, still they remain insensible, refusing to believe that He who knew their hearts could forgive sins, wherefore the Lord proves to them the cure of the soul by that of the hotly, showing time invisible by the visible, that which is more difficult by that which is easier, although they did not look upon it as such. For the Pharisees thought it more difficult to heal the body, as being more open to view; but the soul more easy to cure, because the cure is invisible; so that they reasoned thus, Lo, He does not now cure the body, but heals the unseen soul; if He had had more power, lie would at once have cured the body, and not have fled for refuge to the unseen world. The Savior, therefore, showing that He can do both, says, which is the easier? as if He said, I indeed by the healing of time body, which is in reality more easy, but appears to you more difficult, will prove to you the health of the soul, which is really more difficult.

PSEUD-CHRYS. And because it is easier to say than to do, there was still manifestly something to say in opposition, for the work was not yet manifested; wherefore He subjoins, But that you may know, &c. as if He said, Since you doubt my word, I will bring on a work which will confirm what was unseen. But He says in a marked manner, On earth to forgive sins, that He might show that He has joined the power of the divinity to the human nature by an inseparable union, because although He was made man, yet He remained the Worth of God; and although by an economy He conversed on the earth with men, nevertheless He was not prevented from working miracles and from giving remission of sins. For his human nature did not in any thing take away from these things which essentially belonged to His Divinity, nor the Divinity hinder the Word of God from becoming on earth, according to the flesh, time Son of Man without change and in truth.

THEOPHYL. Again, He Says, Take up your bed, to prove the greater certainty of the miracle, showing that it is not a mere illusion; and at time same time to show that He not only healed, but gave strength; thus He not only turns away souls from sin, but gives them the power of working out the commandments.

BEDE; A carnal sign therefore is given, that the spiritual sign may be proved, although it belongs to the same power to do away with the distempers of both soul and body, whence it follows: And immediately he arose, took up the bed, and went forth before them all.

CHRYS. Further, He first healed by the remission of sins that which He had come to seek, that is, a soul, so that when they faithlessly doubted, then He might bring forward a work before them, and in this way His word might be confirmed by the work, and a hidden sign be proved by an open one, that is, the health of the soul by the healing of the body.

BEDE; We are also informed, that many sicknesses of body arise from sins, and therefore perhaps sins are first remitted, that the causes of sickness being taken away, health may be restored. For men are afflicted by fleshly troubles for five causes, in order to increase their merits, as Job and the Martyrs; or to preserve their lowliness, as Paul by the messenger of Satan; or that they may perceive amid correct their sins, as Miriam, the sister of Moses, and this paralytic; or for the glory of God, as the man born blind and Lazarus; or as the beginnings of the pains of damnation, as Herod and Antiochus. But wonderful is the virtue of the divine power, where without the least interval of time, by time command of the Savior, a speedy health accompanies His words. Wherefore there follows: Insomuch that they were all amazed. Leaving the greater thing, that is, the remission of sins, they only wonder at that which is apparent, that is, the health of the body.

THEOPHYL. This is not however the paralytic, whose cure is related by John, for he had no man with him , this one had four; he is cured in the pool of the sheep market, but this one in a house. It is the same man, however, whose cure is related by Matthew and Mark. But mystically, Christ is still in Capernaum, in the house of consolation.

BEDE; Moreover, whilst the Lord is preaching in the house, there is not room for them , not even at the door, because whilst Christ is preaching in Judea, the Gentiles are not yet able to enter to hear Hum, to whom, however, though placed without, he directed the words of His doctrine by His preachers.

Catena Aurea: Commentary on the Gospel of St. Mark

PSEUDO-JEROME; Again, the palsy is a type of the torpor, in which man lies slothful in the softness of the flesh, though desiring health.

THEOPHYL. If therefore I, having the powers of my mind unstrung, remain, whenever I attempt any thing good without strength, as a palsied man, and if I be raised on high by the four Evangelists, and be brought to Christ, and there hear myself called son, then also are my sins quitted by me; for a man is called the son of God because he works the commandments.

BEDE; Or else, because there are four virtues, by which a man is through an assured heart exalted so that he merits safety; which virtues some call prudence, fortitude, temperance, and justice. Again, they desire to bring the palsied man to Christ, but they are impeded on every side by the crowd which is between them, because often the soul desires to be renewed by the medicine of Divine grace, but through the sluggishness of the groveling body is held back by the hindrance of old custom. Oftentimes amidst the very sweetnesses of secret prayer, and, as it may be called, the pleasant converse with God, a crowd of thoughts, cutting off the clear vision of the mind, shuts out Christ from its sight. Let us not then remain in the lowest ground, where the crowds are bustling, but aim at the roof of the house, that is, the sublimity of the Holy Scripture, and meditate on the law of the Lord.

THEOPHYL. But how should I be borne to Christ, if the roof be not opened. For the roof is the intellect, which is set above all those things which are within us; here it has much earth about it in the tiles which are made of clay, I mean, earthly things: but if these be taken away, the virtue of the intellect within us is freed from its load. After this let it be let down, that is, humbled. For it does not teach us to be puffed up, because our intellect has its load cleared away, but to be humbled still more.

BEDE; Or else, the sick man is let down after the roof is opened, because, when the Scriptures are laid open to us, we arrive at the knowledge of Christ, that is, we descend to His lowliness, by the dutifulness of faith. But by the sick man being let down with his bed, it is meant that Christ should be known by man, whilst yet in the flesh. But by rising from the bed is meant the soul's rousing itself from carnal desires, in which it was lying in sickness. To take up the bed is to bridle the flesh itself by the bands of continence, and to separate it from earthly pleasures, through the hope of heavenly rewards. But to take up the bed and to go home is to return to paradise. Or else the man, now healed, who had been sick carries back home his bed, when the soul, after receiving remission of sins, returns, even though encompassed with the body, to its internal watch over itself.

THEOPHYL. It is necessary to take up also one's bed, that is the body, to the working of good. For then shall we be able to arrive at contemplation, so that our thoughts should say within us, never have we seen in this way before, that is never understood as we have done since we have been cured of the palsy; for he who is cleansed from sin, sees more purely.

13. And he went forth again by the sea side; and all the multitude resorted unto him, and he taught them.

14. And as he passed by, he saw Levi the son of Alphaeus sitting at the receipt of custom, and said unto him, Follow me. And he

arose and followed him.

15. And it came to pass, that as Jesus sat at meat in his house, many Publicans and sinners sat also together with Jesus and his disciples; for there were many, and they followed him.

16. And when the Scribes and Pharisees saw him eat with Publicans and sinners, they said unto his disciples, How is it that he eats and drinks with Publicans and sinners?

17. When Jesus heard it, he said unto them, They that are whole have no need of the physician, but they that are sick: I came not to call the righteous, but sinners to repentance.

BEDE; After that the Lord taught at Capernaum, He went to the sea, that He might not only set in order the life of men in towns, but also might preach the Gospel of the kingdom to those who dwelt near the sea, and might teach them to despise the restless motions of those things which pass away like the waves of the sea, and to overcome them by the firmness of faith; wherefore it is said, And he went forth again to the sea, and all the multitude, &c.

THEOPHYL. Or else, after the miracle, He goes to the sea, as if wishing to be alone, but the crowd runs to Him again, that you might learn, that the more you fly from glory, the more she herself pursues you; but if you follow her, she will fly from you. The Lord passing on from thence called Matthew; wherefore there follows, And as he passed by, he saw Levi the son of Alpheus sitting, &c.

CHRYS. Now this is the same publican who is named by all the Evangelists; Matthew by Matthew; simply Levi by Luke; and Levi, the son of Alphaeus, by Mark; for he was the son of Alphaeus. And you may find persons with two names in other parts of Scripture; as Moses' father in law is sometimes called Jethro, sometimes Raguel.

BEDE; So also the same person is called Levi and Matthew; but Luke and Mark, on account of their reverence and the honor of the Evangelist, are unwilling to put the common name, while Matthew is a just accuser of himself, and calls himself Matthew and publican he wishes to show to his hearers that no one who is converted should despair of his salvation, since he himself was suddenly changed from a publican into an Apostle. But he says that he was sitting at the 'teloneum', that is, the place where the customs are looked after and administered. For 'telos' in Greek is the same as 'vectigal,' customs, in Latin.

THEOPHYL. For he sat at the receipt of custom, either, as is often done, exacting from some, or making up accounts, or doing some actions of that sort, which publicans are wont to do in their abodes, yes this man, who was raised on high from this state of life that he might leave all things and follow Christ. Wherefore it goes on, And he says to him, Follow me, &c.

BEDE; Now to follow is to imitate, and therefore in order to imitate the poverty of Christ, in the feeling of his soul even more than in outward condition, he who used to rob his neighbor's wealth, now leaves his own. And not only did he quit the gain of the customs, but he also despised the peril, which might come from the princes of this world, because he left the accounts of the customs imperfect and unsettled. For the Lord Himself, Who externally, by human language, called Him to follow, inflamed him inwardly by divine inspiration to follow Him the moment that He called him.

PSEUDO-JEROME; Thus then Levi, which means Appointed, followed from the custom-house of human affairs, the Word, Who says, He who does not quit all that he has, cannot be my disciple.

THEOPHYL. But he who used to plot against others becomes so benevolent, that he invites many persons to eat with him. Wherefore it goes on; And it came to pass, that as Jesus sat at meat in his house.

BEDE; The persons here called publicans are those who exact the public customs, or men who farm the customs of the exchequer or of republics; moreover, those also, who follow after the gain of this world by business, are called by the same name. They who had seen that the publican, converted from his sins to better things, had found a place of pardon, even for this reason themselves also do not despair of salvation. And they come to Jesus, not remaining in their former sins, as the Pharisees and Scribes complain, but in penitence, as the following words of the Evangelist show, saying, For there were many who followed him. For the Lord went to the feasts of sinners, that he might have an opportunity of teaching them, and might set before his entertainers spiritual meats, which also is carried on in mystical figures. For he who receives Christ into his inward habitation is fed with the highest delights of overflowing pleasures. Therefore the Lord enters willingly, and takes up His abode in the affection of him who has believed on Him; and this is the spiritual banquet of good works, which the rich cannot have, and on which the poor feast.

THEOPHYL. But the Pharisees blame this, making themselves pure. Whence there follows: And when the Scribes and Pharisees saw him eat, &c.

BEDE; If by the election of Matthew and calling of the publicans, the faith of the Gentiles is expressed, who formerly were intent on the gains of this world; certainly the haughtiness of the Scribes and Pharisees intimates the envy of the Jewish people, who are vexed at the salvation of the Gentiles. It goes on: When Jesus heard it, he said to them, They that are whole need not the physician, but they that are sick. The aims at the Scribes and Pharisees, who, thinking themselves righteous, refused to keep company with sinners. He calls Himself the physician, Who, by a strange mode of healing, was wounded on account of our iniquities, and by His wound we are healed. And He calls those whole and righteous, who, wishing to establish their own righteousness, are not subject to the righteousness of God. Moreover He calls those rich and sinners, who, overcome by the consciousness of their own frailty, and seeing that they cannot be justified by the Law, submit their necks to the grace of Christ by repentance. Wherefore it is added, For I came not for all the righteous, but sinners, &c.

THEOPHYL. Not indeed that they should continue sinners, but be converted to that repentance.

18. And the disciples of John and of the Pharisees used to fast:

and they come and say to him, Why do the disciples of John and of the Pharisees fast, but your disciples fast not?

19. And Jesus said unto them, Can the children of the bride-chamber fast, while the bridegroom is with them? as long as they have the bridegroom with them, they cannot fast.

20. But the days will come, when the bridegroom shall be taken away from them, and then shall they fast in those days.

21. No man also sews a piece of new cloth on an old garment: else the new piece that filled it up takes away from the old, and the rent is made worse.

22. And no man puts new wine into old bottles: else the new wine does burst the bottles, and the wine is spilled, and the bottles will be marred: but new wine must be put into new bottles.

GLOSS. As above, the Master was accused to the disciples for keeping company with sinners in their feasts, so now, on the other hand, the disciples are complained of to the Master for their omission of fasts, that so matter for dissension might arise amongst them. Wherefore it is said, And the disciples of John and the Pharisees used to fast.

THEOPHYL. For the disciples of John being in an imperfect state, continued in Jewish customs.

AUG. But it may be thought that he added Pharisees, because they joined with the disciples of John in saying this to the Lord, whilst in Matthew relates that the disciples of John alone said it: but the words which follow rather show that those who said it spoke not of themselves, but of others. For it goes on, And they come and say unto him, Why do the disciples, &c. For these words show, that the guests who were there came to Jesus, and had said this same thing to the disciples, so that in the words which he uses, they came, he speaks not of those same persons, of whom he had said, And the disciples of John and the Pharisees were fasting. But as they were fasting, those persons who remembered it, come to him. Matthew then says this, And there came to him the disciples of John, saying, because the Apostles also were there, and all eagerly, as each could, objected these things.

CHRYS. The disciples of John, therefore, and of the Pharisees, being jealous of Christ, ask Him, whether He alone of all men with His disciples could, without abstinence and toil, conquer in the fight of the passions.

BEDE; But John did not drink wine and strong drink, because he who has no power by nature, obtains more merit by abstinence. But why should the Lord, to whom it naturally belonged to forgive sins, shun those whom he could make more pure, than those who fast? But Christ also fasted, lest He should break the precept, He ate with sinners, that you might see His grace, and acknowledge His power. It goes on; And Jesus said to them, Can the children, &c.

AUG. Mark here calls them children of the nuptials, whom Matthew calls children of the bridegroom; for we understand the children of the nuptials to be not only those of the bride-groom, but also of the bride.

PSEUD-CHRYS. He then calls Himself a bridegroom, as if about to be betrothed to the Church. For the betrothal is giving an earnest, namely, that of the grace of the Holy Ghost, by which the world believed.

THEOPHYL. He also calls Himself a bridegroom, not only as betrothing to Himself virgin minds, but because the time of His first coming is not a time of sorrow, nor of sadness to believers, neither does it bring with it toil, but rest. For it is without any works of the law, giving rest by baptism, by which we easily obtain salvation without toil. But the sons of the nuptials or of the Bridegroom are the Apostles; because they, by the grace of God, are made worthy of every heavenly blessing, by the grace of God, and partakers of every joy.

PSEUD-CHRYS. But intercourse with Him, He says, is far removed from all sorrow, when He adds, As long as they have the bridegroom with them, they cannot fast. He is sad, from whom some good is far removed; but be who has it present with him rejoices, and is not sad.

But that He might destroy their elation of heart, and show that He intended not His own disciples to be licentious, He adds, But the days will come when the bridegroom shall be taken, &c. as if He said, The time will come, when they will show their firmness; for when the Bridegroom shall be taken from them, they will fast as longing for His coming, and in order to unite to Him their spirits, cleansed by bodily suffering. He shows also that there is no necessity for His disciples to fast, as having present with them the Bridegroom of human nature, Who every where executes the words of God, and Who gives the seed of life. The sons of the Bridegroom also cannot, because they are infants, be entirely conformed to their Father, the Bridegroom, Who, considering their infancy, deigns to allow them not to fast: but when the Bridegroom is gone, they will fast, through desire of Him; when they have been made perfect, they will be united to the Bridegroom in marriage, and will always feast at the king's banquet.

THEOPHYL. We must also understand, that every man whose works are good is the son of the Bridegroom; he has the Bridegroom with him, even Christ, and fasts not, that is, does no works of repentance, because he does not sin: but when the Bridegroom is taken away by the man's falling into sin, then lie fasts and is penitent, that he may cure his sin.

BEDE; But in a mystical sense, it may thus be expressed; that the disciples of John and the Pharisees fast, because every man who boasts of the works of the law without faith, who follows the traditions of men, and receives the preaching of Christ with his bodily ear, and not by the faith of the heart, keeps aloof from spiritual goods, and wastes away with a fasting soul. But he who is incorporated into the members of Christ by a faithful love cannot fast, because he feasts upon His Body and Blood. It goes on, No one sews a piece of rough that is new cloth on an old garment: else the new piece that fills it up takes away from the old, and the rent is made worse.

PSEUD-CHRYS. As if He said, because these are preachers of the New Testament, it is not possible that they should serve old laws; but you who follow old customs, fitly observe the fasts of Moses. But for these, who are about to hand down to men new and wonderful observances, it is not necessary to observe the old traditions, but to be virtuous in mind; some time or other however they will observe fasting with other Virtues. But this fasting is different from time fasting of the law, for that was one of restraint, this of goodwill; on account of the fervor of the Spirit, Whom they cannot yet receive, Wherefore it goes on, And no one puts new wine into old bottles: else the new wine does burst the bottles, and the wine is spilled, and the bottles will be marred: but new Wine must be put in new bottles.

BEDE; For He compares His disciples to old bottles, who would burst at spiritual precepts, rather than be held in restraint by them. But they will be new bottles, when after the ascension of the Lord, they are renewed by desiring His consolation, and then new wine will come to the new bottles, that is, the fervor of the Holy Ghost will fill the hearts of spiritual men. A teacher must also take heed not to commit the hidden things of new mysteries to a soul, hardened in old wickedness.

THEOPHYL. Or else the disciples are likened to old garments on account of the infirmity of their minds, on which it was not fitting to impose the heavy command of fasting.

BEDE; Neither was it fitting to sew on a new piece; that is, a portion of doctrine which teaches a general fast from all the joy of temporal delights; for if this be done, the teaching is rent, and agrees not with the old part. But by a new garment is intended good works, which are done externally, and by the new wine, is expressed the fervor of faith, hope, and charity, by which we are reformed in our minds.

23. And it came to pass, that he went through the corn fields on the sabbath day; and his disciples began, as they went, to pluck the ears of corn.

24. And the Pharisees said to him, Behold, why do they on the sabbath day that which is not lawful?

25. And he said to them, Have you never read what David did, when he had need, and was an hungered, he, and they that were with him?

26. How he went into the house of God, in the days of Abiathar the High Priest, and did eat the show-bread, which is not lawful to eat but for the priests, and gave also to them which were with him?

27. And he said to them, The sabbath was made for man, and not man for the sabbath:

28. Therefore the Son of man is Lord also of the sabbath.

PSEUD-CHRYS. The disciples of Christ, freed from the figure, and united to the truth, do not keep the figurative feast of the sabbath, wherefore it is said, And it came to pass, that he went through the corn fields on the sabbath day; and his disciples began, as they went, to pluck the ears of corn.

BEDE; We read also in the following part, that they who came and went away were many, and that they had not time enough to take their food, wherefore, according to man's nature, they were hungry.

CHRYS. But being hungry, they no ate simple food, not for pleasure, but on account of the necessity of nature. The Pharisees however, serving the figure and the shadow, accused the disciples of doing wrong. Wherefore there follows, But the Pharisees said to him, Behold, why do they on the sabbath day that which is not lawful.

AUG. For it was a precept in Israel, delivered by a written law, that no one should detain a thief found in his fields unless he tried to take something away with him. For the man, who had touched nothing else but what he had eaten, they were commanded to allow to go away free and unpunished. Wherefore the Jews accused our Lord's disciples, who were plucking the ears of corn, of breaking the sabbath, rather than of theft.

PSEUD-CHRYS. But our Lord brings forward David, to whom it once happened to eat though it was forbidden by the law, when he touched the Priest's food, that by his example, he might do away with their accusation of the disciples. For there follows, Have you never read, &c.

THEOPHYL. For David, when flying from the face of Saul, went to the Chief Priest, and ate the show-bread, and took away the sword of Goliath, which things had been offered to the Lord. But a question has been raised how the Evangelist called Abiathar at this time High Priest, when the Book of Kings calls him Abimelech.

BEDE; There is, however, no discrepancy, for both were there, when David came to ask for bread, and received it: that is to say, Abimelech, the High Priest, and Abiathar his son; but Abimelech having been slain by Saul, Abiathar fled to David, and became the Companion of all his exile afterwards. When he came to the throne, he himself also received the rank of High Priest, amid the son became of much greater excellence than the falter, and therefore was worthy to be mentioned as the High Priest, even during his father's life-time It goes on: And he said to them, the sabbath was made for man, and not man for the sabbath.

For greater is the care to be taken of the health and life of a man, than the keeping of the sabbath. Therefore the sabbath was ordered to be observed in such a way, that, if there were a necessity, he should not be guilty, who broke the sabbath-day; therefore it was not forbidden to circumcise on the sabbath, because that was a necessary work. And the Maccabees, when necessity pressed on them, fought on the Sabbath-day. Wherefore, His disciples being hungry, what was not allowed in the law became lawful through their necessity of hunger; as now, if a sick man break a fast, he is not held guilty in any way.

It goes on: Therefore the Son of man is Lord, &c. As if he said, David the king is to be excused for feeding on the food of the priests, how much more the Son of man, the true King and Priest, and Lord of the sabbath, is free from fault, for pulling ears of corn on the sabbath-day.

PSEUD-CHRYS. He calls himself properly, Lord of the sabbath, and Son of man, since being the Son of God, he deigned to be called Son of man, for the sake of men. Now the law has no

Catena Aurea: Commentary on the Gospel of St. Mark

authority over the Lawgiver and Lord, for more is allowed the king, than is appointed by the law. The law is given to the weak indeed, but not to the perfect and to those who work above what the law enjoins.

BEDE; But in a mystical sense the disciples pass through the corn fields, when the holy doctors look with the care of a pious solicitude upon those whom they have initiated in the faith, and who, it is implied, are hungering for time best of all things, the salvation of men. But to pluck the ears of corn means to snatch men away from the eager desire of earthly things. And to rub with the hands is by examples of virtue to put from the purity of their minds the concupiscence of the flesh, as men do husks.

To eat the grains is when a man, cleansed from the filth of vice by the months of preachers, is incorporated amongst the members of the Church. Again, fitly are the disciples related to have done this, walking before the face of the Lord, for it is necessary that the discourse of the doctor should come first, although the grace of visitation from on high, following it, must enlighten the heart of the hearer. And well, on the sabbath-day, for the doctors themselves in preaching labor for the hope of future rest, and teach their hearers to toil over their tasks for the sake of eternal repose.

THEOPHYL. Or else, because when they have rest from their passions, then are they made doctors to head others to virtue, plucking away from them earthly things.

BEDE; Again, if they walk through the corn fields with the Lord, who rejoice in meditating upon His sacred words. They hunger, when they desire to find in them the bread of life; and they hunger on sabbath days, as soon as their minds are in a soothing rest, and they rejoice in freedom from troubled thoughts; they pluck the ears of corn, and by rubbing, cleanse them, till they come to what is fit to eat, when by meditation they take to themselves the witness of the Scriptures, to which they arrive by reading, and discuss them continually, until they find in them the marrow of love; this refreshment of the mind is truly unpleasing to fools, but is approved by the Lord.

Mark 3

1. And he entered again into the synagogue; and there was a man there which had a withered hand.

2. And they watched him, whether he would heal him on the sabbath day; that they might accuse him.

3. And he said to the man which had the withered hand, Stand forth.

4. And he said to them, Is it lawful to do good on the sabbath days, or to do evil? to save life, or to kill? But they held their peace.

5. And when he had looked round about on them with anger, being grieved for the hardness of their hearts, he said to the man, Stretch forth your hand. And he stretched it out: and his hand was restored whole as the other.

THEOPHYL. After confounding the Jews, who had blamed His disciples, for pulling the ears of corn on the sabbath day, by the example of David, the Lord now further bringing them to the truth, works a miracle on the sabbath; showing that, if it is a pious deed to work miracles on the sabbath for the health of men, it is not wrong to do on the sabbath things necessary for the body: he says therefore, And he entered again into the synagogue; and there was a man there which had a withered hand.

And they watched him, whether he would heal him on the sabbath-day; that they might accuse him.

BEDE; For, since He had defended the breaking of the sabbath, which they objected to His disciples, by an approved example, now they wish, by watching Him, to calumniate Himself, that they might accuse Him of a transgression, if He cured on the sabbath, of cruelty or of folly, if He refused. It goes on: And he said to the man which had the withered hand, Stand in the midst.

PSEUD-CHRYS. He placed him in the midst, that they might be frightened at the sight, and on seeing him compassionate him, and lay aside their malice.

BEDE; And anticipating the calumny of the Jews, which they had prepared for Him, He accused them of violating the precepts of the law, by a wrong interpretation. Wherefore there follows: And he said to them, Is it lawful to do good on the sabbath-day, or to do evil? And this He asks, because they thought that on the sabbath they were to rest even from good works, whilst the law commands to abstain from bad, saying, You shall do no servile work therein; that is, sin: for Whosoever commits sin is the servant of sin. What He first says, to do good on the sabbath-day or to do evil, is the same as what He afterwards adds, to save a life or to lose it; that is, to cure a man or not. Not that God, Who is in the highest degree good, can be the author of perdition to us, but that His not saving is in the language of Scripture to destroy.

But if it be asked, wherefore the Lord, being about to cure time body, asked about the saving of the soul, let him understand either that in the common way of Scripture the soul is put for the man; as it is said, All the souls that came out of the loins of Jacob; or because He did those miracles for time saving of a soul, or because the healing itself of the hand signified the saving of the soul.

AUG. But someone may wonder how Matthew could have said, that they themselves asked the Lord, if it was lawful to heal on the sabbath-day; when Mark rather relates it that they were asked by our Lord, Is it lawful to do good on the sabbath-day, or to do evil? Therefore we must understand that they first asked the Lord, if it was lawful to heal on the sabbath-day, then that understanding their thoughts, and that they were seeking an opportunity to accuse Him, He placed in the middle him whom He was about to cure, and put those questions, which Mark and Luke relate. We must then suppose, that when they were silent, He propounded the parable of the sheep, and concluded, that it was lawful to do good on time sabbath-day. It goes on: But they were silent.

PSEUD-CHRYS. For they knew that He would certainly cure him. It goes on: And looking round about upon them with anger. His looking round upon them in anger, and being saddened at the blindness of their hearts, is fitting for His humanity, which He deigned to take upon Himself for us. He connects the working of the miracle with a word, which proves that the man is cured by His voice alone. It follows therefore, And he stretched it out, and his hand was restored. Answering by all these things for His disciples, and at time same time showing that His life is above the law.

BEDE; But mystically, the man with a withered hand shows the human race, dried up as to its fruitfulness in good works, but now cured by the mercy of the Lord; the hand of man, which in our first parent had been dried up when He plucked the fruit of the forbidden tree, through time grace of the Redeemer, Who stretched His guiltless hands on the tree of the cross, has been restored to health by the juices of good works. Well too was it in the synagogue that the hand was withered; for where the gift of knowledge is greater there also the danger of inexcusable guilt is greater.

PSEUDO-JEROME; Or else it means the avaricious, which, being able to give had rather receive, and love robbery rather than making gifts. And they are commanded to stretch forth their hands, that is, let him that stole steal no more, but rather let him labor, working with his hand the thing which is good, that he may have to give to him that needs.

THEOPHYL. Or, he has his right hand withered, whom does not the works which belong to the right side; for from the time that our hand is employed in forbidden deeds, from that time it is withered to the working of good. But it will be restored whenever it stands firm in virtue; wherefore Christ said, Arise, that is, from sin, and stand in the midst; that thus it may stretch itself forth neither too little or too much.

6. And the Pharisees went forth, and straightway took counsel with the Herodians against him, how they might destroy him.

7. But Jesus withdrew himself with his disciples to the sea: and a great multitude from Galilee followed him, and from Judea,

Catena Aurea: Commentary on the Gospel of St. Mark

8. And from Jerusalem, and from Judea, and from beyond Jordan; and they about Tyre and Sidon, a great multitude, when they had heard what great things He did, came to him.

9. And he spoke to his disciples, that a small ship should wait on him, because of the multitude, lest they should throng him.

10. For he had healed many; insomuch that they pressed upon him for to touch him, as many as had plagues.

11. And unclean spirits, when they saw him, fell down before him, and cried, saying, You ard the Son of God.

12. And he straitly charged them that they should not make him known.

BEDE; The Pharisees, thinking it a crime that at the word of the Lord the hand which was diseased was restored to a sound state, agreed to make a pretext of the words spoken by our Savior; wherefore it is said, And the Pharisees went forth, and straightway took counsel with the Herodians against him, how they might destroy him. As if every one amongst them did not greater things on the sabbath day, carrying food, reaching forth a cup, and whatever else is necessary for meals. Neither could He, Who said and it was done, be convicted of toiling on the sabbath day.

THEOPHYL. But the soldiers of Herod the king are called Herodians, because a certain new heresy had sprung up, which asserted that Herod was the Christ. For the prophecy of Jacob intimated, that when the princes of Judah failed, then Christ should come; because therefore in the time of Herod none of the Jewish princes remained, and he, an alien, was the sole ruler, some thought that he was the Christ, and set on foot this heresy. These, therefore, were with the Pharisees trying to kill Christ.

BEDE; Or else he calls Herodiamus the servants of Herod the Tetrarch, who on account of the hatred which their Lord had for Joimum, pursued with treachery and hate the Savior also, Whom John preached it goes on, But Jesus withdrew himself with his disciples to the sea; He fled from their treachery, because the hour of His passion had not yet come, and no place away from Jerusalem was proper for His Passion. By which also he gave an example to His disciples, when they suffer persecution in one city, to thee to another.

THEOPHYL. At the same time again, he goes away, that by quitting the ungrateful he might do good to more, for many followed him, and he healed them. For there follows, And great multitude from Galilee, &c. Syrians and Sidonians, being foreigners, receive benefit from Christ; but His kindred the Jews persecute Him: thus there is no profit in relationship, if there be not a similarity in goodness.

BEDE; For the strangers followed Him, because they saw the works of His powers, and in order to hear the words of His teaching. But the Jews, induced solely by their opinion of His powers, in a vast multitude come to hear Him, and to beg for His aiding health; wherefore there follows, And he spoke to his disciples, that they should wait, &c.

THEOPHYL. Consider then how he hid His glory, for he begs

for a little ship, lest the crowd should hurt Him, so that entering into it, he might remain unharmed. it follows, As many as had scourges, &c. But he means by scourges, diseases, for God scourges us, as a father does His children.

BEDE; Both therefore fell down before the Lord, those who had the plagues of bodily diseases, and those who were vexed by unclean spirits. The sick did this simply with the intention of obtaining health, but the demoniacs, or rather the devils within them, because under the mastery of a fear of God they were compelled not only to fall down before Him, but also to praise His majesty; wherefore it goes on, And they cried out, saying, You are the Son of God. And here we must wonder at the blindness of the Arians, who, after the glory of His resurrection, deny the Son of God, Whom the devils confess to be the Son of God, though still clothed with human flesh.

There follows, And he straitly charged them, that they should not make him known. For God said to the sinner, Why do you preach my laws? A sinner is forbidden to preach the Lord, lest any one listening to his preaching should follow him in his error, for the devil is an evil master, who always mingles false things with true, that the semblance of truth may cover the witness of fraud. But not only devils, but persons healed by Christ, and even Apostles, are ordered to be silent concerning Him before the Passion, lest by the preaching of the majesty of His Divinity, the economy of His Passion should be retarded. But allegorically, in the Lord's coming out of the synagogue, and them retiring to the sea, The prefigured the salvation of the Gentiles, to whom The deigned to come through their faith, having quitted the Jews on account of their perfidy. For the nations, driven about in divers by-paths of error, are fitly compared to the unstable sea.

Again, a great crowd from various provinces followed Him, because He has received with kindness many nations, who came to Him through the preaching of the Apostles. But the ship waiting upon the Lord in the sea is the Church, collected from amongst the nations; and He goes into it lest the crowd should throng Him, because flying from the troubled minds of carnal persons, The delights to come to those who despise the glory of this world, and to dwell within them. Further, there is a difference between thronging the Lord, and touching Him; for they throng Him, when by carnal thoughts and deeds they trouble peace, in which truth dwells; but he touches Him, who by faith and love has received Him into his heart; wherefore those who touched Him are said to have been saved.

THEOPHYL. Morally again, the Herodians, that is, persons who love the lusts of the flesh, wish to slay Christ. For the meaning of Herod is, 'of skin.' But those who quit their country, that is, a carnal mode of living, follow Christ, and their plagues are healed, that is, the sins which wound their conscience. But Jesus in us is our reason, which commands that our vessel, that is, our body, should serve Him, lest the troubles of worldly affairs should press upon our reason.

13. And he goes up into a mountain, and calls to him whom he would: and they came to him.

Catena Aurea: Commentary on the Gospel of St. Mark

14. And he ordained twelve, that they should be with him, and that he might send them forth to preach,

15. And to have power to heal sicknesses, and to cast out devils:

16. And Simon he surnamed Peter;

17. And James the son of Zebedee, and John the brother of James; and he surnamed them Boanerges, which is, The sons of thunder:

18. And Andrew, and Philip, and Bartholomew, and Matthew, and Thomas, and James the son of Alpheus, and Thaddeus, and Simon the Canaanite,

19. And Judas Iscariot, which also betrayed him.

BEDE; After having forbidden the evil Spirits to preach Him, The chose holy men, to cast out the unclean spirits, and to preach the Gospel; wherefore it is said, And he went up in to a mountain, &c.

THEOPHYL. Luke, however, says that He went up to pray, for after the showing forth of miracles He prays, teaching us that we should give thanks, when we obtain anything good, and refer it to divine grace.

PSEUD-CHRYS. The also instructs the Prelates of the Church to pass the night in prayer before they ordain, that their office be not impeded. When therefore, according to Luke, it was day, He called whom He would; for there were many who followed Him.

Collected Out of the Works of the Fathers

BEDE; For it was not a matter of their choice and zeal, but of Divine condescension and grace, that they should be called to the Apostleship. The amount also in which the Lord chose His Apostles, shows the lofty righteousness in which they were to be instructed, and which they were about to preach to men.

PSEUDO-JEROME; Or spiritually, Christ is the mount, from which living waters flow, and milk is procured for the health of infants; whence the spiritual feast of fat things is made known, and whatever is believed to be most highly good is established by time grace of that Mountain. Those therefore who are highly exalted in merits and in words are called up into a mountain, that the place may correspond to the loftiness of their merits. It goes on: And they came to him, &c. For the Lord loved the beauty of Jacob, that they might sit upon twelve thrones, judging the twelve tribes of Israel, who also is bands of threes and fours watch around the tabernacle of the Lord, and carry the holy words of the Lord, bearing them forward on their actions, as men do burdens on their shoulders.

BEDE; For as a sacrament of this the children of Israel once used to encamp about time Tabernacle, so that on each of the four sides of the square three tribes were stationed. Now three times four are twelve, and in three bands of four the Apostles were sent to preach, that through the four quarters of time whole world they might baptize the nations in the name of the Father, the Son, and the Holy Ghost.

It goes on: And he gave them power, &c. That is, in order that time greatness of their deeds might bear witness to the greatness of their heavenly promises, and that they, who preached unheard-of things, might do unheard-of actions.

THEOPHYL. Further, He gives the names of the Apostles, that the true Apostles might be known, so that men might avoid the false. And therefore it continues: And Simon he surnamed Cephas.

AUG. But let no one suppose that Simon now received his name and was called Peter, for thus he would make Mark contrary to John, who relates that it had been long before said to him, You shall be called Cephas. But Mark gives this account by way of recapitulation; for as he wished to give the names of the twelve Apostles, and was obliged to call him Peter, his object was to intimate briefly, that he was not called this originally, but that the Lord gave him that name.

BEDE; And the reason that the Lord willed that he fled should at first he called otherwise, was that from the change in itself of the name, a mystery might be conveyed to us. Peter then in Latin or in Greek means the same thing as Cephas in Hebrew, and in each language the name is drawn from a stone. Nor can it be doubted that is the rock of which Paul spoke, And this rock was Christ. For as Christ was the true light, and allowed also that the Apostles should be called the light of the world, so also to Simon, who believed on the rock Christ, He gave the name of Rock.

PSEUDO-JEROME; Thus from obedience, which Simon signifies, the ascent is made to knowledge, which is meant by Peter. It goes on: And James the son of Zebedee, and John his brother.

BEDE; We must connect this with what went before, He goes up into a mountain, and calls.

PSEUDO-JEROME; Namely, James who has supplanted all the desires of the flesh, and John, who received by grace what others held by labor. There follows: And he surnamed them, Boanerges.

PSEUD-CHRYS. The calls the sons of Zebedee by this name, because they were to spread over the world the mighty and illustrious decrees of the Godhead.

PSEUDO-JEROME; Or by this the lofty merit of the three mentioned above is shown, who merited to hear in the mountain the thunders of the Father, when he proclaimed in thunder through a cloud concerning the Son, This is my beloved Son; that they also through the cloud of the flesh and the fire of the word, might as it were scatter the thunderbolts in rain on the earth, since the Lord turned the thunderbolts into rain, so that mercy extinguishes what judgment sets on fire.

It goes on: And Andrew, who manfully does violence to perdition, so that he had ever ready within him his own death, to give as an answer, and his soul was ever in his hands.

BEDE; For Andrew is a Greek name, which means 'manly', from that is, man, for he manfully adhered to the Lord. There follows, And Philip.

PSEUDO-JEROME; Or, 'the mouth of a lamp,' that is, one who

can throw light by his mouth upon what he has conceived in his heart, to whom the Lord gave the opening of a mouth, which diffused light. We know that this mode of speaking belongs to holy Scripture; for Hebrew names are put down in order to intimate a mystery. There follows: And Bartholomew, which means, the son of him who suspends the waters; of him, that is, who said, I will also command the clouds that they rain no rain upon it. But the name of son of God is obtained by peace and loving one's enemy; for, Blessed are the peacemakers, for they are the sons of God. And, Love your enemies, that you may be the sons of God. There follows: And Matthew, that is, 'given,' to whom it is given by the Lord, not only to obtain remission of sins, but to be enrolled in the number of the Apostles. And Thomas, which means, 'abyss;' for men who have knowledge by the power of God, put forward many deep things. It goes on: And James the son of Alphaeus, that is, of 'the learned' or 'the thousandth,' beside whom a thousand will fall. This other James is he, whose wrestling is not against flesh and blood, but against spiritual wickedness. There follows, And Thaddeus, that is, 'corculum,' which means 'he who guards the heart,' one who keeps his heart in all watchfulness.

BEDE; But Thaddeus is the same person, as Luke calls in the Gospel and in the Acts, Jude of James, for he was the brother of James, the brother of the Lord, as he himself has written in his Epistle.

There follows, And Simon the Canaanite, and Judas Iscariot, who betrayed him. He has added this by way of distinction from Simon Peter, and Jude the brother of James. Simon is called the Canaanite from Cana, a village in Galilee, and Judas, Scariotes, from the village from which he had his origin, or he is so called from the tribe of Issachar.

THEOPHYL. Whom he reckons amongst the Apostles, that we may learn that God does not repel any man for wickedness, which is future, but counts him worthy on account of his present virtue.

PSEUDO-JEROME; But Simon is interpreted, 'laying aside sorrow;' for blessed are they that mourn, for they shall be comforted. And he is called Canaanite, that is, Zealot, because the zeal of the Lord ate him up. But Judas Iscariot is one who does not do away his sins by repentance. For Judas means 'boaster,' or vain-glorious. And Iscariot, 'the memory of death.' But many are the proud and vain-glorious confessors in the Church, as Simon Magus, and Arius, and other heretics, whose deathlike memory is celebrated in the Church, that it may be avoided.

19. - And they went into an house.

20. And the multitude comes together again, so that they could not so much as eat bread.

21. And when his friends heard of it, they went out to lay hold on him: for they said, He is beside himself.

22. And the Scribes which came down from Jerusalem said, He has Beelzebub, and by the prince of the devils casts he out devils.

BEDE; The Lord leads the Apostles, when they were elected,

into a house, as if admonishing them, that after having received the Apostleship, they should retire to look on their own consciences.

Wherefore it is said, And they came into a house, and the multitude came together again, so that they could not eat bread.

PSEUD-CHRYS. Ungrateful indeed were the multitudes of princes, whom their pride hinders from knowledge, but the grateful multitude of the people came to Jesus.

BEDE; And blessed indeed the concourse of the crowd, flocking together, whose anxiety to obtain salvation was so great, that they left not the Author of Salvation even an hour free to take food. But Him, whom a crowd of strangers loves to follow, his relations hold in little esteem: for it goes on: And when his friends heard of it, they went out to lay hold upon him. For since they could not take in the depth of wisdom, which they heard, they thought that He was speaking in a senseless way, wherefore it continues, for they said, he is beside himself.

THEOPHYL. That is, He has a devil and is mad, and therefore they wished to lay hold upon Him, that they might shut Him up as one who had a devil. And even His friends wished to do this, that is, His relations, perchance His countrymen, or His brethren. But it was a silly insanity in them, to conceive that the Worker of such great miracles of Divine Wisdom had become mad.

BEDE; Now there is a great difference between those who do not understand the word of God from slowness of intellect, such as those, who are here spoken of, and those who purposely blaspheme, of whom it is added, And the Scribes which came down from Jerusalem, &c. For what they could not deny, they endeavor to pervert by a malicious interpretation, as if they were not the works of God, but of a most unclean spirit, that is, of Beelzebub, who was the God of Ekron. For 'Beel' means Baal himself, and 'zebub' a fly; the meaning of Beelzebub therefore is the man of flies, on account of the filth of the blood which was offered, from which most unclean rite, they call him prince of the devils, adding, and by the prince of the devils casts he out devils.

PSEUDO-JEROME; But mystically, the house to which they came, is the early Church. The crowds which prevent their eating bread are sins and vices; for he who eats unworthily, eats and drinks damnation to himself.

BEDE; The Scribes also coming down from Jerusalem blaspheme. But the multitude from Jerusalem, and from other regions of Judea, or of the Gentiles, followed the Lord, because so it was to be at the time of His Passion, that a crowd of the people of the Jews should lead Him to Jerusalem with palms and praises, and the Gentiles should desire to see Him; but the Scribes and Pharisees should plot together for His death.

23. And he called them to him, and said to them in parables, How can Satan cast out Satan?

24. And if a kingdom be divided against itself, that kingdom cannot stand.

25. And if a house be divided against itself, that house cannot stand.

26. And if Satan rise up against himself, and be divided, he cannot stand, but has an end.

27. No man can enter into a strong man's house, and spoil his goods, except he will first bind the strong man; and then he will spoil his house.

28. Verily I say to you, All sins shall be forgiven to the sons of men, and blasphemies wherewith soever they shall blaspheme:

29. But he that shall blaspheme against the Holy Ghost has never forgiveness, but is in danger of eternal damnation:

30. Because they said, He has an unclean spirit.

PSEUD-CHRYS. The blasphemy of the Scribes having been detailed, our Lord shows that what they said was impossible confirming His proof by an example. Wherefore it says And having called them together to him, He said to them in parables, How can Satan, cast out Satan?

As if He had said, A kingdom divided against itself by civil war must be desolated, which is exemplified both

in a house and in a city. Wherefore also if Satan's kingdom be divided against itself, so that Satan expels Satan from men, the desolation of the kingdom of the devils is at hand. But their kingdom consists in keeping men under their dominion. If therefore they are driven away from men, it amounts to nothing less than the dissolution of their kingdom. But if they still hold their power over men, it is manifest that the kingdom of evil is still standing, and Satan is not divided against himself.

GLOSS. And because He has already shown by an example that a devil cannot cast out a devil, He shows how he can be expelled, saying,

No man can enter into a strong man's house, &c.

THEOPHYL. The meaning of the example is this: The devil is the strong man; his goods are the men into whom he is received; unless therefore a man first conquers the devil, how can he deprive him of his goods, that is, of the men whom he has possessed? So also I who spoil his goods, that is, free men from suffering by his possession, first spoil the devils and vanquish them, and am their enemy. How then can you say that I have Beelzebub, and that being the friend of the devils, I cast them out?

BEDE; The Lord has also bound the strong man, that is, the devil: which means, he has restrained him from seducing the elect, and entering into his house, the world; The has spoiled his house , and his goods, that is men, because He has snatched them from the snares of the devil, and has united them to His Church. Or, He has spoiled his house, because the four parts of the world, over which the old enemy had sway, He has distributed to the Apostles and their successors, that they may convert the people to the way of life.

But the Lord shows that they committed a great sin, in crying out that that which they knew to be of God, was of the devil, when

He subjoins, Verily I say to you, All sins are forgiven, &c. All sins and blasphemies are not indeed remitted to all men, but to those who have gone through a repentance in this life sufficient for their sins; thus neither is Novatus right, who denied that any pardon should be granted to penitents, who had lapsed in time of martyrdom; nor Origen, who asserts that after the general judgment, after the revolution of ages, all sinners will receive pardon for their sins, which error the following words of the Lord condemn, when He adds, But he that shall blaspheme against the Holy Ghost, &c.

PSEUD-CHRYS. He says indeed, that blasphemy concerning Himself was pardonable, because He then seemed to be a man despised and of the most lowly birth, but, that contumely against God has no remission. Now blasphemy against the Holy Ghost is against God, for the operation of the Holy Ghost is the kingdom of God; and for this reason, He says, that blasphemy against the Holy Ghost cannot be remitted. Instead, however, of what is here added, But will be in danger of eternal damnation, another Evangelist says, Neither in this world, nor in the world to come. By which is understood, the judgment which is according to the law, and that which is to come. For the law orders one who blasphemes God to be slain, and in the judgment of the second law he has no remission. However, he who is baptized is taken out of this world; but the Jews were ignorant of the remission which takes place in baptism. He therefore who refers to the devil miracles, and the casting out of devils which belong to the Holy Ghost alone, has no room left him for remission of his blasphemy.

Neither does it appear that such a blasphemy as this is remitted, since it is against the Holy Ghost. Wherefore he adds, explaining it, Because they said, He has an unclean spirit.

THEOPHYL. We must however understand, that they will not obtain pardon unless they repent. But since it was at the flesh of Christ that they were offended, even though they did not repent, some excuse was allowed them, and they obtained some remission.

PSEUDO-JEROME; Or this is meant; that he will not deserve to work out repentance, so as to be accepted, who, understanding who Christ was, declared that He was the prince of the devils.

BEDE; Neither however are those, who do not believe the Holy Spirit to be God, guilty of an unpardonable blasphemy, because they were persuaded to do this by human ignorance, not by devilish malice.

AUG. Or else impenitence itself is the blasphemy against the Holy Ghost which has no remission. For either in his thought or by his tongue, he speaks a word against the Holy Ghost, the forgiver of sins, who treasures up for himself an impenitent heart. But He subjoins, Because they said, He has an unclean spirit, that he might show that His reason for saying it, was their declaring that He cast out a devil by Beelzebub, not because there is a blasphemy, which cannot be remitted, since even this might be remitted through a right repentance; but the cause why this sentence was put forth by the Lord, after mentioning the unclean spirit, (who as our Lord shows was divided against himself,) was, that the Holy Ghost even makes those whom He brings together undivided, by His remitting those sins, which divided them from Himself, which gift of remission is resisted by no one, but him who has the hardiness of an impenitent heart. For in another place, the Jews said of the Lord, that He had a devil, without however His saying anything there about the blasphemy against the Spirit; and the reason is, that they did not there cast in His teeth the unclean spirit, in such a way, that that spirit could by their own words be shown to be divided against Himself, as Beelzebub was here shown to be, by their saying, that it might be he who cast out devils.

31. There came then his brethren and his mother, and, standing without, sent to him, calling him.

32. And the multitude sat about him, and they said to him, Behold, your mother and your brethren without seek for you.

33. And he answered them, saying, Who is my mother, or my brethren?

34. And he looked round about on them which sat about him, and said, Behold my mother and my brethren!

35. For whoever shall do the will of God, the same is my brother, and my sister, and mother.

THEOPHYL. Because the relations of the Lord had come to seize upon Him, as if beside Himself, His mother, urged by the sympathy of her love, came to Him; wherefore it is said, And there came to him his mother, and, standing without, sent to him, calling him.

CHRYS. From this it is manifest that His brethren and His mother were not always with Him; but because He was beloved by them, they come from reverence and affection, waiting without. Wherefore it goes on, And the multitude sat about him, &c.

BEDE; The brothers of the Lord must not be thought to be the sons of the ever-virgin Mary, as Helvidius says, nor the sons of Joseph by a former marriage, as some think, but rather they must be understood to be His relations.

PSEUD-CHRYS. But another Evangelist says, that His brethren did not believe on Him. With which this agrees, which says, that they sought Him, waiting without, and with this meaning the Lord does not mention them as relations. Wherefore it follows, And he answered them, saying, Who is my mother. or my brethren? But He does not here mention His mother and His brethren altogether with reproof, but to show that a man must honor his own soul above all earthly kindred; wherefore this is fitly said to those who called Him to speak with His mother and relations, as if it were a more useful task than the teaching of salvation.

BEDE; Being asked therefore by a message to go out, He declines, not as though He refused the dutiful service of His mother, but to show that He owes more to His Father's mysteries than to His mother's feelings. Nor does He rudely despise His brothers, but, preferring His spiritual work to fleshly relationship, He teaches us that religion is the bond of the heart rather than that of the body. Wherefore it goes on, And looking round about on them which sat about him, he said, Behold my mother and my brethren.

CHRYS. By this, the Lord shows that we should honor those who are relations by faith rather than those who are relations by blood. A man indeed is made the mother of Jesus by preaching Him; for He, as it were, brings forth the Lord, when he pours Him into the heart of his hearers.

PSEUDO-JEROME; But let us be assured that we are His brethren and This sisters, if we do the will of the Father; that we may be joint-heirs with Him, for He discerns us not by sex but by our deeds. Wherefore it goes on: Whoever shall do the will of God, &c.

THEOPHYL. The does not therefore say this, as denying His mother, but as showing that He is worthy of honor, not only because she bore Christ, but on account of her possessing every other virtue.

BEDE; But mystically, the mother and brother of Jesus means the synagogue, (from which according to the flesh He sprung,) and the Jewish people who, while the Savior is teaching within, come to Him, and are not able to enter, because they cannot understand spiritual things. But the crowd eagerly enter, because when the Jews delayed, the Gentiles flocked to Christ; but His kindred, who stand without wishing to see the Lord, are the Jews who obstinately remained without, guarding the letter, and would rather compel the Lord to go forth to them to teach carnal things, than consent to enter in to learn spiritual things of Him. If therefore not even His parents when standing without are acknowledged, how shall we be acknowledged, if we stand without? For the word is within and the light within.

Mark 4

1. And he began again to teach by the sea side: and there was gathered to him a great multitude, so that he entered into a ship, and sat in the sea; and the whole multitude was by the sea on the land.

2. And he taught them many things by parables, and said to them in his doctrine,

3. Hearken; Behold, there went out a sower to sow:

4. And it came to pass, as he sowed, some fell by the way side, and the fowls of the air came and devoured it up.

5. And some fell on stony ground, where it had not much earth; and immediately it sprang up, because it had no depth of earth.

6. But when the sun was up, it was scorched; and because it had no root, it withered away.

7. And some fell among thorns, and the thorns grew up, and choked it, and it yielded no fruit.

8. And other fell on good ground, and did yield fruit that sprang up and increased; and brought forth, some thirty, and some sixty, and some an hundred.

9. And he said to them, He that has ears to hear, let him

hear.

10. And when he was alone, they that were about him with the twelve asked of him the parable.

11. And he said to them, to you it is given to know the mystery of the kingdom of God: but to them that are without, all these things are done in parables:

12. That seeing they may see, and not perceive; and hearing they may hear, and not understand; lest at any time they should he converted, and their sins should be forgiven them.

13. And he said to them, Know you not this parable? and how then will you know an parables?

14. The sower sows the word.

15. And these are they by the way side, where the word is sown; but when they have heard, Satan comes immediately, and takes away the word that was sown in their hearts.

16. And these are they likewise which are sown on stony ground; who, when they have heard the word, immediately receive it with gladness;

17. And have no root in themselves, and so endure but for a time: afterward, when affliction or persecution arises for the word's sake, immediately they are offended.

18. And these are they which are sown among thorns; such as hear the word,

19. And the cares of this world, and the deceitfulness of riches, and the lusts of other things entering in, choke the word, and it becomes unfruitful.

20. And these are they which are sown on good ground; such as hear the word, and receive it, and bring forth fruit, some thirty-fold, some sixty, and some an hundred.

THEOPHYL. Although the Lord appears in the transactions mentioned above to neglect His mother, nevertheless He honors her; since on her account He goes forth about the borders of the sea: wherefore it is said, And Jesus began to teach again by the sea-side, &c.

BEDE; For if we look into the Gospel of Matthew, it appears that this same teaching of the Lord at the sea, was delivered on the same day as the former. For after the conclusion of the first sermon, Matthew immediately subjoins, saying, The same day went Jesus out of the house, and sat by the sea-side.

PSEUDO-JEROME; But He began to teach at the sea, that the place of His teaching might point out the bitter feelings and instability of His hearers.

BEDE; After leaving the house also, He began to teach at the sea, because, quitting the synagogue, He came to gather together the multitude of the Gentile people by the Apostles. Wherefore it continues: And there was gathered to him a great multitude, so that he entered into a ship, and sat in the sea.

CHRYS. Which we must understand was not done without a purpose, but that He might not leave anyone behind Him, but have all His hearers before His face.

BEDE; Now this ship showed in a figure the Church, to be built in the midst of the nations, in which the Lord consecrates fir Himself a beloved dwelling-place. It goes on: And he taught them many things by parables.

PSEUDO-JEROME; A parable is a comparison made between things discordant by nature, under some similitude. For parable is the Greek for a similitude, when we point out by some comparisons what we would have understood. In this way we say an iron man, when we desire that he should be understood to be hardy and strong; when to be swift, we compare him to winds and birds. But He speaks to the multitudes in parables, with His usual providence, that those who could not take in heavenly things, might conceive what they heard by an earthly similitude.

CHRYS. For He rouses the minds of His hearers by a parable, pointing out objects to the sight, to make His discourse more manifest.

THEOPHYL. And in order to rouse the attention of those

who heard, the first parable that He proposes is concerning the seed, which is the word of God. Wherefore it goes on, And he said to them in his doctrine. Not in that of Moses, nor of the Prophets, because He preaches His own Gospel. Hearken: behold, there went out a sower to sow. Now the Sower is Christ.

CHRYS. Not that He went out in space, Who is present in all space, and fills all, but in the form and economy by which He is made more near to us through the clothing of flesh. For since we were not able to go to Him, because sins impeded our path, He went out to us. But He went out, preaching in order to sow the worth of piety, which He spoke abundantly. Now He does not needlessly repeat the same word, when He says, A sower went out to sow, for sometimes a sower goes out that he may break up land for tillage, or to pull up weeds, or for some other work. But this one went out to sow.

BEDE; Or else, He went out to sow, when after calling to His faith the elect portion of the synagogue, He poured out the gifts of His grace in order to call the Gentiles also.

CHRYS. Further, as a sower does not make a distinction in the ground which is beneath him, but simply and without distinction puts in the seed, so also He Himself addresses all. And to signify this, The says, And as he sowed, come fell by the way-side.

THEOPHYL. Take notice, that He says not that He threw it in the way, but that it fell, for a sower, as far as he can, throws it into good ground, but if the ground be bad, it corrupts the seed. Now the way is Christ; but infidels are by the way-side, that is, out of Christ.

BEDE; Or else, the way is a mind which is a path for bad thoughts, preventing the seed of the word from growing in it. And therefore whatever good seed comes in contact with such a way, perishes, and is carried off by devils. Wherefore there follows, And the fowls of the air came and devoured it up. And well are the devils called fowls of the air, either because they are of a heavenly and spiritual origin, or because they dwell in the air. Or else, those who are about the way are negligent and slothful men. It goes on: And some fell on stony ground. He calls stone, the hardness of a wanton mind; He calls ground, the inconstancy of a soul in its obedience; and sun, the heat of a raging persecution.

Therefore the depth of earth, which ought to have received the seed of God, is the honesty of a mind trained in heavenly discipline, and regularly brought up in obedience to the Divine words. But the stony places, which have no strength for fixing the root firmly, are those breasts which are delighted only with the sweetness of the word which they hear, and for a time with the heavenly promises, but in a season of temptation fall away, for there is too little of healthful desire in them to conceive the seed of life.

THEOPHYL. Or, the stony persons are those who adhering a little to the rock, that is, to Christ, up to a short time, receive the word, and afterwards, falling back, cast it away. It goes on: And some fell among thorns; by which are marked souls which care for many things. For thorns are cares.

CHRYS. But further He mentions good ground, saying, And other fell on good ground. For the difference of the fruits follows the quality of the ground. But great is the love of the Sower for men, for the first He commends, and rejects not the second, and gives a place to the third.

THEOPHYL. Sec also how the bad are the greatest number, and the few are those who are saved, for the fourth part of the ground is found to be saved.

CHRYS. This, however, the greater portion of the seed is not lost through the fault of the owner, but of the earth, which received it, that is, of the soul, which hears. And indeed the real husbandman, if he sowed in this way, would be rightly blamed; for he is not ignorant that rock, or the road, or thorny ground, cannot become fertile. But in spiritual things it is not so; for there it is possible that stony ground may become fertile; and that the road should not be trodden down, and that the thorns may be destroyed, for if this could not take place, he would not have sown there. By this therefore He gives to us hope of repentance. It goes on, And he said to them, He that has ears to hear, let him hear.

BEDE; As often as this is inserted in the Gospel or in the Apocalypse of John, that which is spoken is mystical, and is pointed out as healthful to be heard and learnt. For the ears by which they are heard belong to the heart, and the ears by which men obey and do what is commanded, are those of an interior sense. There follows, And when he was alone, the twelve that were with him asked of him the parable; and he said to them,

To you it is given to know the mystery of the kingdom of God, but to them that are without all things are done in parables.

PSEUD-CHRYS. As if He said to them, You that are worthy to be taught all things which are fitted for teaching, shall learn the manifestation of parables; but I use parables with them who are unworthy to learn, because of their wickedness. For it was right that they who did not hold fast their obedience to that law which they had received, should not have any share in a new teaching, but should be estranged from both; for He showed by the obedience of His disciples, that, on the other hand, the others were become unworthy of mystical doctrine. But afterwards, by bringing in a voice from prophecy, He confounds their wickedness, as having been long before reproved; wherefore it goes on, that seeing they might see, and not perceive, &c. as if He said, that the prophecy might be fulfilled which foretells these things.

THEOPHYL. For it was God Who made them to see, that is, to understand what is good. But they themselves see not, of their own will making themselves not to see, lest they should be converted and correct themselves, as if they were displeased at their own salvation. It goes on, Lest at any time they should be converted, and their sins be forgiven them.

PSEUD-CHRYS. Thus, therefore, they see and they do not see, they hear and do not understand, for their seeing and hearing comes to them from God's grace, but their seeing and not understanding comes to them from their willingness to receive grace, and closing their eyes, and pretending that they could not see; neither do they acquiesce in what was said, and so are not changed as to their sins by hearing and seeing, but rather are made worse.

THEOPHYL. Or we may understand in a different way His speaking to the rest in parables, that seeing they might not perceive, and hearing, not understand. For God gives sight and understanding to men who seek for them, but the rest He blinds, lest it become a greater accusation against them, that though they understood, they did not choose to do what they ought. Wherefore it goes on, Lest at any time they should be, &c.

AUG. Or else they deserved this, their not understanding., and yet this in itself was done in mercy to them, that they might know their sins, and, being converted, merit pardon.

BEDE; To those then who are without, all things are done in parables, that is, both the actions and the words of the

Savior because neither in those miracles which He was working, nor in those mysteries which He preached, were they able to acknowledge Him as God. Therefore they are not able to attain to the remission of their sins.

PSEUD-CHRYS. But His speaking to them only in parables, and yet not leaving off speaking to them entirely, shows that to those who are placed near to what is good, though they may have no good in themselves, still good is shown disguised. But when a man approaches it with reverence and a right heart, he wins for himself an abundant revelation of mysteries; when on the contrary his thoughts are not sound, he will he neither made worthy of those things which are easy to many men, nor even of hearing them. There follows, And he said to them, Know you not this parable, how then shall you know all parables?

PSEUSDO-JEROME; For it was necessary that they to whom h ho spoke in parables should ask for what they do not understand, and learn by the Apostle whom they despised, the mystery of the kingdom which they themselves had not.

GLOSS. And for this reason, the Lord in saying these things, shows that they ought to understand both this first, and all following miracles. Wherefore explaining it, He goes on, The sower sows the word.

CHRYS. And indeed the prophet has compared the teaching of the people to the planting of a vine; in this place however it is compared to sowing, to show that obedience is now shorter and more easy, and will sooner yield fruit.

BEDE; But in this exposition of the Lord there is embraced the whole range of those who might hear the words of truth, but are unable to attain to salvation. For there are some to whom no faith, no intellect, nay no opportunity of trying its usefulness, can give a perception of the word which they hear; of whom He says, And these are by the wayside. For unclean spirits take away at once the word committed to their hearts, as birds carry away the seed of the trodden way.

There are some who both experience its usefulness and feel a desire for it, but some of them the calamities of this world frighten, and others its prosperity allures, so that they do not attain to that which they approve.

Of the first of whom He says, And these are they who fell on stony ground; of the latter, And these are they which are sown among thorns. But riches are called thorns, because they tear the soul with the piercing of its own thoughts, and after bringing it to sin, they, as one may say, make it bleed by inflicting a wound.

Again He says, And the toil of this world, and the deceitfulness of riches; for the man who is deceived by an empty desire of riches must soon he afflicted by the toils of continual cares. He adds, And the lusts of other things; because, whoever despises the commandments of God, and wanders away lustfully seeking other things, is unable to attain to the joy of beatitude. And concupiscences of this sort choke the word, because they do not allow a good desire to enter into the heart, and, as it were, stifle the entrance of vital breath. There are, however, excepted from these different classes of men, the Gentiles who do not even have grace to hear the words of life.

THEOPHYL. Further, of those who receive the seed as they ought there are three degrees. Wherefore it goes on, And these are they who are sown on good ground. Those who bear fruit an hundred-fold are those who lead a perfect and an obedient life, as virgins and hermits. Those who bear fruit sixty-fold are those who are in the mean as continent persons and those who are living in convents. Those who bear thirty-fold are those who though weak indeed, bear fruit according to their own virtue, as laymen and married persons.

BEDE; Or he bears thirty-fold, who instills into the minds of the elect faith in the Holy Trinity; sixty-fold, who teaches the perfection of good works; a hundred-fold, who shows the rewards of the heavenly kingdom. For in counting a hundred, we pass on to the fight hand; therefore that number is fitly made to signify everlasting happiness. But the good ground is the conscience of the elect, which does the contrary to all the former three, which both receives with willingness the seed of the word committed to it, and keeps it when received up to the season of fruit.

PSEUDO-JEROME; Or else the fruits of the earth are contained in thirty, sixty, and a hundred-fold, that is, in the Law, the Prophets, and the Gospel.

21. And he said to them, Is a candle brought to be put under a bushel, or under a bed? and not to be set on a candlestick?

22. For there is nothing hid, which shall not be manifested; neither was any thing kept secret, but that it should come abroad.

23. If any man have ears to hear, let him hear.

24. And he said to them, Take heed what you hear: with what measure you mete, it shall be measured to you: and to you that hear shall more be given.

25. For he that has, to him shall be given: and he that has not, from him shall be taken even that which he has.

CHRYS. After the question of the disciples concerning the parable, and its explanation, He well subjoins, And he said to them, Is a candle brought, &c. As if he said, A parable is given, not that it should remain obscure, and hidden as if under a bed or a bushel, but that it should be manifested to those who are worthy. The candle within us is that of our intellectual nature, and it shines either clearly or obscurely according to the proportion of our illumination. For if meditations which feed the light, and the recollection with which such a light is kindled, are neglected, it is presently extinguished.

PSEUDO-JEROME; Or else the candle is the discourse concerning the three sorts of seed. The bushel or the bed is the hearing of the disobedient. The Apostles are the candlestick, whom the word of the Lord has enlightened; wherefore it goes on, For there is nothing hidden, &c. The hidden and secret thing is the parable of the seed, which comes forth to light, when it is spoken of by the Lord.

THEOPHYL. Or else the Lord warns His disciples to be as light, in their life and conversation; as if He said, As a candle is put so as to give light, so all will look to your life. Therefore be diligent to lead a good life; sit not in corners, but be you a candle. For a candle gives light, not when placed under a bed, but on a candlestick; this light indeed must be placed on a candlestick, that is, on the eminence of a godly life, that it may be able to give light to others. Not under a bushel, that is, in things pertaining to the palate, nor under a bed, that is, in idleness. For no one who seeks after the delights of his palate and loves rest can be a light shining over all.

BEDE; Or, because the time of our life is contained under a certain measurement of Divine Providence, it is rightly compared to a bushel. But the bed of the soul is the body, in which it dwells and reposes for a time. He therefore who hides the word of God under the love of this transitory life, and of carnal allurements, covers his candle with a bushel or a bed. But be puts his light on a candlestick, who employs his body in the ministry of the word of God; therefore under these words He typically teaches them a figure of preaching. Wherefore it goes on, For there is nothing hidden, which shall not be revealed, nor is there any thing made secret, which shall not come abroad. As if He said, Be not afraid of the Gospel, but amidst the darkness of persecution raise the light of the word of God upon the candlestick of your body, keeping fixedly in your mind that day, when the Lord will throw light upon the hidden places of darkness, for then everlasting praise awaits you, and everlasting punishment your adversaries.

CHRYS. Or else, There is nothing hid; as if He said, If you conduct your life with care, accusation will not be aide to obscure your light.

THEOPHYL. For each of us, whether he have done good or evil, is brought to light in this life, much more in that which is to come. For what can be more hidden than God, nevertheless He Himself is manifested in the flesh. It continues, If any man have ears to ear, let him hear.

BEDE; That is, if any man have a sense for understanding. the word of God, let him not withdraw himself, let him not turn his ear to fables, but let him lend his ear to search those things which truth has spoken, his hands for fulfilling them, his tongue for preaching them. There follows, And he said to them, Take heed what you hear.

THEOPHYL. That is, that none of those things which are said to you by me should escape you. With what measure you mete, it shall be measured to you, that is, whatsoever degree of application you bring, in that degree you will receive profit.

BEDE; Or else, If you diligently endeavor to do all the good which you can, and to teach it to your neighbors, the mercy of God will come in, to give you both in the present life a sense to take in higher things, and a will to do better things, and will add for the future an everlasting reward. And therefore it is subjoined, And to you shall more be given.

PSUEDO-JEROME; According. to the measure of his faith the understanding of mysteries is divided to every man, and the virtues of knowledge will also be added to them. It goes on: For he that has, to him shall be given; that is, he who has faith shall have virtue, and he who has obedience to the word, shall also have the understanding of the mystery. Again, he who, on the other hand, has not faith, fails in virtue; and he who has not obedience to the word, shall not have the understanding of it; and if he does not understand he might as well not have heard.

PSEUD-CHRYS Or else, he who has the desire and wish to hear and to seek, to him shall be given. But be who has not the desire of hearing. divine things even what he happens to have of the written law is taken from him.

BEDE; For sometimes a clever reader by neglecting his mind, deprives himself of wisdom, of which he tastes the sweetness, who, though slow in intellect, works more diligently.

CHRYS. Again it may be said, that he has not, who has not truth. But our Lord says that he has, because he has a lie, for every one whose understanding believes a lie, thinks that he has something.

26. And he said, So is the kingdom of God, as if a man should cast seed into the ground;

27. And should sleep, and rise night and day, and the seed should spring and grow up, he knows not how.

28. For the earth brings forth fruit of herself; first the blade, then the ear, after that the full corn in the ear.

29. But when the fruit is brought forth, immediately he puts in the sickle, because the harvest is come.

PSEUD-CHRYS. A parable occurred, a little above, about the three seeds which perished in various ways, and the one which was saved; in which last He also shows three differences, according to the proportion of faith and practice Here however, He puts forth a parable concerning those only who are saved. Wherefore it is said, And he said, So is the kingdom of God, as if a man should cast seed into the ground, &c.

PSEUDO-JEROME; The kingdom of God is the Church which is ruled by God, and herself rules over men, amid treads down the powers which are contrary to her, and all wickedness.

PSEUD-CHRYS. Or else He calls by the name of kingdom of God, faith in Him, and in the economy of His Incarnation; which kingdom indeed is as if a man should throw seed. For He Himself being God and the Son of God, having without change been made man, has cast seed upon time earth, that is, He has enlightened the whole world by the word of divine knowledge.

PSEUDO-JEROME; For the seed is the word of life, the ground is the human heart, and the sleep of the man means the death of the Savior. The seed springs up night and day, because after the sleep of Christ, the number of Christians, through calamity and prosperity, continued to flourish more and more in faith, and to wax greater in deed.

PSEUD-CHRYS. Or Christ himself is the man who rises, for He sat waiting with patience, that they who received seed should bear fruit. He rises, that is, by, the word of His love, He makes us grow to the bringing forth fruit, by the armor of righteousness on the right hand, by which is meant the day, and on the left, by which is meant the night of persecution; for by these the seed springs up and does not wither.

THEOPHYL. Or else Christ sleeps, that is, ascends into

heaven, where, though He seem to sleep, yet He rises by night, when through temptations He raises us up to the knowledge of Himself; and in the day time, when on account of our prayers, He sets in order our salvation.

PSEUDO-JEROME; But when He says, He knows not how, He is speaking in a figure; that is, He does not make known to us, who amongst us will produce fruit to the end.

PSEUD-CHRYS. Or else He says, He knows not, that He may show free-will of those who receive the word, for He commits a work to our will, and does not work the whole Himself alone, lest the good should seem involuntary. For the earth brings forth fruits of its own accord, that is, she is brought to hear fruit without being compelled by a necessity contrary to inner will. First the blade.

PSEUDO-JEROME; That is, fear. For the fear of God is the beginning of wisdom. Then the full corn in the ear; that is, charity, for charity is the fulfilling of the Law.

PSEUD-CHRYS. Or, first it produces the blade, in the law of nature, by degrees growing up to advancement; afterwards it brings forth the ears, which are to be collected into a bundle, and to be offered on an altar to the Lord, that is, in the law of Moses; afterwards the full-fruit, in the Gospel. Or because we must not only put forth leaves by obedience, but also learn prudence, and, like the stalk of corn, remain upright without minding the winds which blow us about. We must also take heed to our soul by a diligent recollection, that, like the ears, we may bear fruit, that is, show forth the perfect operation of virtue.

THEOPHYL. For we put forth the blade, when we show a principle of good; then the ear, when we can resist temptations; then comes the fruit, when a man works something perfect. It goes on: and when it has brought forth the fruit, immediately he sends the sickle, because the harvest is come.

PSEUDO-JEROME; The sickle is death or the judgment, which cuts down all things; the harvest is the end of the world.

GREGORY; Or else; Man casts seed to the ground, when he places a good intention in his heart; and he sleeps, when he already rests in the hope which attends on a good work. But he rises night and day because he advances amidst prosperity and adversity, though he knows it not for he is as yet unable to measure his increase, and yet virtue, once conceived, goes on increasing. When therefore we conceive good desires, we put seed into the ground; when we begin to work rightly, we are the blade. When we increase to the perfection of good works, we arrive at the ear; when we are firmly fixed in the perfection of the same working, we already put forth the full corn in the ear.

30. And he said, Whereto shall we liken the kingdom of God? or with what comparison shall we compare it?

31. It is like a grain of mustard seed, which, when it is sown in the earth, is less than all the seeds that be in the earth:

32. But when it is sown, it grows up, and becomes greater than all herbs, and shoots out great branches; so that the fowls of the air may lodge under the shadow of it.

33. And with many such parables spoke he the word to them, as they were able to hear it.

34. But without a parable spoke he not to them: and when they were alone, he expounded all things to his disciples.

GLOSS. After having narrated the parable concerning the coming forth of the fruit from the seed of the Gospel, he here subjoins another parable, to show the excellence of the doctrine of the Gospel before all other doctrines. Wherefore it is said, And he said, Whereto shall liken the kingdom of God?

THEOPHYL. Most brief indeed is the word of faith; Believe in God, and you shall he saved. But the preaching of it has been spread far and wide over the earth, and increased so, that time birds of heaven, that is, contemplative men, sublime in understanding and knowledge, dwell under it. For how many wise men among the Gentiles, quitting their wisdom, have found rest in the preaching of the Gospel! Its preaching then is greater than all.

CHRYS. And also because the wisdom spoken amongst the perfect expands, to a extent greater than all other sayings, that which was told to men in short discourses, for there is nothing greater than this truth.

THEOPHYL. Again, it put forth great boughs, for the Apostles were divided off as the boughs of a tree, some to Rome, some to India, some to other parts of the world

PSEUDO-JEROME; Or else, that seed is very, small in fear, but great when it has grown into charity, which is greater than all herbs; for God is love, whilst all flesh is grass. But the boughs which it puts forth are those of mercy and compassion, since under its shade the poor of Christ, who are meant by the living creatures of the heavens, delight to dwell.

BEDE; Again, the man who sows is by many taken to mean the Savior Himself, by others, man himself sowing in his own heart.

CHRYS. Then after this, Mark, who delights in brevity, to show the nature of the parables, subjoins, And with many such parables spoke he the word to them as they could hear him.

THEOPHYL. For since the multitude was unlearned, he instructs them from objects of food and familiar names, and for this reason he adds, But without a parable spoke he not to them, that is, in order that they might be induced to approach and to ask Him. It goes on And when they were alone, he expounded all things to his disciples, that is, all things about which they were ignorant and asked Him, not simply all, whether obscure or not.

PSEUDO-JEROME; For they were worthy to hear mysteries apart, in the most secret haunt of wisdom, for they were men, who, removed from the crowds of evil thoughts, remained in the solitude of virtue; and wisdom is received in a time of quiet.

35. And the same day, when the even was come, he said to them, Let us pass over to the other side.

36. And when they had sent away the multitude, they took him even as he was in the ship. And there were also with him other little ships.

37. And there arose a great storm of wind, and the waves beat into the ship, so that it was now full.

38. And he was in the hinder part of the ship, asleep on a pillow: and they awake him, and say to him, Master, care you not that we perish?

39. And he arose, and rebuked the wind, and said to the sea, Peace, be still. And the wind ceased, and there was a great calm.

40. And he said to them, Why are you so fearful? how is

it that you have no faith?

41. And they feared exceedingly, and said one to another, What manner of man is this, that even the wind and the sea obey him?

PSEUDO-JEROME; After His teaching, they come from that place to the sea, and are tossed by the waves. Wherefore it is said, And the same day, when the even was come, &c.

REMIG. For the Lord is said to have had three places of refuge, namely, the ship, the mountain, and the desert. As often as He was pressed upon by the multitude, he used to fly to one of these. When therefore the Lord saw many crowds about Him, as man, He wished to avoid their importunity, and ordered His disciples to go over to the other side. There follows: And sending away the multitudes, they took him, &c.

CHRYS. The Lord took the disciples indeed, that they might be spectators of the miracle which was coining, but He took them alone, that no others might see that they were of such little faith. Wherefore, to show that others went across separately, it is said, And there were also with him other ships. best again the disciples might be proud of being alone taken, He permits them to be in danger; and besides this, in order that they might learn to bear temptations manfully.

Wherefore it goes on, And there arose a great storm of

wind; and that He might impress upon them a greater sense of the miracle which was to be done, He gives time for their fear, by sleeping.

Wherefore there follows, And he was himself in the hinder part of the ship, &c. For if He had been awake, they would either not have feared, nor have asked Him to save them when the storm arose, or they would not have thought that He could do any such things.

THEOPHYL. Therefore He allowed them to fall into the fear of danger, that they might experience His power in themselves, who saw others benefited by Him. But He was sleeping upon the pillow of the ship, that is, on a wooden one.

CHRYS. Showing His humility, and thus teaching us many lessons of wisdom. But not yet did the disciples who remained about Him know His glory; they thought indeed that if He arose He could command the winds, but could by no means do so reposing or asleep. And therefore there follows, And they awake him, and say to him, Master, care you not that we perish?

THEOPHYL. But He arising, rebukes first the wind, which was raising the tempest of the sea, and causing the waves to swell, and this is expressed in what follows, And he arose, and rebuked the wind; then He commands the sea; wherefore it goes on, And he said to the sea, Peace, be still.

GLOSS. For from the troubling of the sea there arises a certain sound, which appears to be its voice threatening danger, and therefore, by a sort of metaphor, He fitly commands tranquillity by a word signifying silence: just as in the restraining of the winds, which trouble the sea with their violence, He uses a rebuke. For men who are in power are accustomed to curb those, who rudely disturb the peace of mankind, by threatening to punish them; by this, therefore, we are given to understand, that, as a king can repress violent men by threats, and by his edicts soothe the murmurs of his people, so Christ, the king of all creatures, by His threats restrained the violence of the winds, and compelled the sea to be silent. And immediately the effect followed, for it continues, And the wind ceased, which He had threatened, and there arose a great calm, that is, in the sea, to which He had commanded silence.

THEOPHYL. He rebuked His disciples, for not having faith; for it goes on, And he said to them, Why are you so fearful? How is it that you have not faith? For if they had had faith, they would have believed that even when sleeping, The could preserve them safe.

There follows, And they feared with a great fear, and said one to another, &c. For they were in doubt about Him, for since He stilled the sea, not with a rod like Moses, nor with prayers as Elisha at the Jordan, nor with the ark as Joshua, the son of Nun, on this account they thought Him truly God, but since He was asleep they thought Him a man.

PSEUDO-JEROME; Mystically, however, the hinder part of the ship is the beginning of the Church, in which the Lord sleeps in the body only for He never sleeps who keeps Israel for the ship with its skins of dead animals keeps in the living, and keeps out the waves, and is bound together by wood, that is, by the cross and the death of the Lord the Church is saved. The pillow is the body of the Lord, on which His Divinity, which is as His head, has come down. But the wind and the sea are devils and persecutors, to whom He says Peace, when he restrains the edicts of impious kings, as He will. The great calm is the peace of the Church after oppression, or a contemplative after an active life.

BEDE; Or else the ship into which He embarked, is taken to mean the tree of His passion, by which the faithful attain to the security of the safe shore. The other ships which are said to have been with the Lord, signify those who are imbued with faith in the cross of Christ, and are not beaten about by the whirlwind of tribulation, or who after the storms of temptation, are enjoying the security of peace. And whilst His disciples are sailing on, Christ is asleep because the time of our Lord's Passion came on His faithful ones, when they were mediating on the rest of His future reign. Wherefore it is related, that it took place late, that not only the sleep of our Lord, but the hour itself of departing light, might signify the setting of the true Sun. Again, when He ascended the cross, of which the stern of the ship was a type, His blaspheming persecutors rose like the waves against Him, driven on by the storms of the devils, by which, however, His own patience is not disturbed, but His foolish disciples are struck with amazement. The disciples awake the Lord, because they sought, with most earnest wishes, the resurrection of Him whom they had seen die. Rising up, He threatened the wind, because when He had triumphed in His resurrection, He prostrated the pride of the devil. He ordered the sea to be still, that is, in rising again, He cast down the rage of the Jews. The disciples are blamed, because after His resurrection, He chid them for their unbelief. And we also when being marked with the sign of the Lord's cross, we determine to quit the world, embark in the ship with Christ; we attempt to cross the sea; but, He goes to sleep, as we are sailing amidst the roaring of the waters, when amidst the strivings of our virtues, or amidst the attacks of evil spirits, of wicked men, or of our own thoughts, the flame of our love grows cold. Amongst storms of this sort, let us diligently strive to awake Him; He will soon restrain the tempest, pour down peace upon us, give us the harbor of salvation.

Mark 5

1. And they came over to the other side of the sea, into the country of the Gadarenes.

2. And when he was come out of the ship, immediately there met him out of the tombs a man with an unclean spirit,

3. Who had his dwelling among the tombs; and no man could bind him, no, not with chains:

4. Because that he had been often bound with fetters and chains, and the chains had been plucked asunder by him, and the fetters broken in pieces: neither could any man tame him.

5. And always, night and day, he was in the mountains, and in the tombs, crying, and cutting himself with stones.

6. But when he saw Jesus afar off, he ran and worshipped him,

7. And cried with a loud voice, and said, What have I to do with you, Jesus, you Son of the most high God? I adjure you by God, that you torment me not.

8. For he said to him, Come out of the man, you unclean spirit.

9. And he asked him, What is your name? And he answered, saying, My name is Legion: for we are many.

10. And he besought him much that he would not send them

away out of the country.

11. Now there was nigh to the mountains a great herd of swine feeding.

12. And all the devils besought him, saying, Send us into the swine, that we may enter into them.

13. And forthwith Jesus gave them leave. And the unclean spirits went out, and entered into the swine: and the herd ran violently down a steep place into the sea, (they were about two thousand;) and were choked in the sea.

14. And they that fed the swine fled, and told it in the city, and in the country. And they went out to see what it was that was done.

15. And they come to Jesus, and see him that was possessed with the devil, and had the legion, sitting, and clothed, and in his right mind: and they were afraid.

16. And they that saw it told them how it befell to him that was possessed with the devil, and also concerning the swine.

17. And they began to pray him to depart out of their coasts.

18. And when he was come into the ship, he that had been possessed with the devil prayed him that he might be with him.

19. However Jesus suffered him not, but said to him, Go home to your friends, and tell them how great things the Lord has done for you, and has had compassion on you.

20. And he departed, and began to publish in Decapolis how great things Jesus had done for him: and all men did marvel.

THEOPHYL. Those who were in the ship inquired among themselves, What manner of man is this? and how it is made known Who He is by the testimony of His enemies. For the demoniac came up confessing that He was the Son of God. Proceeding to which circumstance the Evangelist says, And they came over to the other side, &c.

BEDE; Geraza is a noted town of Arabia, across the Jordan, near mount Galaad, which the tribe of Manasseh held, not far from the lake of Tiberias, into which the swine were precipitated.

PSEUD-CHRYS. Nevertheless the exact reading contains neither Gadarenes, nor Gerasines, but Gergesenes. For Gadara is a city of Judea, which has no sea at all about it; and Geraza is a city of Arabia, having neither lake nor sea near it. And that the Evangelists may not be thought to have spoken so manifest a falsehood, well acquainted as they were with the parts around Judea, Gergese, from which come the Gergesenes was an ancient city, now called Tiberias, around which is situated a considerable lake. It continues, And when he was come out of the ship, immediately there met him, &c.

AUG. Though Matthew says that there were two, Mark and Luke mention one, that you may understand that one of them was a more illustrious person, concerning whose state that country was much afflicted.

CHRYS. Or else, Mark and Luke relate what was most worthy of compassion, and for this reason they put down more at length what had happened to this man; for there follows, no man could bind him, no, not with chains. They therefore simply said, a man possessed of a devil, without taking heed to the number; or else, that he might show the greater virtue in the Worker; for He who had cured one such, might cure many others. Nor is there any discrepancy shown here, for they did not say that there was one alone, for then they would have contradicted Matthew. Now devils dwelt in tombs, wishing to convey a false opinion to many, that the souls of the dead were changed to devils.

GREG. NYSS. Now the assembly of the devils had prepared itself to resist time divine power. But when He was approaching Who had power over all things, they proclaim aloud His eminent virtue.

Wherefore there follows, But when he saw Jesus afar off, he ran and worshipped him, saying, &c.

CYRIL; See how the devil is divided between two passions, fear amid audacity; he hangs back and prays, as if meditating a question; he wishes to know what he had to do with Jesus, as though be would say, Do you cast me out from men, who are mine?

BEDE; And how great is the impiety of the Jews, to say that He cast out devils by the prince of the devils, when the very devils confess that they have nothing in common with Him.

CHRYS. Then praying to Him, he subjoins, I adjure you by God, that you torment me not. For he considered being cast out to be a torment, or else he was also invisibly tortured. For however bad the devils are, they know that there awaits them at last a punishment for their sins; but that the time of their last punishment was not yet come, they full well knew, especially as they were permitted to mix among men. But because Christ had come upon them as they were doing such dreadful deeds, they thought that, such was the heinousness of their crimes, He would not wait for the last times, to punish them; for this reason they beg that they may not be tormented.

BEDE; For it is a great torment for a devil to cease to hurt a man, and the more severely he possesses him, the more reluctantly he lets him go. For it goes on, For he said to him, Come out of the man, you unclean spirit.

CYRIL; Consider the unconquerable power of Christ; He makes Satan shake, for to him the words of Christ are fire and flame; as the Psalmist says, The mountains melted at the presence of the Lord, that is, great and proud powers.

There fellows, And he asked him, What is your name?

THEOPHYL. The Lord indeed asks, not that He Himself required to know, but that the rest might know that there was a multitude of devils dwelling in him.

PSEUD-CHRYS. Lest he should not be believed, if He affirmed there were many, He wishes that they themselves should confess it; wherefore there follows, And he said to him, Legion, for we are many. He gives not a fixed number, but a multitude, for such accuracy in the number would not help us to understand it.

BEDE; But by the public declaration of the scourge which the madman suffered, the virtue of the Healer appears more gracious. And even the priests of our time, who know how to cast out devils by the grace of exorcism, are wont to say that the sufferers cannot be cured at all, unless they in confession openly declare, as far as they are able to know, what they have suffered from the unclean spirits in sight, in hearing, in taste, in touch, or any other sense of body or soul, whether awake or asleep. It goes on, And he besought him much that he would not send them away out of the country.

PSEUD-CHRYS Luke however says, into the abyss. For the abyss is the separation of this world, for devils observe to be sent into outer darkness, prepared for the devil and his angels. This Christ might have done, but He allows them to remain in this world, lest the absence of a tempter should deprive men of the crown of victory.

THEOPHYL. Also that by fighting with us, they may make us more expert. It goes on, Now there was there about the mountain a great herd of swine feeding.

AUG. What Mark here says, that the herd was about the mountain, and what Luke calls on the mountain, are by no means inconsistent. For the herd of swine was so large, that some part were on the mountain, the rest around it. It goes on: And the devils besought him, saying, send us into the swine, that we may enter in to them.

Catena Aurea: Commentary on the Gospel of St. Mark

REMIG. The devils entered not into the swine of their own will, but their asking for this concession, was, that it might be shown that they cannot hurt men without Divine permission. They did not ask to be sent into man, because they saw that He, by whose power they were tortured, bore a human form. Nor did they desire to be sent into the flocks, for they are clean animals offered up in the temple of God. But they desired to be sent into the swine, because no animal is more unclean than a hog, and devils always delight in filthiness. It goes on: And forthwith Jesus gave them leave.

BEDE; And He gave them leave, that by the killing of the swine, the salvation of men might be furthered.

PSEUD-CHRYS. He wished to show publicly the fury which devils entertain against men, and that they would inflict much worse things upon men, if they were not hindered by Divine power because, again, His compassion would not allow this to his shown on men, He permitted them to enter into the swine that on them the fury and power of the devils might be made known. There follows: And the unclean spirits went out.

TITUS; But the herdsmen also took to flight, lest they should perish with the swine, and spread the same fear amongst the inhabitants of the town. Wherefore there follows: And they that fed them, &c. The necessity of their loss, however, brought these men to the Savior; for frequently when God makes men suffer loss in their possessions, he confers a benefit on their souls.

Wherefore it goes on: And they came to Jesus, and see him that was tormented by the devil, &c. that is, at the feet of Him from whom he had obtained health; a man, whom before, not even chains could bind, clothed and in his right mind, though he used to be continually naked; and they were amazed; wherefore it says, And they were afraid. This miracle then they find omit partly by sight, partly by words; wherefore there follows: And they that saw it told them.

THEOPHYL. But amazed at the miracle, which they had heard, they were afraid, and for this reason they beseech Him to depart out of their borders; which is expressed in what follows: And they began to pray him to depart out of their coasts; for they feared lest some time or other they should suffer a like thing: for, saddened at the loss of their swine, they reject the presence of the Savior.

BEDE; Or else, conscious of their own frailty, they judged themselves unworthy of the presence of the Lord. It goes on: And when he was going to the ship, he that had been tormented, &c.

THEOPHYL. For he feared lest sometime or other the devils should find him, and enter into him a second time. But the Lord sends him back to his house, intimating to him, that though He himself was not present, yet His power would keep him; at the same time also that he might be of use in the healing of others; where fore it goes on: And he did not suffer him, and said to him, Go home to your friends, &c. See the humility of the Savior. He said not, Proclaim all things which I have done to you, but, all that the Lord has done; do you also, when you have done any good thing, take it not to yourself, but refer it to God.

CHRYS. But although He bade others, whom he healed, to tell it to no one, he nevertheless fitly bids this one proclaim it, since all that region, being possessed by devils, remained without God.

THEOPHYL. He therefore began to proclaim it, and all wonder, which is that which follows: And he began to publish.

BEDE; Mystically, however, Gerasa or Gergese, as some read it, is interpreted casting out a dweller or a stranger approaching, because the people of the Gentiles both expelled the enemy from the heart, and he who was afar off is made near.

PSEUDO-JEROME; Here again the demoniac is the people of the Gentiles, in a most hopeless case, bound neither by the law of nature, nor of God, nor by human fear.

BEDE; Who dwelt in the tombs, because they delighted in dead works, that is, in sins; who were ever raging night and day, because whether in prosperity or in adversity, they were never free from the service of malignant spirits: again, by time foulness of their works, they lay as it were in the tombs, in their lofty pride, they wandered over the mountains, by words of most hardened infidelity, they as it were cut themselves with stones. But he said, My name is Legion, because the Gentile people were enslaved to divers idolatrous forms of worship. Again, that the unclean spirits going out from man enter into swine, which they east headlong into the sea, implies that now that time people of the Gentiles are freed from the empire of demons, they who have not chosen to believe in Christ, work sacrilegious rites in hidden places.

THEOPHYL. Or by this it is signified that devils enter into those men, who live like swine, rolling themselves in the slough of pleasure; they drive them headlong into the sea down the precipice of perdition, into the sea of an evil life where they are choked.

PSEUDO-JEROME; Or they are choked in hell without any touch of mercy by the rushing on of an early death; which evils many persons thus avoid, for by the scourging of the fool, the wise is made more prudent.

BEDE; But that the Lord did not admit him, though He wished to be without Him, signifies, that every one after the remission of his sins should remember that he must work to obtain a good conscience, and serve the Gospel for the salvation of others, that at last he may rest in Christ.

GREG. For when we have perceived ever so little of the Divine knowledge, we are at once unwilling to return to human affairs, and seek for the quiet of contemplation; but the Lord commands that the mind should first toil hard at its work, and afterwards should refresh itself with contemplation.

PSEUDO-JEROME; But the man who is healed preached in Decapolis, where the Jews, who hang on the letter of the Decalogue, are being turned away from the Roman rule.

21. And when Jesus was passed over again by ship to the other side, much people gathered to him: and He was nigh to the sea.

22. And, behold, there comes one of the rulers of the synagogue,

Catena Aurea: Commentary on the Gospel of St. Mark

Jairus by name; and when he saw him, he fell at his feet,

23. And besought him greatly, Saying, My little daughter lies at the point of death: I pray you, come and lay your hands on her, that she may be healed; and she shall live.

24. And Jesus went with him; and much people followed him, and thronged him.

25. And a certain woman, which had an issue of blood twelve years,

26. And had suffered many things of many physicians, and had spent all that she had, and was nothing bettered, but rather grew worse,

27. When she had heard of Jesus, came in the press behind, and touched his garment.

28. For she said, If I may touch but his clothes, I shall be whole.

29. And straightway the fountain of her blood was dried up; and she felt in her body that she was healed of that plague.

30. And Jesus, immediately knowing in himself that virtue had gone out of him, turned him about in the press, and said, Who touched my clothes?

31. And his disciples said to him, You see the multitude thronging you, and say you, Who touched me?

32. And he looked round about to see her that had done this thing.

33. But the woman fearing and trembling, knowing what was done in her, came and fell down before him, and told him all the truth.

34. And he said to her, Daughter, your faith has made you whole; go in peace, and be whole of your plague.

THEOPHYL. After the miracle of the demoniac, the Lord works another miracle, namely, in raising up the daughter of the ruler of the synagogue; the Evangelist, before narrating this miracle, says, And when Jesus was passed over again by ship to the other side, much people gathered to him.

AUG. But we must understand, that what is added of the daughter of the ruler of the synagogue, took place when Jesus had again crossed the sea in a ship, though how long after does not appear; for if there were not an interval, there could be no time for the taking place of that which Matthew relates, concerning the feast at his own house; after which event, nothing follows immediately, except this concerning the daughter of the chief of the synagogue. For he has so put it together, that the transition itself shows that the narrative follows the order of time. It goes on, There comes one of the rulers of the synagogue, &c.

PSEUD-CHRYS. He has recorded the name on account of the Jews of that time, that it might mark the miracle. It goes on, And when he saw him, he fell at his feet, and besought him greatly,

&c. Matthew indeed relates that the chief of the synagogue reported that his daughter was dead, but Mark says that she was very sick, and that afterwards it was told to the ruler of the synagogue, when our Lord was about to go with him, that she was dead. The fact then, which Matthew implies, is the same, namely, that He raised her from the dead; and it is for the sake of brevity, that he says that she was dead, which was evident from her being raised.

AUG. For he attaches himself not to the words of the father, but to what is of most importance, his wishes; for he was in such despair, that his wish was that she should return to life, not thinking that she could be found alive, whom he had left dying.

THEOPHYL. Now this man was faithful in part, inasmuch as he fell at the feet of Jesus, but in that he begged of Him to come, he did not show as much faith as lie ought. For he ought to have said, Speak the word only, and my daughter shall be healed. There follows, And he went away with him, and much people followed him, and thronged him;

and a woman, which had an issue of blood twelve years, &c.

CHRYS. This woman, who was celebrated and known to all, did not dare to approach the Savior openly, nor to come to Him, because, according to the law, she was unclean; for this reason she touched Him behind, and not in front, for that she dare not do, but only ventured to touch the hem of His garment. It was not however the hem of the garment, but her frame of mind that made her whole.

There follows, For she said, If I may but touch his clothes, I shall be whole.

THEOPHYL. Most faithful indeed is this woman, who hoped for healing from His garments. For which reason she obtains health; wherefore it goes on, And straightway the fountain of her blood was dried up, and she felt in her body that she was healed.

PSEUD-CHRYS. Now the virtues of Christ are by His own will imparted to those men, who touch Him by faith. Wherefore there follows, And Jesus, immediately knowing in himself that virtue had gone out of him, turned him about in the press, and said, who touched my clothes? The virtues indeed of the Savior do not go out of Him locally or corporally, nor in any respect pass away from Him. For being incorporeal, they go forth to others and are given to others; they are not however separated from Him, from whom they are said to go forth, in the same way as sciences are given by the teacher to his pupils. Therefore it says, Jesus, knowing in himself the virtue which had gone out of him, to show that with His knowledge, and not without His being aware of it, the woman was healed.

But He asked, Who touched me? although He knew her who touched Him, that He might bring to light the woman, by her coming forward, and proclaim her faith, and lest the virtue of His miraculous work should be consigned to oblivion. It goes on, And his disciples said to him, You see the multitude thronging you, and say you, Who touched me? But the Lord asked, Who touched me, that is in thought and faith, for the crowds who throng Me cannot be said to touch Me, for they do not come near to Me in thought and in faith.

There follows, And he looked round about to see her that had done this thing.

THEOPHYL. For the Lord wished to declare the woman, first to give His approbation to her faith, secondly to urge the chief of the synagogue to a confident hope that He could thus cure his child, and also to free the woman from fear. For the woman feared because she had stolen health; wherefore there follows, But the woman fearing and trembling, &c.

BEDE; Observe that the object of His question was that the woman should confess the truth of her long want of faith, of her sudden belief and healing, and so herself be confirmed in faith, and afford an example to others. But he said to her, Daughter, your faith has made you whole; go in peace, and be whole of your plague. He said not, Your faith is about to make you whole, but has made you whole, that is, in that you have believed, you have already been made whole.

CHRYS. He calls her daughter because she was saved by her faith; for faith in Christ makes us His children.

THEOPHYL. But He said to her, Go in peace, that is, in rest, which means, go and have rest, for up to this time you have been in pains and torture

PSEUD-CHRYS. Or else He says, Go in peace, sending her away into that which is the final good, for God dwells in peace, that you may know, that she was not only healed in body but also from the causes of bodily pain, that is, from her sins

PSEUDO-JEROME. Mystically, however, Jairus comes after the healing of the woman, because when the fullness of the Gentiles has come in, then shall Israel be saved. Jairus means either illuminating, or illuminated, that is, the Jewish people having cast off the shadow of the letter, enlightened by the Spirit and enlightening others, falling at the feet of the Word that is humbling itself before the Incarnation of Christ, prays for her daughter, for when a man lives himself, he makes others live also. Thus Abraham, and Moses, and Samuel, intercede for the people who are dead, and Jesus comes upon their prayers.

BEDE; Again, the Lord going to the child, who is to be healed, is thronged by the crowd, because though He gave healthful advice to the Jewish nation, he is oppressed by the wicked habits of that carnal people; but the woman with an issue of blood, cured by the Lord, is the Church gathered together from the nations, for the issue of blood may be either understood of the pollution of idolatry, or of those deeds, which are accompanied by pleasure to flesh and blood. But whilst the word of the Lord decreed salvation to Judea, the people of the Gentiles by an assured hope seized upon the health, promised and prepared for others.

THEOPHYL. Or else, by the woman, who had a bloody flux, understand human nature; for sin rushed in upon it, which since it killed the soul, might be said to spill its blood. It could not be cured by many physicians, that is, by the wise men of this world, and of the Law and the Prophets; but the moment that it touched the hem of Christ's garment, that is, His flesh, it was healed, for whoever believes the Son of man to be Incarnate is he who touches the hem of His garment.

BEDE; Wherefore one believing woman touches the Lord, whilst the crowd throngs Him, because He, who is grieved by divers heresies, or by wicked habits, is worshipped faithfully with the heart of the Catholic Church alone. But the Church of the Gentiles came behind Him; because though it did not see the Lord present in time flesh, for the mysteries of His Incarnation had been gone through, yet it attained to the grace of His faith, and so when by partaking of His sacraments, it merited salvation from its sins, as it were the fountain of its blood was dried up by the touch of His garments. And the Lord looked round about to see her who had done this, because He judges that all who deserve to be saved are worthy of His look and of His pity.

35. While he yet spoke, there came from the ruler of the synagogue's house certain which said, Your daughter is dead: why trouble you the Master any further?

36. As soon as Jesus heard the word that was spoken, he said to the ruler of the synagogue, Be not afraid, only believe.

37. And he suffered no man to follow him, save Peter, and James, and John the brother of James.

38. And he comes to the house of the ruler of the synagogue, and sees the tumult, and them that wept and wailed greatly.

39. And when he was come in, he said to them, Why make you this ado, and weep? the damsel is not dead, but sleeps.

40. And they laughed him to scorn. But when he had put them all out, he takes the father and the mother of the damsel, and them that were with him, and enter in where the damsel was lying.

41. And he took the damsel by the by and, and said unto her, Talitha cumi; which is, being interpreted, Damsel, I say to you, arise.

42. And straightway the damsel arose, and walked; for she was of the age of twelve years. And they were astonished with a great astonishment.

43. And he charged them straitly that no man should know it; and commanded that something should be given her to eat.

THEOPHYL. Those who were about the ruler of the synagogue, thought that Christ was one of the prophets, and for this reason they thought that they should beg of Him to come and pray over the damsel. But because she had already expired, they thought that He ought not to be asked to do so. Therefore it is said, While he yet spoke, there came messengers to the ruler of the synagogue, which said, Your daughter is dead; why trouble you the Master any further?

But the Lord Himself persuades the father to have confidence. For it goes on, As soon as Jesus heard the word which was spoken, he said to the ruler of the synagogue, Be not afraid; only believe.

AUG. It is not said that he assented to his friends who brought the tidings and wished to prevent the Master from coming, so that our Lord's saying, Fear not, only believe, is not a rebuke for his want of faith, but was intended to strengthen the belief which he had already. But if the Evangelist had related, that the ruler of the synagogue joined the friends who came from his house, in saying that Jesus should not be troubled, the words which Matthew relates him to have said, namely, that the damsel was dead, would then have been contrary to what was in his mind.

It goes on, And he suffered no man to follow him, save Peter, and James, and John the brother of James.

THEOPHYL. For Christ in His lowliness would not do any thing for display. It goes on, And he comes to the house of the ruler of the synagogue, and sees the tumult, and them that wept and wailed greatly.

PSEUD-CHRYS. But He Himself commands them not to wail, as if the damsel was not dead, but sleeping; wherefore it says, And when he was come in, he said to them, Why make you this ado, and weep? the damsel is not dead, but sleeps.

PSEUDO-JEROME; It was told the ruler of the synagogue, Your daughter is dead. But Jesus said to him, She is not dead, but sleeps. Both are true, for the meaning is, She is dead to you, but to Me she is asleep.

BEDE; For to men she was dead, who were unable to raise her up; but to God she was asleep, in whose purpose both the soul was living, and the flesh was resting, to raise again. Whence it became a custom amongst Christians, that the dead, who, they doubt not, will rise again, should be said to sleep. It goes on, And they laughed him to scorn.

THEOPHYL. But they laugh at Him, as if unable to do anything farther; and in this He convicts them of bearing witness involuntarily, that she was really dead whom He raised up, and therefore, that it would be a miracle if He raised her.

BEDE; Because they chose rather to laugh at than to believe in this saying concerning her resurrection, they are deservedly excluded from the place, as unworthy to witness His power in raising her, and the mystery of her rising; wherefore it goes on, But when he had put them all out, he takes the father and the mother of the damsel, and them that were with him, and enters in where the damsel was lying.

CHRYS. Or else, to take away all display, He suffered not all to he with Him; that, however He might leave behind Him witnesses of His divine power, He chose His three chief disciples and the father and mother of the damsel, as being necessary above all. And He restores life to the damsel both by His hand, and by word of mouth. Wherefore it says, And he took the damsel by the hand, and said unto her, Talitha cumi; which is, being interpreted, Damsel, I say unto you, Arise.

For the hand of Jesus, having a quickening power, quickens the dead body, and His voice raises her as she is lying; wherefore it follows, And straightway the damsel arose and walked.

JEROME; Some one may accuse the Evangelist of a falsehood in his explanation, in that he has added, I say to you, when in

Hebrew, Talitha cumi only means, Damsel, arise; but He adds, I say unto thee, Arise, to express that His meaning was to call and command her. It goes on, For she was of the age of twelve years.

GLOSS. The Evangelist added this, to show that she was of an age to walk. By her walking she is shown to have been not only raised up but also perfectly cured. It continues, And they were astonished with a great astonishment.

CHRYS. To show that He had raised her really, and not only to the eve of fancy

BEDE; Mystically; the woman was cured of a bloody flux, and immediately after the daughter of the ruler of the synagogue is reported to be dead, because as soon as the Church of the Gentiles is washed from the stain of vice, and called daughter by the merits of her faith, at once the synagogue is broken up on account of its zealous treachery and envy; treachery, because it did not choose to believe in Christ; envy, because it was vexed at the faith of the Church. What the messengers told the ruler of the synagogue, Why trouble you the Master anymore, is said by those in this day who, seeing the state of the synagogue, deserted by God, believe that it cannot be restored, and therefore think that we are not to pray that it should he restored. But if the ruler of the synagogue, that is, the assembly of the teachers of the Law, determine to believe, the synagogue also, which is subjected to them, will be saved.

Further, because the synagogue lost the joy of having Christ to dwell in it, as its faithlessness deserved, it lies dead as it were, amongst persons weeping and wailing. Again, our Lord raised the damsel by taking hold of her hand, because the hands of the Jews, which are full of blood, must first be cleansed, else the synagogue, which is dead, cannot rise again. But in the woman with the bloody flux, and the raising of the damsel, is shown the salvation of the human race, which was so ordered by the Lord, that first some from Judea, then the fullness of the Gentiles, might come in, and so all Israel might be saved. Again, the damsel was twelve years old, and the woman had suffered for twelve years, because the sinning of unbelievers was contemporary with the beginning of the faith of believers; wherefore it is said, Abraham believed on God, and it was counted to him for righteousness.

GREG. Morally again, our Redeemer raised the damsel in the house, the young man without the gate, Lazarus in the tomb; he still lies dead in the house, whose sin is concealed; he is carried without the gate, whose sin has broken forth into the madness of an open deed; he lies crushed under the mound of the tomb, who in the commission of sin, lies powerless beneath the weight of habit.

BEDE; And we may remark, that lighter and daily errors may he cured by the remedy of a lighter penance. Wherefore the Lord raises the damsel, lying in the inner chamber with a very easy cry, saying, Damsel, arise; but that he who had been four days dead might quit the prison of the tomb, he groaned in spirit, He was troubled, He shed tears. In proportion, then, as the death of the soul presses the more heavily, so much the more ardently must the fervor of the penitent press forward. But this too must be observed, that a public crime requires a public reparation; wherefore Lazarus, when called from the sepulcher, was placed before the eyes of the people: but slight sins require to be washed out by a secret penance, wherefore the damsel lying in the house is raised up before few witnesses, and those are desired to tell no man. The crowd also is cast out before the damsel is raised; for if a crowd of worldly thoughts be not first cast out from the hidden parts of the heart, the soul, which lies dead within, cannot rise. Well too did she arise and walk, for the soul, raised from sin, ought not only to rise from the filth of its crimes, but also to make advances in good works, and soon it is necessary that it should be filled with heavenly bread, that at is, made partaker of the Divine Word, and of the Altar.

Mark 6

1. And he went out from thence, and came into his own country; and his disciples follow him.

2. And when the sabbath day was come, he began to teach in the synagogue: and many hearing him were astonished, saying, From whence has this man these things? and what wisdom is this which is given unto him, that even such mighty works are wrought by his hands?

3. Is not this the carpenter, the son of Mary, the brother of James, and Joses, and of Juda, and Simon? and are not his sisters here with us? And they were offended at him.

4. But Jesus said to them, A prophet is not without honor, but in his own country, and among his own kin, and in his own house.

5. And he could there do no mighty work, save that be laid his hands upon a few sick folk, and healed them.

6. And he marveled because of their unbelief.

THEOPHYL. After the miracles which have been related, the Lord returns into His own country, not that He was ignorant that they would despise Him, but that they might have no reason to say, If you had come, we had believed You; wherefore it is said, And he went out from thence, and came in to his own country.

BEDE; He means by His country, Nazareth, in which He was

brought up. But how great the blindness of the Nazarenes! they despise Him, Who by His words and deeds they might know to be the Christ, soley on account of His kindred. It goes on, And when the sabbath day was come, he began to teach in the synagogue: and many hearing him were astonished, saying, From whence has this man these things? and what wisdom is this which it given unto him, that even such mighty works are wrought by his hands? By wisdom is meant His doctrine, by powers, the cures and miracles which He did.

It goes on, Is not this the carpenter, the son of Mary?

AUG. Matthew indeed says that He was called the son of a carpenter; nor are we to wonder, since both might have been said, for they believed Him to be a carpenter, because He was the son of a carpenter.

PSEUDO-JEROME; Jesus is called the son of a workman, of that one, however, whose work was the morning and the sun, that is, the first and second Church, as a figure of which the woman and the damsel are healed.

BEDE; For although human things are not to be compared with divine, still the type is complete, because the Father of Christ works by fire and spirit. It goes on, The brother of James, Joses, Jude, and of Simon. And are not his sisters here with us? They bear witness that His brothers and sisters were with Him, who nevertheless are not to be taken for the sons of Joseph or of Mary, as heretics say, but rather, as is usual in Scripture, we must understand them to be His relations, as Abraham and Lot are called brothers, though Lot was brother's son to Abraham. And they were offended at him. The stumbling and the error of the Jews is our salvation, and the condemnation of heretics. For so much did they despise the Lord Jesus Christ, as to call Him a carpenter, and son of a carpenter.

It goes on, And Jesus said to them, A prophet is not without honor, but in his own country. Even Moses bears witness that the Lord is called a Prophet in the Scripture, for predicting His future Incarnation to the sons of Israel, he says, A Prophet shall the Lord raise up to you of your brethren. But not only He Himself, Who is Lord of prophets, but also Elias, Jeremiah, and the remaining lesser prophets, were worse received in their own country than in strange cities, for it is almost natural for men to envy their fellow-townsmen; for they do not consider the present works of the man, but they remember the weakness of His infancy.

PSEUDO-JEROME; Oftentimes also the origin of a man brings him contempt, as it is written, Who is the son of Jesse? for the Lord has respect to the lowly; as to the proud, He beholds them afar off.

THEOPHYL. Or again, if the prophet has noble relations, his countrymen hate them, and on that account do not honor the prophet. There follows, And he could there do no mighty work, &c. What, however, is here expressed by He could not, we must take to mean, He did not choose, because it was not that He was weak, but that they were faithless; He does not therefore work any miracles there, for He spared them, lest they should be worthy of greater blame, if they believed not, even with miracles before their eyes. Or else, for the working of miracles, not only the power of the Worker is necessary, but the faith of the recipient, which was wanting in this case: therefore Jesus did not choose to work any signs there.

There follows, And he marveled at their unbelief.

BEDE; Not as if He Who knows all things before they are done, wonders at what He does not expect or look forward to but knowing the hidden things of the heart, and wishing to intimate to men that it was wonderful, He openly shows that He wonders. And indeed the blindness of the Jews was wonderful, for they neither believed what the prophets said of Christ, nor would in their own persons believe in Christ, Who was born amongst them. Mystically again; Christ is despised in His own house and country, that is, amongst the people of the Jews, and therefore He worked few miracles there, lest they should become altogether inexcusable. But He performs greater miracles every day amongst the Gentiles, not so much in the healing of their bodies, as in the salvation of their souls.

6. - And he went round about the villages, teaching.

7. And he called to him the twelve, and began to send them forth by two and two; and gave them power over unclean spirits;

8. And commanded them that they should take nothing for their journey, save a staff only; no scrip, no bread, no money in their purse:

9. But be shod with sandals; and not put on two coats.

10. And He said to them, In what place soever you enter into an house, there abide till you depart from that place.

11. And whoever shall not receive you, nor hear you, when you depart thence, shake off the dust under your feet for a testimony against them. Verily I say to you, It shall be more tolerable for Sodom and Gomorrha in the day of judgment, than for that city.

12. And they went out, and preached that men should repent.

13. And they cast out many devils, and annointed with oil many that were sick, and healed them.

THEOPHYL. The Lord not only preached in the cities, but also in villages, that we may learn not to despise little things, nor always to seek for great cities, but to sow the word of the Lord, in abandoned and lowly villages. Wherefore it is said, And he went round about the villages, teaching.

BEDE; Now our kind and merciful Lord and Master did not grudge His servants and their disciples His own virtues, and as He Himself had healed every sickness and every infirmity, so also He gave the same power to His disciples. Wherefore it goes on: And he called to him the twelve, and began to send them forth by two and two; and gave them power over unclean spirits. Great is the difference between giving and receiving. Whatever He does is done in His own power, as Lord; if they do anything, they confess their own weakness and the power of the Lord, saying in the name of Jesus, Arise, and walk.

THEOPHYL. Again He sends the Apostles two and two that

they might become more active; for, as say's the Preacher, Two are better than one. But if He had sent more than two, that there would not have been a sufficient number to allow of their being sent to many villages.

GREG. Further, the Lord sent the disciples to preach, two and two, because there are two precepts of charity, namely, the love of God, and of our neighbor, and charity cannot be between less than two; by this therefore He implies to us, that he who has not charity towards his neighbor, ought in no way to take upon himself the office of preaching. There follows, And he commanded them, that they should take nothing for their journey, save a staff only; no scrip, no bread, no money in their purse:

but be shod with sandals; and not put on two coats.

BEDE; For such should be the preacher's trust in God, that, though He takes no thought for supplying his own wants in this present world, yet he should feel most certain that these will not be left unsatisfied lest whilst his mind is taken up with temporal things, he should provide less of eternal things to others.

PSEUDO-CHRYS. The Lord also gives them this command, that they might show by their mode of life, how far removed they were from the desire of riches.

THEOPHYL. Instructing them also by this means not to be fond of receiving gifts, in order too that these, who saw them preach poverty, might be reconciled to it when they saw that the Apostles themselves possessed nothing.

AUG. Or else; according to Matthew, the Lord immediately subjoined, The workman is worthy of his meat, which sufficiently proves why He forbade their carrying or possessing such things, not because they were not necessary, but because he sent them in such a way as to show, that they were due to them from the faithful, to whom they preached the Gospel. From this it is evident, that the Lord did not mean by this precept that the Evangelists ought to live only on the gifts of those to whom they preach the Gospel, else the Apostle transgressed this precept when He procured his livelihood, the labor of his own hands, but He meant that He had given them a power, in virtue of which, they might be assured, these things were due to them.

It is also often asked, how it comes that Matthew and Luke have related that the Lord commanded His disciples no to carry even a staff, whilst Mark says, And he commanded them that they should take nothing for their journey, save a staff only. Which question is solved, by supposing that the word 'staff' has a meaning in Mark, who says that it ought to be carried, different from that which it bears in Matthew and Luke, who affirm the contrary.

For in a concise way one might say, Take none of the necessaries of life with you, nay, not a staff, save a staff only; so that the saying, nay not a staff; may mean, nay not the smallest thing; but that which is added, save a staff only, may mean that, through the power received by them from the Lord, of which a rod is the ensign, nothing, even of those things which they do not carry, will be wanting to them. The Lord therefore said both, but because one Evangelist has not given both, men suppose, that he who has said that the staff, in one sense, should be taken, is contrary to him who again has declared, that, in another sense, it should be left behind: now however that a reason has been given, let no one think so.

So also when Matthew declares that shoes are not to be worn on the journey, he forbids anxiety about them, for the reason why men are anxious about carrying them, is that they may not be without them. This is also to be understood of the two coats, that no man should be troubled about having only that with which He is clad, from anxiety lest He should need another, when he could always obtain one from the power given by the Lord.

In like manner Mark, by saying that they are to be shod with sandals or soles, warns us that this mode of protecting the foot has a mystical signification, that the foot should neither be covered above nor be naked on the ground, that is, that the Gospel should neither be hid, nor rest upon earthly comforts; and in that He forbids their possessing or taking with them, or more expressly their wearing, two coats, He bids them walk simply, not in duplicity. But whoever thinks that the Lord could not in the same discourse say some things figuratively, others in a literal sense, let him look into His other discourses, and he shall see, how rash and ignorant is his judgment.

BEDE; Again, by the two tunics, He seems to me to mean two sets of clothes; not that in places like Scythia, covered with the ice and snow, a man should be content with only one garment, but by coat, I think a suit of clothing is implied, that being clad with one, we should not keep another through anxiety as to what may happen.

PSEUD-CHRYS. Or else, Matthew and Luke neither allow shoes nor staff; which is meant to point out the highest perfection. But Mark bids themselves take a staff and be shod with sandals, which is spoken by permission.

BEDE; Again, allegorically; under the figure of a scrip is pointed out the burdens of this world, by bread is meant temporal delights, by money in the purse, the hiding of wisdom; because he who receives the office of a doctor, should neither be weighed down by the burden of worldly affairs, nor be made soft by carnal desires, nor hide the talent of the word committed to him under the ease of an inactive body. It goes on, And he said unto them, In what place soever you enter into a house, there abide till you depart from that place. Where He gives a general precept of constancy, that they should look to what is due to the tie of hospitality, adding, that it is inconsistent with the preaching of the kingdom of heaven to run about from house to house.

THEOPHYL. That is, lest they should be accused of gluttony in passing from one to another. It goes on, And whoever shall not receive you, &c. This the Lord commands them, that they might show that they had walked a long way for their sakes, and to no purpose. Or, because they received nothing from them, not even dust, which they shake off, that it might be a testimony against them, that is, by way of convicting them.

PSEUD-CHRYS. Or else, that it might be a witness of the toil of the way, which they sustained for them; or as if the dust of the sins of the preachers was turned against themselves. It goes on, And they went and preached that men should repent.

And they cast out many devils, and anointed with oil many that were sick, and healed them. Mark alone mentions their anointing with oil. James however, in his canonical Epistle, says a thing similar. For oil both refreshes our labors, and gives us light and joy; but again, oil signifies the mercy of the unction of God, the healing of infirmity, and the enlightening of the heart, the whole of which is worked by prayer.

THEOPHYL. It also means, the grace of the Holy Ghost, by which we are eased from our labors, and receive light and spiritual joy.

BEDE; Wherefore it is evident from the Apostles themselves, that it is an ancient custom of the holy Church that persons possessed or afflicted with any disease whatever, should be anointed with oil consecrated by priestly blessing.

14. And king Herod heard of him; (for his name was spread abroad) and he said, That John the Baptist was risen from the dead, and therefore mighty works do show forth themselves in him.

15. Others said, That it is Elias. And others said, That it is a prophet, or as one of the prophets.

16. But when Herod heard thereof, he said, It is John, whom I beheaded: he is risen from the dead.

GLOSS. After the preaching of the disciples of Christ, and the working of miracles, the Evangelist subjoins an account of the report, which arose amongst the people; wherefore he says, And king Herod heard of him.

PSEUD-CHRYS. This Herod is the son of the first Herod, under whom Joseph had led Jesus into Egypt. But Matthew calls him Tetrarch, and Luke mentions him as ruling over one fourth of his father's kingdom; for the Romans after the death of his father divided his kingdom into four parts. But Mark calls him a king, either after the title of his father, or because it was on consonant to his own wish.

PSEUDO-JEROME; It goes on, For his name spread abroad. For it is not right that a candle should be placed under a bushel. And they said, that is, some of the multitude, that John the Baptist was risen from the dead, and therefore mighty works do show themselves forth in him.

BEDE; Here we are taught how great great the envy of the Jews. For, lo, they believe that John, of whom it was said that he did no miracle, could rise from the dead, and that, without the witness of anyone. But Jesus, approved of God by miracles and signs, whose resurrection, Angels and Apostles, men and women, preached, they chose to believe was carried away by stealth, rather than suppose that He had risen again. And these men, in saying that John was risen from the dead, and that therefore mighty works were wrought in him, had just thoughts of the power of the resurrection, for men, when they shall have risen from the dead, shall have much greater power, than they possessed, when still weighed down by the weakness of the flesh. There follows, But others said that it was Elias.

Catena Aurea: Commentary on the Gospel of St. Mark

THEOPHYL; For John confuted many men, when he said, You generation of vipers. It goes on, But other said, that it is a prophet or as one of the prophets.

PSEUD-CHRYS. It seems to me that this prophet means that one of whom Moses said, God will raise up a prophet to you of your brethren. They were right indeed, but because they feared to say openly, This is the Christ, they used the voice of Moses, veiling their own surmise through fear of their rulers. There follows, But when Herod heard thereof; he said, It is John, whom I beheaded: He is risen from the dead. Herod expressly says, this in irony.

THEOPHYL. Or else, Herod, knowing that he without a cause had slain John, who was a just man, thought that he had risen from the dead, and had received through his resurrection the power of working miracles.

AUG. But in these words Luke bears witness to Mark to this point at least, that others and not Herod said that John had risen but Luke had represented Herod as hesitating and has put down his words as if he said, John have I beheaded, but who is this of hear such things? We must however suppose, that after this hesitation, he had confirmed in his own mind what others had said, for he says to his children, as Matthew relates, This is John the Baptist, he has risen from the dead. Or else these words are to be spoken, so as to indicate that he is still hesitating, particularly as Mark who had said above that others had declared that John had risen from the dead, afterwards however is not silent as to Herod's plainly saying, It is John, whom I beheaded: he is risen from the dead. Which words also may be spoken in two ways, either they may be understood as those of a man affirming or doubting.

17. For Herod himself had sent forth and laid hold upon John, and bound him in prison for Herodias' sake, his brother Philip's wife: for he had married her.

18. For John had said unto Herod, It is not lawful for you to have your brother's wife.

19. Therefore Herodias had a quarrel against him, and would have killed him; but she could not;

20. For Herod feared John, knowing that he was a just man and a holy, and observed him; and when he heard him, he did many things, and heard him gladly.

21. And when a convenient day was come, that Herod on his birthday made a supper to his lords, high captains, and chief estates of Galilee;

22. And when the daughter of the said Herodias came in, and danced, and pleased Herod and them that sat with him, the king said unto the damsel, Ask of me whatsoever you wilt, and I will give it you.

23. And he swore unto her, Whatever you shall ask of me, I will give it you, to the half of my kingdom.

24. And she went forth, and said unto her mother, What shall I ask? And she said, The head of John the Baptist.

25. And she came in straightway with haste unto the king, and asked, saying, I will that you give me by and by in a charger the head of John the Baptist.

26. And the king was exceeding sorry; yet for his oath's sake, and for their sakes which sat with him, he would not reject her.

27. And immediately the king sent an executioner, and commanded his head to be brought: and he went and beheaded him in the prison,

28. And brought his head in a charger, and gave it to the damsel: and the damsel gave it to her mother.

29. And when his disciples heard of it, they came and took up his corpse, and laid it in a tomb.

THEOPHYL. The Evangelist Mark, taking occasion from what went before, here relates the death of the Forerunner, saying, For Herod himself had sent John and laid hold upon John, and bound him in prison for Herodias' sake his brother Philip's wife: for he had married her.

BEDE; Ancient history relates, that Philip the son of Herod the great, under whom the Lord fled into Egypt, the brother of this Herod, under whom Christ suffered, married Herodias, the daughter of king Aretas; but afterwards that his father in-law, after certain disagreements had arisen with his son in-law, had taken his daughter away, and, to the grief of her former husband, had given her in marriage to his enemy; therefore John the Baptist rebukes Herod and Herodias for contracting an unlawful union, and because it was not allowed for a man to marry his brother's wife during his lifetime.

THEOPHYL. The law also commanded a brother to marry his brother's wife, if he died without children; but in this case there was a daughter which made the marriage criminal: there follows, Therefore Herodias had a quarrel against him, and would have killed him but she could not.

BEDE; For Herodias was as afraid, lest Herod should repent at some time, or be reconciled to his brother Philip, and so the unlawful marriage be divorced. It goes on, For Herod feared John, knowing that he was a just man, and a holy.

GLOSS. He feared him, I say, because he revered him, for he knew him to be just in his dealings with men, and holy towards God, and he took care that Herodias should not slay him. And when he heard him, he did many things, for he thought that he spoke by the Spirit of God, and heard him gladly, because He considered that what he said was profitable.

THEOPHYL. But see how great the fury of lust, for though Herod had such an awe and fear of John, he forgets it all, that he may minister to his fornication.

REMIG. For his lustful will drove him to lay hands on a man, whom he knew to be just and holy. And by this we may see how a less fault became the cause to him of a greater; as it is said, He which is filthy, let him be filthy still. It goes on, And when a convenient day was come, that Herod on his birthday made a supper to his lords, high captains, and chief estates of Galilee.

BEDE, The only men whom we read of, as celebrating their birthdays with festive joys are Herod and Pharaoh, but each, with an evil presage, stained his birthday with blood; Herod, however, with so much the greater wickedness, as he slew the holy and guiltless teacher of truth, and that, by the wish, and at the instance of a female dancer. For there follows, And when the daughter of the said Herodias came in, and danced, and pleased Herod and them that sat with him, the king said to the damsel, Ask of me whatever you will, and I will give it you.

THEOPHYL. For during the banquet, Satan danced in the person of the damsel, and the wicked oath is completed. For it goes on, And he swore to her, Whatever you shall ask of me, I will give it you, to the half of my kingdom.

BEDE; His oath does not excuse his murder, for per-chance his reason for swearing was, that he might find an opportunity for slaying, and if she had demanded the death of his father and mother, he surely would not have granted it. It goes on, And she went forth, and said to her mother, What shall I ask? And He said, The head of John the Baptist. Worthy is blood to be asked as the reward of such a deed as dancing.

It goes on, And she came in straightway with haste, &c.

THEOPHYL. The malignant woman begs that the head of John he given to her immediately, that is, at once, in that very hour, for she feared lest Herod should repent. There follows, And the king was exceeding sorry.

Collected Out of the Works of the Fathers

BEDE; It is usual with Scripture, that the historian should relate events as they were when believed by all, thus Joseph is called the father of Jesus by Mary herself. So now also Herod is said to be exceeding sorry, for so the guests thought, since the hypocrite bore sadness on his face, when he had joy in his heart; and he excuses his wickedness by his oath, that he might be impious under pretense of piety. Wherefore there follows For his oath's sake, and for their sakes who sat with him, he would not reject her.

THEOPHYL. Herod not being his own master, but full of lust, fulfilled his oath, and slew the just man, it would have been better however to break his oath, than to commit so great a sin.

BEDE; In that again which is added, And for their sakes who sat with him, he wishes to make all partakers in his guilt, that a bloody feast might be set before luxurious and impure guests. Wherefore it goes on, But sending an executioner, he commanded his head to be brought in a charger.

THEOPHYL. 'Spiculator' is the name for the public servant commissioned to put men to death.

BEDE; Now Herod was not ashamed to bring before his guests the head of a murdered man; but we do not read of such an act of madness in Pharoah. From both examples, however, it is proved to be more useful, often to call to mind the coming day of our death, by fear and by living chastely, than to celebrate the day of our birth with luxury. For man is born in the world to toil, but the elect pass by death out of the world to repose. It goes on, And he beheaded him in prison, &c.

Catena Aurea: Commentary on the Gospel of St. Mark

GREG. I cannot, without the greatest wonder, reflect that he, who was filled even in his mother's womb with the spirit of prophecy, and then was the greatest that had arisen amongst those born of women, is sent into prison by wicked men, is beheaded for the dancing of a girl, and though a man of so great austerity, meets death through such a foul instrument. Are we to suppose that there was something evil in his life, to have wiped away by so incomprehensible a death? When, however, could he commit a silo even in his eating, whose food was only locusts and wild honey? How could he offend in his conversation, who never quitted the wilderness? How is it that Almighty God so despises in this life those whom He has so sublimely chosen before all ages, if it be not for the reason, when is plain to the piety of the faithful, that He thus sinks them into the lowest place, because he sees how he is rewarding them in the highest, and outwardly He throws them down amongst things despised, because inwardly he draws them up even to incomprehensible things. Let each then infer from us what they shall suffer, whom he rejects, if he so grieves those whom he loves.

BEDE; There follows, And when his disciples heard of it, they came and took up his corpse, and laid it in a tomb. Josephus relates, that John was brought bound into the castle of Macheron, and there slain; and, ecclesiastical history says that he was buried in Sebaste, a city of Palestine, once called Samaria. But the beheading of John the Baptist signifies the lessening of that fame, by which he was thought to be Christ by the people, as the raising of our Savior on the cross typifies the advance of the faith, in that He Himself, who was first looked upon as a prophet by the multitude, was recognized as the Son of God by all the faithful; wherefore John, who was destined to decrease, was born when the daylight begins to wax short; but the Lord at that season of the year in which the day begins to lengthen.

THEOPHYL. In a mystical way, however, Herod, whose name means, 'of skin,' is the people of the Jews, and the wife to whom he was wedded means vain glory, whose daughter even now encircles the Jews with her dance, namely, a false understanding of the Scriptures; they indeed beheaded John, that is, the word of prophecy, and, hold to him without Christ, his head.

PSEUDO-JEROME; Or else, The head of the law, which is Christ, is cut off from his own body, that is, the Jewish people, and is given to a Gentile damsel, that is, the Roman Church, and the damsel gives it to her adulterous mother, that is, to the synagogue, when in the end we believe. The body of John is buried, his head is put in a dish; thus the human Letter is covered over, the Spirit is honored, and received on the altar.

30. And the apostles gathered themselves together to Jesus, and told him all things, both what they had done, and what they had taught.

31. And he said to them, Come you yourselves apart into a desert place, and rest a while: for there were many coming and going, and they had no leisure so much as to eat.

32. And they departed into a desert place by ship privately.

33. And the people saw them departing, and many knew him, and ran afoot thither out of all cities, and out went them, and

came together to him.

34. And Jesus, when he came out, saw many people, and was moved with compassion toward them, because they were as sheep not having a shepherd: and he began to teach them many things.

GLOSS. The Evangelist, after relating the death of John, gives an account of those things which Christ did with His disciples after the death of John, saying, And the Apostles gathered themselves together to Jesus, and told him all things, both what they had done, and what they had taught.

PSEUDO-JEROME; For they return to the fountain-head whence the streams flow; those who are sent by God, always offer up thanks for those things which they have received.

THEOPHYL. Let us also learn, when we are sent on any mission, not to go far away, and not to overstep the bounds of the office committed, but to go often to him, who sends us, and report all that we have done and taught; for we must not only teach but act.

BEDE; Not only do the Apostles tell the Lord what they themselves had done and taught, but also his own and John's disciples together tell him what John had suffered, during the time that they were occupied in teaching, as Matthew relates. It goes on: And he said to them, Come you yourselves apart, &c.

AUG. This is said to have taken place, after the passion of John, therefore what is first related took place last, for it was by these events that Herod was moved to say, This is John the Baptist, whom I beheaded.

THEOPHYL. Again, He goes to a desert place from His humility. But Christ makes His disciples rest, that men who are set over others may hear, that they who labor in any work or in the word deserve rest, and ought not to labor continually.

BEDE; How arose the necessity for giving rest to His disciples, He shows, when He adds, For there were many coming and going, and they had no leisure so much as to eat; we may then see how great was the happiness of that time, both from the toil of the teachers, and from the diligence of the learners. It goes on, And embarking into a ship, they departed into a desert place privately. The disciples did not enter into the ship alone, but taking up the Lord with them, they went to a desert place, as Matthew shows. Here He tries the faith of the multitude, and by seeking a desert place. He would see whether they care to follow Him. And they follow Him, and that not on horseback, nor in carriages, but laboriously coming on foot, they show how great is their anxiety for their salvation.

There follows, And the people saw them departing, and many knew him, and ran afoot thither out of all cities, and out went them. In saying that they out went them on foot, it is proved that the disciples with the Lord did not reach the other bank of the sea, or of the Jordan, but they went to the nearest places of the same country, where the people of those parts could come to them on foot.

THEOPHYL. So do you not wait for Christ till He Himself call you, but outrun Him, and come before Him. There follows, And Jesus when he came out saw much people, and was moved with compassion towards them, because they were as sheep having no shepherd. The Pharisees being ravenous wolves did not feed the sheep, but devoured them; for which reason they gather themselves to Christ, the trite Shepherd, who gave them spiritual food, that is, the word of God. Wherefore it goes on, And he began to teach them many things. For seeing that those who followed Him on account of His miracles were tired from the length of the way, He pitied them, and wished to satisfy their wish by teaching them.

BEDE; Matthew says that he healed their sick, for the real way of pitying the poor is to open to them the way of truth by teaching them, and to take away their bodily pains.

PSEUDO-JEROME; Mystically, however, the Lord took apart those whom He chose, that though living amongst evil men, they might not apply their minds to evil things, as Lot in Sodom, Job in the land of Uz, and Obadiah in the house of Ahab.

BEDE; Leaving also Judea, the holy preachers, in the desert of the Church, overwhelmed by the burden of their tribulations amongst the Jews, obtained rest by the imparting of the grace of faith to the Gentiles.

PSEUDO-JEROME; Little indeed is the rest of the saints here on earth, long is their labor, but afterwards, they are bidden to rest from their labors. But as in the ark of Noah, the animals that were within were sent forth, and they that were without rushed in, so is it in the Church, Judas went, the thief came to Christ.

But as long as men go back from the faith, the Church can have no refuge from grief; for Rachel weeping for her children would not be comforted. Moreover, this world is not the happiest, in which the new wine is drank, when the new song will be sung by men made anew, when this mortal shall have put in immortality.

BEDE; But when Christ goes to the deserts of the Gentiles, many bands of the faithful leaving the walls of their cities, that is their old manner of living, follow Him.

35. And when the day was now far spent, His disciples came to him, and said, This is a desert place, and now the time is far passed:

36. Send them away, that they may go into the country round about, and into the villages, and buy themselves bread: for they have nothing to eat.

37. He answered and said to them, Give you them to eat. And they say to him, Shall we go and buy two hundred pennyworth of bread, and give them to eat?

38. He said to them, How many loaves have you? go and see. And when they knew, they say, Five, and two fishes.

39. And he commanded them to make all sit down by companies on the green grass.

40. And they sat down in ranks, by hundreds, and by fifties.

41. And when He had taken the five loaves and the two fishes,

He looked up to heaven, and blessed, and broke the loaves, and gave them to His disciples to set before them; and the two fishes divided he among them all.

42. And they did all eat, and were filled.

43. And they took up twelve baskets full of the fragments, and of the fishes.

44. And they that did eat of the loaves were about five thousand men.

THEOPHYL. The Lord, placing before them, first, what is most profitable, that is, the food of the word of God, afterwards also gave the multitude food for their bodies; in beginning to relate which the Evangelist says, And to when on, the day was now far spent, his disciples came to him, and said, This is a desert place.

BEDE; The time being far spent, points out that it was evening. Wherefore Luke says, But the day had begun to decline.

THEOPHYL. See now, how those who are disciples of Christ grow in love to man, for they pity the multitudes, and come to Christ to intercede for them. But the Lord tried them, to see whether they would know that His power was great enough to feed them.

Wherefore it goes on, He answered and said to them, Give you them to eat.

BEDE; By these words He calls on His Apostles, to break bread for the people, that they might be able to testify that they had no bread, and thus the greatness of the miracle might become more known.

THEOPHYL. But the disciples thought that He did not know what was necessary for the feeding of so large a multitude, for their answer shows that they were troubled. For it goes on, And they said to him, Shall we go and buy two hundred pennyworth of bread, and give them to eat?

AUG. This in the Gospel of John is the answer of Philip, but Mark gives it as the answer of the disciples, wishing it to be understood that Philip made this answer as a mouthpiece of the others; although he might put the plural number for the singular, as is usual. It goes on, And he said to them, How many loaves have you? go and see. The other Evangelists pass over this being done by the Lord. It goes on, And when they knew, they say, Five, a two fishes. This, which was suggested by Andrew, as we learn from John, the other Evangelists, using the plural for the singular, have put into the mouth of the disciples.

It goes on, And he commanded them enter to make all sit do down by companies upon the green grass,

and they sat down in ranks by hundreds and by fifties. But we need not be perplexed, though Luke says that they were ordered to sit down by fifties, and Mark by hundreds and fifties, for, one was mentioned a part, the other the whole. Mark, who mentions the hundreds, fills up what the other has left out.

THEOPHYL. We are given to understand that they lay down in

parties, separate from one another, for what is translated by companies, is repeated twice over in the Greek, as though it were by companies and companies. It goes on, And when he had taken the five loaves and the two fishes, he looked up to heaven, and blessed, and broke the loaves, and gave them to his disciples to set before them, and the two fishes divided he among them all.

CHRYS. Now it was with fitness that He looked up to heaven, for the Jews, when receiving manna in the desert, presumed to say of God, Can he give bread? To prevent this therefore before He performed the miracle, He referred to His Father what He was about to do.

THEOPHYL. He also looks up to heaven that He may teach us to seek our food from God, and not from the devil, as they do who unjustly feed on other man labors. By this also He intimated to the crowd, that He could not be opposed to God, since He called upon God. And He gives the bread to His disciple's to set before the multitude, that by handling the bread they might see that it was an undoubted miracle. It goes on: And they did all eat, and were filled:

and they took up twelve baskets full of the fragments.

Twelve baskets of fragments remained over and above, that each of the Apostles, carrying a basket on his shoulder, might recognize the unspeakable Worker of the miracle. For it was a proof of overflowing power not only to feed so many men, but also to leave such a superabundance of fragments. Even though Moses gave manna, yet what was given to each was measured by his necessity, and what was over and above was overrun with worms. Elias also fed the woman, but gave her just what was enough for her; but Jesus, being the Lord, makes his gifts with superabundant profusion.

BEDE; Again, in a mystical sense, the Savior refreshes the hungry crowds at the day's decline, because, either, now that the end of the world approaches, or now that the Sun of justice has set in death for us, we are saved from wasting away in spiritual hunger. He calls the Apostles to Him at the breaking of bread, intimating that daily by them our hungry souls are fed, that is, by their letters and examples. By the five loaves are figured the Five Books of Moses, by the two fishes the Psalms and Prophets.

THEOPHYL. Or the two fishes are the discourses of fishermen that is, their Epistles and Gospel.

BEDE; There are five senses in the outward man which shows that by the five thousand men are meant those who, living in the world, know how to make a good use of external things.

GREG. The different ranks in which those who ate lie down, mark out the divers churches which make up the one Catholic. But the Jubilee rest is contained in the mystery of the number fifty, and fifty must be doubled before it reaches up to a hundred. As then the first step is to rest from doing evil, that afterwards the soul may rest more fully from evil thoughts, some lie down in parties of fifty, others of a hundred.

BEDE; Again, those men lie down on grass and are fed by the food of the Lord, who have trodden under foot their concupiscences by continence, and apply themselves diligently to hear and fulfill the words of God. The Savior, however, does not create a new sort of food; for when He came in the flesh He preached no other things than were predicted, but showed how pregnant with mysteries of grace were the writings of the Law and the Prophets. He looks up to heaven, that He may teach us that there we must look for grace. He breaks and distributes to the disciples that they may place the bread before the multitudes, because He has opened the mysteries of prophecy to holy doctors, who are to preach them to the whole world. What is left by the crowd is taken up by the disciples, because the more sacred mysteries, which cannot be received by the foolish, are not to be passed by with negligence, but to be inquired into by the perfect. For by the twelve baskets, the Apostles and the following Doctors are typified, externally indeed despised by men, but inwardly full of healthful food. For all know that carrying baskets is a part of the work of shaves.

PSEUDO-JEROME; Or, in the gathering of the twelve baskets full of fragments, is signified the time, when they shall sit on thrones, judging all who are left of Abraham, Isaac, and Jacob, the twelve tribes of Israel, when the remnant of Israel shall be saved.

45. And straightway he constrained his disciples to get into the ship, and to go to the other side before unto Bethsaida, while he sent away the people.

46. And when He had sent them away, he departed into a mountain to pray.

47. And when evening was come, the ship was in the midst of

the sea, and He alone on the land.

48. And he saw them toiling in rowing; for the wind was contrary to them: and about the fourth watch of the night he came to them, walking upon the sea, and would have passed by them.

49. But when they saw him walking upon the sea, they supposed it had been a spirit, and cried out:

50. For they all saw him, and were troubled. And immediately He talked with them, and said to them, Be of good cheer: it is I; be not afraid.

51. And he went up into them into the ship; and the wind ceased: and they were sore amazed in themselves beyond measure, and wondered.

52. For they considered not the miracle of the loaves: for their heart was hardened.

GLOSS. The Lord indeed by the miracle of the loaves showed that He is the Creator of the world: but now by walking on the waves He proved that He had a body free from the weight of all sin, and by appeasing the winds and by calming the rage of the waves, He declared Himself to be the Master of the elements. Wherefore it is said, And straight way he constrained his disciples to yet into the ship, and to go to the other side before to Bethsaida, while he sent away the people.

PSEUD-CHRYS. He dismisses indeed the people, with His

blessing and with some cures. But He constrained His disciples, because they could not without pain separate themselves from Him, and that, not only on account of the very great affection which they had for Him, but also because they were at a loss how He would join them.

BEDE; But it is with reason that we wonder how Mark says, that after the miracles of the loaves the disciples crossed the sea of Bethsaida, when Luke relates that the miracle was done in the parts of Bethsaida, unless we understand that Luke means by the desert which is Bethsaida not the country immediately around the town, but the desert places belonging to it. But when Mark says that they should go before unto Bethsaida, the town itself is meant. It goes on: And when he had sent them away he departed into a mountain to pray.

PSEUD-CHRYS. This we must understand of Christ, in that He is man; He does it also to teach us to he constant prayer.

THEOPHYL. But when He had dismissed the crowd, He goes up to pray, for prayer requires rest and silence.

BEDE; Not every man, however, prays goes up into a mountain, but he alone prays well, who seeks God in prayer. But he who prays for riches or worldly labor, or for the death of his enemy, sends up from the lowest depths his vile prayers to God. John says, When Jesus therefore perceived that they would come and take him by force and make him a king, he departed again into a mountain himself alone.

It goes on; and when even was come the ship was in the midst of the sea, and he alone on the land.

THEOPHYL; Now the Lord permitted His disciples to be in danger, that they might learn patience; wherefore He did not immediately come to their aid, but allowed them to remain in danger all night, that He might teach them to wait patiently, and not to hope at once for help in tribulations, For there follows, And he saw them toiling in rowing, for the wind was contrary unto them; and about the fourth watch of the night, he comes to them walking upon the sea.

PSEUD-CHRYS. Holy Scripture reckons four watches in the night, making each division three hours ; wherefore by the fourth watch it means that which is after the ninth hour that is, in the tenth or some following hour. There follows, And would have passed them by.

AUG. But how could they understand this, except from His going a different way, wishing to pass them as strangers; for they were so far from recognizing Him, as to take Him for a spirit. For it goes on: But when they saw him walking upon the sea, they supposed it had been a spirit, and cried out.

THEOPHYL. See again how Christ, though He was about to put an end to their dangers puts them in greater fear. But He immediately reassured them by His voice, for it continues, And immediately he talked with them, and said to them It is I be not afraid.

CHRYS. As soon then as they knew Him. His voice, their fear left them. How then could He wish to pass them, whose fears He so reassures, if it were not that His wish to pass them would wring from them that cry, which called for His help?

BEDE ; But Theodorus who, as Bishop of Phanara, wrote that the Lord had no bodily weight in His flesh, and walked on the sea without weight; but the Catholic faith declares that I He had weight according to the flesh. For Dionysius says, We know not how without plunging in His feet, which had bodily weight and the gravity of matter, He could walk on the wet and unstable substance

THEOPHYL. Then by entering into the ship, the Lord restrained the tempest. For it continues, And he went up to them into the ship, and the wind ceased. Great indeed is the miracle of our Lord's walking on the sea, but the tempest and the contrary wind were there as well, to make the miracle greater. For the Apostles, not understanding g from the miracle of the five loaves the power of Christ, now more fully knew it from the miracle of the sea. Wherefore it goes on, And they were sore amazed in themselves. For they understood not concerning the loaves .

BEDE; The disciples indeed, who were still carnal , were amazed at the greatness of His virtue, they could not yet however recognize in Him the truth of the divine Majesty. Therefore it goes on, For their hearts were hardened. But mystically, the toil of the disciples in rowing, and the contrary wind, mark out the labors of the Holy Church, who amidst the beating waves of the world, and the blasts of unclean spirits, strives to teach the repose of her celestial country.

And well is it said that the ship was in the midst of the sea, and

He alone on land, for sometimes the Church is afflicted by a pressure from the Gentiles so overwhelming, that her Redeemer seems to have entirely deserted her, but the Lord sees His own, toiling on the sea, for, lest they faint in tribulations, He strengthens them by the look of His love, and sometimes frees themselves by a visible assistance. Further, in the fourth watch He came to them as daylight approached, for when man lifts up his mind to the light of guidance from on high, the Lord will he with him, and the dangers of temptations will he laid asleep.

PSEUD-CHRYS. Or else, the first watch means the time up to the deluge; the second, up to Moses; the third, up to the coming of the Lord; in the fourth the Lord came and spoke to His disciples.

BEDE; Often then does the love of heaven seem to have deserted the faithful in tribulation, so that it may be thought that Jesus wishes to pass by His disciples, as it were, toiling in the sea. And still do heretics suppose that the Lord was a phantom, and did not take upon Him real flesh from the Virgin.

PSEUDO-JEROME; And He says to them, Be of good cheer, it is I, because we shall see Him as He is. But the wind and the storm ceased when Jesus sat down, that is, reigned in the ship, which is the Catholic Church.

BEDE; In whatever heart, also, He is present by the grace of His love, there soon all the strivings of vices, and of the adverse world, or of evil spirits, are kept under and put to rest.

53. And after they had passed over, they came into the land of

Gennesaret, and drew to the shore.

54. And when they were come out of the ship, straightway they knew him,

55. And ran through that the region round about, and began to carry about in beds those that were sick, where they heard he was.

56. And whithersoever he entered, into villages, or cities, or country, they laid the sick in the streets, and besought him that they might touch if it were but the border of his garment: and as many as touched him were made whole.

GLOSS. The Evangelist, having shown the danger which the disciples had sustained in their passage, and their deliverance from it, now shows the place to which they sailed, saying, And when they had passed over, they came into the land of Gennesaret, and drew to the shore.

THEOPHYL. The Lord remained at the above-mentioned place for some time. Therefore the Evangelist subjoins, And when they had come out of the ship, straightway they knew him, that is, the inhabitants of the country.

BEDE; But they knew Him by report, not by His features; or through the greatness of His miracles, even His person was known to some. See too how great was the faith of the men of the land of Gennesaret, so that they were not content with the healing of those who were present, but sent to other towns round about, that all might hasten to the Physician; wherefore there follows, And ran through the whole region round about, and began to carry about in beds those that were sick, where they heard he was.

THEOPHYL. For they did not call Him to their houses that He might heal them, but rather the sick themselves were brought to Him. Wherefore it also follows, And whithersoever he entered into villages, or cities, or country try, &c. For the miracle which had been wrought on the woman with an issue of blood, had reached the ears of many, and caused in them that great faith, by which they were healed. It goes on, And as many as touched him were made whole.

BEDE; Again, in a mystical sense, do they understand by the hem of His garment the slightest of His commandments, for whoever shall transgress it shall be called the least in the kingdom of heaven, or else His assumption of our flesh, by which we have come to the Word of God, and afterwards, shall have the enjoyment of His majesty.

PSEUDO-JEROME; Furthermore that which is said, And as many as touched him were made whole, shall be fulfilled, when grief and mourning shall fly away.

Catena Aurea: Commentary on the Gospel of St. Mark

Mark 7

1. Then came together unto him the Pharisees, and certain of the Scribes, which came from Jerusalem.

2. And when they saw some of his disciples eat bread with defiled, that is to say, with unwashed, hands, they found fault.

3. For the Pharisees, and all the Jews, except they wash their hands off, eat not, holding the tradition of the elders.

4. And when they come from the market, except they wash, they eat not. And many other things there be, which they have received to hold, as the washing of cups, and pots, brasen vessels, and of tables.

5. Then the Pharisees and Scribes asked him, Why walk not you disciples according to the tradition of the elders, but eat bread with unwashed hands?

6. He answered and said unto them, Well has Esaias prophesied of you hypocrites, as it is written, This people honor me with their lips, but their heart is far from me.

7. However in vain do they worship me, teaching for doctrines the commandments of men.

8. For laying aside the commandment of God, you hold the tradition of men, as the washing of pots and cups: and many other such like things you do.

9. And he said unto them, Full well you reject the commandment of God, that you may keep your own tradition.

10. For Moses said, Honor your father and your mother; and, Whoever curse father or mother, let him die the death:

11. But you say, If a man shall say to his father or mother, It is Corban, that is to say, a gift, by whatever you might be profited by me; he shall be free.

12. And you suffer him no more to do ought for his father or his mother;

13. Making the word of God of none effect through your tradition, which you have deliverd: and many such like things do you.

BEDE; The people of the land of Gennesareth, who seem to be unlearned men, not only come themselves, but also bring their sick to the Lord, that they may but succeed in touching the hem of His garment. But the Pharisees and Scribes, who ought to have been the teachers of the people, run together to the Lord, not to seek for healing but to move captions questions; wherefore it ms said, Then there came together to him the Pharisees and certain of the Scribes, coming from Jerusalem;

and when they saw some of his disciples eat bread with common, that is, with unwashed hands, they found fault.

THEOPHYL. For the disciples of the Lord, who were taught

only the practice of virtue, used to eat in a simple way, without washing their hands; but the Pharisees, wishing to find an occasion of blame against them, took it up; they did not indeed, blame them as transgressors of the law, but for transgressing the traditions of the elders.

Wherefore it goes on: For the Pharisees and all the Jews, except they wash their hands oft, eat not, holding the tradition of the elders.

BEDE; For taking the spiritual words of the Prophets in a carnal sense, they observed, by washing the body alone, commandments which concerned the chastening of the heart and deeds, saying, Wash you, make you clean; and again, Be you clean that bear the vessels of the Lord. It is therefore a superstitious human tradition, that men who are clean already, should wash oftener because they eat bread, and that they should not eat on leaving the market, without washing. But it is necessary for those who desire to partake of the bread which comes down from heaven, often to cleanse their evil deeds by alms, by tears, and the other fruits of righteousness. It is also necessary for a man to wash thoroughly away the pollutions which he has contracted from the cares of temporal business, by being afterwards intent on good thoughts and works. In vain, however, do the Jews wash their hands, and cleanse themselves after the market, so long as they refuse to be washed in the font of the Savior; in vain do they observe the washing of their vessels, who neglect to wash away the filthy sins of their bodies and of their hearts.

It goes on: Then the Scribes and Pharisees asked him, Why walk not your disciples after the tradition of the elder's, but eat bread with common hands?

JEROME; Wonderful is the folly of the Pharisees and Scribes; they accuse the Son of God, because He keeps not the traditions and precepts of men. But common is here put for unclean; for the people of the Jews, boasting that they were the portion of God, called those meats common, which all made use of.

PSEUDO-JEROME; He beats back the vain words of the Pharisees with His arguments, as men drive back dogs with weapons, by interpreting Moses and Isaiah, that we too by the word of Scripture may conquer the heretics, who oppose us; wherefore it goes on: Well has Esaias prophesied of you hypocrites; as it is written, This people honors me with their lips, but their heart is far from me.

PSEUD-CHRYS. For since they unjustly accused the disciples not of transgressing the law, but the commands of the elders, He sharply confounds them, calling them hypocrites, as looking with reverence upon what was not worthy of it. He adds, however, the words of Isaiah the prophet, as spoken of them; as though He would say, As those men, of whom it is said, that they honor God with their lips, whilst their heart is far from him, in vain pretend to observe the dictates of piety, whilst they honor the doctrines of men, so you also neglect your soul, of which you should take care, and blame those who live justly.

PSEUDO-JEROME; But Pharisaical tradition, as to tables and vessels, is to be cut off, and cast away. For they often make the commands of God yield to the traditions of men; wherefore it continues, For laying aside the commandments of God, you hold to the traditions of men, as the washing of pots and cups.

PSEUD-CHRYS. Moreover, to convict them of neglecting the reverence due to God, for the sake of the tradition of the elders which was opposed to the Holy Scriptures. He subjoins, For Moses said, Honor your father and your mother; and Whoever curse father or mother, let him die the death.

BEDE; The sense of the word honor in Scripture us not so much the saluting and paying court to men, as alms-giving, and bestowing gifts; honor, says the Apostle, widows who are widows indeed.

PSEUD-CHRYS. Notwithstanding the existence of such a divine law, and the threats against such as break it, you lightly transgress the commandments of God, observing the traditions of the Elders. Wherefore there follows, But you say, If a man shall say to his father or mother, It is Corban, that is to say, a gift, by whatever you might be profited by me; understand, he will be freed from the observation of the foregoing command.

Wherefore it continues, And you suffer him no more to do ought for his father or his mother.

THEOPHYL. For the Pharisees, wishing to devour the offerings, instructed sons, when their parents asked for some of their property, to answer them, what you have asked of us is corban, that is, a gift, I have already offered it up to the Lord; thus the parents would not require it, as being offered up to the Lord, (and in that way profitable for their own salvation). Thus they deceived the sons into neglecting their parents, whilst they themselves devoured the offerings; with this therefore the Lord reproaches them, as transgressing the law of God for the sake of gain.

Wherefore it goes on, Making the word of God of none effect through your traditions, which you have delivered: and many such like things do you; transgressing, that is, the commands of God, that you may observe the traditions of men.

PSEUD-CHRYS. Or else it may he said, that the Pharisees taught young persons, that if a man offered a gift in expiation of the injury done to his father or mother, he was free from sin, as having given to God the gifts which are owed to a parent; and in saying this, they did not allow parents to be honored.

BEDE; The passage may in a few words have this sense, Every gift which I have to make, will go to do you good; for you compel children, it is meant, to say to their parents, that gift which I was going to offer to God, I expend on feeding you, and does you good, oh father and mother, speaking this ironically. Thus they would be afraid to accept what had been given into the hands of God, and might prefer a life of poverty to living on consecrated property.

PSEUDO-JEROME; Mystically, again, the disciples eating with unwashed hands signifies the future fellowship of the Gentiles with the Apostles. The cleansing and washing of the Pharisees is barren; but the fellowship of the Apostles, though without washing, has stretched out its branches as far as the sea.

Catena Aurea: Commentary on the Gospel of St. Mark

14. And when he had called all the people to him, he said unto them, Hearken unto me every one of you, and understand:

15. There is nothing from without a man, that entering into him can defile him: but the things which come out of him, those are they that defile the man.

16. If any man have ears to hear, let him hear.

17. And when he was entered into the house from the people, his disciples asked him concerning the parable.

18. And he said to them, Are you so without understanding also? Do you not perceive, that whatever thing from without enters into the man, it cannot defile him;

19. Because it enters not into his heart, but into the belly, and goes out into the draught, purging all meats?

20. And he said, That which comes out of the man, that defiles the man.

21. For from within, out of time heart of men, proceed evil thoughts, adulteries, fornications, murders,

22. Thefts, covetousness, wickedness, deceit, lasciviousness, an evil eye, blasphemy, pride, foolishness:

23. All these evil things come from within, and defile the man.

PSEUD-CHRYS. The Jews regard and murmur about only the

bodily purification of the law; our Lord wishes to bring in the contrary. Wherefore it is said, And when he had called all the people to him, he said to them. Hearken in unto me every one, and understand;

there is nothing from without a man, that entering into sin can defile him but the things which come out of a man, those are they which defile a man; that is, which make him unclean. The things of Christ have relation to the inner man but those which are of the law are visible and external, to which, as being bodily, the cross of Christ was shortly to put an end.

THEOPHYL. But the intention of the Lord in saying this was to teach men, that the observing of meats, which the law commands, should not be taken in a carnal sense, and from this He began to unfold to them the intent of the law.

PSEUD-CHRYS. Again he subjoins, If any man have ears to hear, let him hear. For He had not clearly shown them, what those things are which proceed out of a man, and defile a man; and on account of this saying, the Apostles thought that the foregoing discourse of the Lord implied some other deep thing;

wherefore there follows: And when he was entered into the house from the people, his disciples asked him concerning the parable; they called it parable, because it was not clear.

THEOPHYL. The Lord begins by chiding them, wherefore there follows, Are you so without understanding also?

BEDE; For that man is a faulty hearer who considers what is

obscure to be a clear speech, or what is clear to he obscurely spoken.

THEOPHYL. Then the Lord shows them what was hidden, saying, Do you not perceive, that whatever thing from without enters into the man, it cannot make him common?

BEDE; For the Jews, boasting themselves to be the portion of God, call common those meats which all men use, as shellfish, hares, and animals of that sort. Not even however what is offered to idols is unclean, in as far as it is food and God's creature; it is the invocation of devils which makes it unclean; and He adds the cause of it saying, Because it enters not into his heart. The principal seat of the soul according to Plato is time brain, hut according to Christ, it is in the heart.

GLOSS. It says therefore into his heart, that is, into his mind, which is the principal part of his soul, on which his whole life depends; wherefore it is necessary, that according to the state of his heart a man should be called clean or unclean, and thus whatsoever does not reach the soul, cannot bring pollution to the man. Meats therefore, since they do not reach the soul, cannot in their own nature defile a man; but an inordinate use of meats, which proceeds from a want of order in the mind, makes men unclean. But that meats cannot reach the mind, He shows by that which He adds, saying, But into the belly, and goes out into the draught, purging all meats. This however He says, without referring to what remains from the food in the body, for that which is necessary for the nourishment and growth of the body remains. But that which is superfluous goes out, and thus as it were purges the nourishment, which remains.

AUG. For some things are joined to others in such a way as both to change and be changed, just as food, losing its former appearance, is both itself turned into our body, and we too are changed, and our strength is refreshed by it. Further a most subtle liquid, after the food has been prepared and digested in our veins, and other arteries, by some hidden channels, called from a Greek word, pores, passes through us, and goes into the draught.

BEDE; Thus then it is not meat that makes men unclean, but wickedness, which works in us the passions which come from within; wherefore it goes on: And he said, That which comes out of a man, that defiles a man.

GLOSS. The meaning of which He points out, when He subjoins, from within, out of the heart of men, proceed evil thoughts. And thus it appears that evil thoughts belong to the mind, which is lucre called the heart, and according to which a man is called good or bad, clean or unclean.

BEDE; From this passage are condemned those men who suppose that thoughts are put into them by the devil, and do not arise from their own evil will. The devil may excite and help on evil thoughts, he cannot be their author.

GLOSS. From evil thoughts, however, evil actions proceed to greater lengths, concerning which it is added, adulteries, that is acts which consist in the violation of another man's bed; fornications, which are unlawful connections between persons, not bound by marriage; murders, by which hurt is inflicted on the person of one's neighbor; thefts, by which his goods are taken from him; covetousness, by which things are unjustly kept; wickedness, which consists in calumniating others; deceit, in overreaching them; lasciviousness, to which belongs any corruption of mind or body.

THEOPHYL. An evil eye, that is, hatred and flattery, for he who hates turns an evil and envious eye on him who he hates, and a flatterer, looking askance at his neighbor's goods, leads him into evil; blasphemies, that is, faults committed against God; pride, that is, contempt of God, when man ascribes to God, which he does, not to God, for it to his own virtue; foolishness, that is, an injury against one's neighbor.

GLOSS. Or, foolishness consists in wrong thoughts concerning God; for it is opposed to wisdom, which is the knowledge of divine things. It goes on, All these evil things come from within inn, and defile the man. For whatever is in the power of a man, is imputed to him as a fault, because all such things proceed from the interior will, by which man is master of his own actions.

24. And from thence he arose, and sent into the borders of Tyre and Sidon, and entered into an house, and would have no man know it: but he could not be hid.

25. For a certain woman, whose young daughter had an unclean spirit, heard of him, and came and fell at his feet:

26. The woman was a Greek, a Syrophenician by nation; and she besought him that he would cast forth the devil out of her daughter.

27. But Jesus said to her, Let the children first be filled: for it is not meet to take the children's bread, and to cast it unto the dogs.

28. And she answered and said to him, Yes, Lord: yet the dogs under the table eat of the children's crumbs.

29. And he said unto her, For this saying go your way; the devil is gone out of your daughter.

30. And when she was come to her house, she found the devil gone out, and her daughter laid upon the bed.

THEOPHYL. After that the Lord had finished His teaching concerning food, seeing that the Jews wore incredulous, He enters into the country of the Gentiles, for the Jews being unfaithful, salvation turns itself to the Gentiles; wherefore it is said, And from thence he arose, and went into the borders of Tyre and Sidon.

PSEUD-CHRYS. Tyre and Sidon were places of the Canaanites, therefore the Lord comes to them, not as to His own, but as to men, who had nothing in common with the fathers to whom the promise was made. And therefore He comes in such a way, that His coming should not be known to the Tyrians and Sidonians. Wherefore it continues: And entered into a house, and would have no man know it. For the time had not come for His dwelling with the Gentiles and bringing them to the faith, for this was not to be, till after His cross and resurrection.

THEOPHYL. Or else His reason for coming in secret was that the Jews should not find occasion of blame against Him, as if He

Catena Aurea: Commentary on the Gospel of St. Mark

bad passed over to the unclean Gentiles. It goes on, But he could not be hid.

PSEUDO-AUG. But if He wished to do so and could not, it appears as if His will was impotent; it is not possible however that our Savior's will should not be fulfilled, nor can He will a thing, which He knows ought not be. Therefore when a thing has taken place, it may be asserted that He has willed it. But we should observe that this happened amongst the Gentiles, to whom it was not time to preach; nevertheless not to receive them, when they came to the faith of their own accord, would have been to grudge them the faith. So then it came to pass that the Lord was not made known by His disciples; others, however, who had seen Him entering the house, recognized Him, and it began to be known that He was there. His will therefore was that He should not be proclaimed by His own disciples, but that others should come to seek Him, and so it took place.

BEDE; Having entered also into the house, He commanded His disciples not to betray who He was to any one in this unknown region, that they, on whom He had bestowed the grace of healing, might learn by His example, as far as they could, to shrink from the glory of human praise in the showing forth of their miracles; yet they were not to cease from the pious work of virtue, when either the faith of the good justly deserved that miracles should be done, or the unfaithfulness of the wicked might necessarily compel them. For He Himself made known His entry into that place to the Gentile woman, and to whomsoever lie would.

PSEUDO-AUG. Lastly, the Canaanitish woman came in to Him,

on hearing of Him; if she had not first submitted herself to the God of the Jews, she would not have obtained their benefit. Concerning her it continues: For a woman, whose daughter had an unclean spirit, as soon as she had heard of him, came in and fell at his feet.

PSEUD-CHRYS. Now by this the Lord wished to show His disciples that He opened the door of faith even to the Gentiles, wherefore also the nation of the woman is described when it is added, The woman was a Gentile, a Syrophenician by nation, that is, from Syria of Phaenice. It goes on: And she besought him that he would cast forth the devil out of her daughter.

AUG. It appears however, that some question about a discrepancy may be raised, because it is said that the Lord was in the house when the woman came to her, asking about her daughter. When, however, Matthew says that His disciples had suggested to Him, Send her away, for she cries after us, he appears to imply nothing less than that the woman uttered supplicating cries after the Lord, as He walked. How then do we infer that she was in the house, except by gathering it from Mark, who says that she came in to Jesus, after having before said that He was in the house? But Matthew in that he says, He answered her not a word, gave its to understand that He went out, during that silence, from the house; thus too the other events are connected together, so that they now in no way disagree.

It continues; But He said unto her, Let the children be first filled.

BEDE; The time will come when even you who are Gentiles will obtain salvation; but it is right that first the Jews who deservedly are wont to he called by the name of children of God's ancient election, should be refreshed with heavenly bread, and that so at length, the food of life should be ministered to the Gentiles. There follows: For it is not meet to take the children's bread, and to cast it to the dogs.

PSEUD-CHRYS. These words He uttered not that there is in Him a deficiency of virtue, to prevent His ministering to all, but because His benefit, if ministered to both Jews and Gentiles who had no communication with each other, might he a cause of jealousy.

THEOPHYL. He calls the Gentiles dogs, as being thought wicked by the Jews; and He means by bread the benefit which the Lord promised to the children, that is, to the Jews. The sense therefore is, that it is not right for the Gentiles first to be partakers of the benefit, promised principally to the Jews. The reason, therefore, why the Lord does not immediately hear, but delays His grace, is, that He may also show that the faith of the woman was firm, and that we may learn not at once to grow weary in prayer, but to continue earnest till we obtain.

PSEUD-CHRYS. In like manner also to show the Jews that He did not confer healing on foreigners in the same degree as to them, and that by the discovery of the woman's faith, the faithfulness of the Jews might be the more laid bare. For the woman did not take it in, but with much reverence assented to what the Lord had said. Wherefore it goes on, And she answered and said unto him, Truth, Lord, but the dogs under the table eat of the children's crumbs.

Collected Out of the Works of the Fathers

THEOPHYL. As if she had said, The Jews have the whole of that bread which comes down from heaven, and you benefit also; I ask for the crumbs, that is, a small portion of the benefit.

PSEUD-CHRYS. Her placing herself therefore in the rank of dogs is a mark of her reverence; as if she said, I hold it as a favor to be even in the position of a dog, and to eat not from another table but from that of the Master himself.

THEOPHYL. Because therefore the woman answered with much wisdom, she obtained what she wanted; wherefore there follows, And he said unto her, &c. He said not, My virtue has made you whole, but for this saying, that is, for your faith, which is shown by this saying, go your way, the devil is gone out of your daughter.

It goes on, And when she was come into her house, she found her daughter laid upon the bed, and the devil gone out.

BEDE; On account then of the humble and faithful saying of her mother, the devil left the daughter; here is given a precedent for catechizing and baptizing infants, seeing that by the faith and the confession of the parents, infants are freed in baptism from the devil, though they can neither have knowledge in themselves, or do either good or evil.

PSEUDO-JEROME; Mystically however the Gentile woman, who prays for her daughter, is our mother the Church of Rome. Her daughter afflicted with a devil, is the barbarian western race, which by faith has been turned from a dog into a sheep. She desires to take the crumbs of spiritual understanding, not the unbroken bread of the letter.

THEOPHYL. The soul of each of us also, when he falls into sin, becomes a woman; and this soul has a daughter who is sick, that is, evil actions; this daughter again has a devil, for evil actions arise from devils. Again, sinners are called dogs, being filled with uncleanness. For which reason we are not worthy to receive the bread of God, or to be made partakers of the immaculate mysteries of God; if however in humility, knowing ourselves to be dogs, we confess our sins, then the daughter, that is, our evil life, shall be healed.

31. And again, departing from the coasts of Tyre and Sidon, he came unto the sea of Galilee, through the midst of the coasts of Decapolis.

32. And they bring unto him one that was deaf, and had an impediment in his speech; and they beseech him to put his hand upon him.

33. And he took him aside from the multitude, and put his fingers into his ears, and he spit, and touched his tongue;

34. And looking up to heaven, he sighed, and said to him, Ephphatha, that is, Be opened.

35. And straightway his ears were opened, and the string of his tongue was loosed, and he spoke plain.

36. And he charged them that they should tell no man: but the more he charged them, so much the more a great deal they

published it;

37. And were beyond measure astonished, saying, He has done all things well: he makes both the deaf to hear, and the dumb to speak.

THEOPHYL. The Lord did, not wish to stay in the parts of the Gentiles, lest He should give the Jews occasion to say, that they esteemed Him a transgressor of the law, because He held communion with the Gentiles, and therefore He immediately returns; wherefore it is said, And again departing from the coasts of Tyre, he came through Sidon, to the sea of Galilee, through the midst of the borders of Decapolis.

BEDE; Decapolis is a region of ten cities, across the Jordan, to the east, over against Galilee . When therefore it is said that the Lord came to the sea of Galilee, through the midst of the borders of Decapolis, it does not mean that He entered the confines of Decapolis themselves; for He is not said to have crossed the sea, but rather to have come to the borders of the sea, and to have reached quite up to the place, which was opposite to the midst of the coasts of Decapolis, which were situated at a distance across the sea.

It goes on, And they bring him one that was deaf and dumb, and they besought him to lay hands upon him.

THEOPHYL. Which is rightly placed after the deliverance of one possessed with a devil, for such an instance of suffering came from the devil. There follows, And he took him aside from the multitude, and put his fingers into his ears.

PSEUD-CHRYS. He takes the deaf and dumb man who was brought to Him apart from the crowd, that He might not do His divine miracles openly; teaching us to cast away vain glory and swelling of heart, for no one can work miracles as he can, who loves humility and is lowly in his conduct. But He puts His fingers into his ears, when He might have cured him with a word, to show that His body, being united to Deity, was consecrated by Divine virtue, with all that He did. For since on account of the transgression of Adam, human nature had incurred much suffering and hurt in its members and senses, Christ coming into the world showed the perfection of human nature in Himself, and on this account opened ears with His fingers, and gave the power of speech by His spittle. Wherefore it goes on, And spit, and touched his tongue.

THEOPHYL. That He might show that all the members of His sacred body are divine and holy, even the spittle which loosed the string of the tongue. For the spittle is only the superfluous moisture of the body, but in the Lord all things are divine. It goes on, And looking up to haven, he groaned, and said to him, Ephphatha, that is, Be opened.

BEDE; He looked up to heaven, that He might teach us that thence is to be procured speech for the dumb, hearing for the deaf, health for all who are sick. And He sighed, not that it was necessary for Him to beg any thing from His Father with groaning, for He, together with the Father, gives all things to them who ask, but that He might give us an example of sighing, when for our own errors and those of our neighbors, we invoke the guardianship of the Divine mercy.

PSEUD-CHRYS. He at the same time also groaned, as taking our cause upon Himself, and pitying human nature, seeing the misery into which it had fallen.

BEDE; But that which He says, Ephphatha, that is, Be opened, belongs properly to the ears, for the ears are to be opened for hearing, but the tongue to be loosed from the bonds of its impediment, that it may be able to speak.

Wherefore it goes on, And straightway his ears were opened, and the string of his tongue was loosed, and he spoke plain. Where each nature of one and the same Christ is manifestly distinct, looking up indeed, into Heaven as man, praying unto God, He groaned, but presently with one word, as being strong in the Divine Majesty, He healed.

It goes on, And be charged them that they should tell to man.

PSEUD-CHRYS. By which He has taught us not to boast in our powers, but in the cross and humiliation. He also bade them conceal the miracle, lest He should excite the Jews by envy to kill Him before the time.

PSEUDO-JEROME; A city, however, placed on a hill cannot be hid, and lowliness always comes before glory . Wherefore it goes on, But the more he charged them, so much the more a great deal they published it.

THEOPHYL. By this we are taught , when we confer benefits on any, by no means to seek for applause and praise; but when we have received benefits, to proclaim and praise our benefactors, even though they be unwilling.

AUG. If however He, as one Who knew the present and the future wills of men, knew that they would proclaim Him the more in proportion as He forbade them, why did He give them this command? If it were not that He wished to prove to men who are idle, how much more joyfully, with how such greater obedience, they whom He commands to proclaim Him should preach, when they who were forbidden could not hold their peace.

GLOSS. From the preaching however of those who were healed by Christ, the wonder of the multitude, and their praise of the benefits of Christ, increased. Wherefore it goes on, And they were beyond measure astonished, saying, He has done all things well; he makes the deaf to hear, and the dumb to speak.

PSEUDO-JEROME; Mystically, Tyre is interpreted narrowness, and signifies Judea, to which the Lord said, "For the bed is grown too narrow," and from which he turns himself to the Gentiles. Sidon means 'hunting,' for our race is like an untamed beast, and 'sea,' which means a wavering inconstancy. Again, the Savior comes to save the Gentiles in the midst of the coasts of Decapolis, which may be interpreted, as the commands of the Decalogue. Further, the human race throughout its many members is reckoned as one man, eaten up by varying pestilence, in the first created man; it is blinded, that is, its eye is evil; it becomes deaf, when it listens to, and dumb when it speaks, evil. And they prayed Him to lay His hand upon him, because many just men, and patriarchs, wished and longed for the time when the Lord should come in the flesh.

BEDE; Or he is deaf and dumb who neither has ears to hear the words of God, nor opens his mouth to speak them, and such must be presented to the Lord for healing, by men who have already learned to hear and speak the divine oracles.

PSEUDO-JEROME; Further, he who obtain healing is always drawn aside from turbulent thoughts, disorderly actions, and incoherent speeches. And the fingers which are put into the ears are the words and the gifts of the Holy Ghost, whom it is said, This is the finger of God. The spittle is heavenly wisdom, which loosens the sealed lips of the human race, so that it can say, I believe in God, the Father Almighty and the rest of the Creed. And looking up to heaven, he groaned, that is, He taught us to groan, and to raise up the treasures of our hearts to the heavens; because by the groaning of hearty compunction, the silly joy of the flesh is purged away. But the ears are opened to hymns, and songs, and psalms; and He looses the tongue, that it may pour forth the good word, which neither threats nor stripes can restrain.

Mark 8

1. In those days the multitude being very great, and having nothing to eat, Jesus called his disciples unto him, and said unto them,

2. I have compassion on the multitude, because they have now been with me three days, and have nothing to eat:

3. And if I send them away fasting to their own houses, they will faint by the way: for divers of them came from far.

4. And his disciples answered him, From whence can a man satisfy these men with bread here in the wilderness.

5. And he asked them, How many loaves have you? And they said, Seven.

6. And he commanded the people to sit down on the ground: and he took the seven loaves, and gave thanks, and broke, and gave to his disciples to set before them; and they did set them before the people.

7. And they had a few small fishes: and he blessed, and commanded to set them also before them.

8. So they did eat, and were filled: and they took up of the broken meat that was left seven baskets.

9. And they that had eaten were about four thousand: and he sent

them away.

THEOPHYL. After the Lord had performed the former miracle concerning the multiplication of the loaves, now again, a fitting occasion presents itself, and He takes the opportunity of working a similar miracle; wherefore it is said, In those days, the multitude being very great, and having nothing to eat, Jesus called his disciples to him and said to them,

I have compassion on the multitude, because they have now been with me three days, and have nothing to eat. For He did not always work miracles concerning the feeding of the multitude, lest they should follow Him for the sake of food; now therefore He would not have performed this miracle if He had not seen that the multitude was in danger.

Wherefore it goes on: And if I send them away fasting to their own houses, they will faint on the way: for divers of them came from far.

BEDE; Why they who came from afar hold out for three days Matthew says more fully: And he went up to a mountain and sat down there, and great multitudes came to him having with them many sick persons, and cast them down at Jesus feet, to be healed them.

THEOPHYL. The disciples cannot yet understand, nor did they believe in His virtue, notwithstanding former miracles, wherefore it continues, And his disciples said to him, From whence can a man satisfy these men with bread here in the wilderness? But the Lord Himself does not blame them teaching us that we should not he grieviously angry with ignorant men and those who do not understand, but bear with their ignorance.

After this it continues, And He asked them, How many loaves have you? and they answered, Seven.

REMIG. Ignorance was not His reason for asking them, but that from their answering seven, the miracle might he noised abroad, and become more known in proportion to the smallness of the number. It goes on: And he commanded the people to sit down on the ground. In the former feeding they lay on grass, in this one on the ground. It continues, And he took the seven loaves, and gave thanks and broke. In giving thanks, He has left us an example, that for all gifts conferred on us from heaven we should return thanks to Him. And it is to be remarked, that our Lord did not give the bread to the people, but to His disciples, and the disciples to the people; for it goes on, and gave to his disciples to set before them; and they did Set them before the people. And not only the bread, but the fish also He blessed, and ordered to he set before them.

For there comes after, And they had a few small fishes: and he blessed, and commanded to set them also before them.

BEDE; In this passage then we should notice, in one and the same our redeemer, a distinct operation of Divinity and our Manhood; thus the error, of Eutyches, who presumes to lay down the doctrine of one only operation in Christ, is to he cast out far from the Christian pale. For who does not here see that the pity of our Lord for the multitude is the feeling and sympathy of humanity; and that at the same time His satisfying four thousand men with seven loaves and a few fishes, is a work of Divine virtue?

It goes on, And they took up of the broken meat that was left seven baskets.

THEOPHYL. The multitudes who ate and were filled did not take with them the remains of the loaves, but the disciples took them up, as they did before the baskets. In which we learn according to the narration, that veve should be content with what is sufficient, and not look for anything beyond. The number of those who ate is put down, when it is said, And they that had eaten were about four thousand: and he sent them away; where we may see that Christ sends no one away fasting, for He wishes all to be nourished by His grace.

BEDE; The typical difference between this feeding and the other of the five loaves and two fishes, is, that there the letter of the Old Testament, full of spiritual grace, is signified, but here the truth and grace of the New Testament, which is to be ministered to all the faithful, is pointed out. Now the multitude remains three days, waiting for the Lord to heal their sick as Matthew relates, when the elect, in the faith of the Holy Trinity, supplicate for sins, with persevering earnestness; or because they turn themselves to the Lord in deed, in word, and in thought.

THEOPHYL. Or by those who wait for three days, He means the baptized; for baptism is called illumination, and is performed by trine immersion. GREG. He does not however wish to dismiss them fasting, lest they should faint by the way; for it is necessary that men should find in what is preached the word of consolation, lest hungering through want of the food of truth, they sink under the toil of this life.

AMBROSE; The good Lord indeed whilst He requires diligence, gives strength; nor will He dismiss the fasting, lest they faint by the way, that is, either in the course of this life, or before they have reached the fountain-head of life, that is, the Father, and have learnt that Christ is of the Father, lest haply, after, receiving that He is born of a virgin, they begin to esteem His virtue not that of God, but of man. Therefore the Lord Jesus divides the food, and His will indeed is the give to all, to deny none; He is the Dispenser of all things, but if you refuse to stretch forth your hand to receive the food, you will faint by the way, nor can you find fault with Him, who pities and divides.

BEDE; But they who return to repentance after the crimes of the flesh, after thefts, violence, and murders, come to the Lord from afar; for in proportion as a man has wandered farther in evil working, so he has ventured farther from Almighty God. The believers amongst the Gentiles came from afar to Christ, but the Jews from near, for they had been taught concerning Him by the letter of the law and the prophets. In the former case, however, of time feeding with five loaves, the multitude lay upon the green grass; here, however, upon the ground, because by the writing of the law, we are ordered to keep under the desires of the flesh, but in the New Testament we are ordered to leave even the earth itself and our temporal goods.

THEOPHYL. Further, the seven loaves are spiritual discourses, for seven is the number which points out the Holy G host, who perfects all things; for our life is perfected in the number of seven days.

PSEUDO-JEROME; Or else, the seven loaves are the gifts of the Holy Spirit, the fragments of the loaves and the mystical understanding of the first week.

BEDE; For our Lord's breaking the bread means the opening of mysteries; His giving of thanks shows how great a joy He feels in the salvation of the human race; His giving the loaves to His disciples that they might set them before the people, signifies that He assigns the spiritual gifts of knowledge to the Apostles, and that it was His will that by their ministry the food of life should be distributed to the Church.

PSEUDO-JEROME. The small fishes blessed are the books of the New Testament, for our Lord when risen asks for a piece of broiled fish; or else in these little fishes, we receive the saints, seeing that in the Scriptures of the New Testament are contained the faith, life, and, sufferings of them who, snatched away from the troubled waves of this world, have given us by their example spiritual refreshment.

BEDE; Again, what was over and above, after the multitude was refreshed, the Apostles take up, because the higher precepts of perfection, to which the multitude cannot attain, belong to those whose life transcends that of the generality of the people of God; nevertheless, the multitude is said to have been satisfied, because though they cannot leave all that they possess, nor come up to that which is spoken of virgins, yet by listening to the commands of the law of God, they attain to everlasting life.

PSEUDO-JEROME; Again, the seven baskets are the Seven Churches. By the four thousand is meant the year of the new dispensation, with its four seasons. Fitly also are there four thousand, that in the number itself it might be taught us that they were filled with the food of the Gospel.

THEOPHYL. Or there are four thousand, that is, men perfect in the four virtues; and for this reason, as being more advanced, they ate more, and left fewer fragments. For in this miracle, seven baskets full remain, but in the miracle of the five loaves, twelve, for there were five thousand men, which means men enslaved to the five senses, and for this reason they could not eat, but were satisfied with little, and many remains of the fragments were over and above.

10. And straightway he entered into a ship with his disciples, and came into the parts of Dalmanutha.

11. And the Pharisees came forth, and began to question with him, seeking of him a sign from heaven, tempting him.

12. And He sighed deeply in his spirit, and said, Why does this generation seek after a sign? verily I say unto you, There shall no sign be given unto this generation.

13. And he left them, and entering into the ship again departed to the other side.

14. Now the disciples had forgotten to take bread, neither had they in the ship with them more than one loaf.

15. And he charged them, saying, Take heed, beware of the leaven of the Pharisees, and of the leaven of Herod.

16. And they reasoned among themselves, saying, It is because we have no bread.

17. And when Jesus knew it, he said unto them, Why reason you, because you have no bread? perceive you not yet, neither understand? have you your heart yet hardened?

18. Having eyes, see you not? and having ears, hear you not? and do you not remember?

19. When I broke the five loaves among five thousand, how many baskets full of fragments took you up? They say unto him, Twelve.

20. And when the seven among four thousand, how many baskets full of fragments took you up? And they said, Seven.

21. And he said unto them, how is it that you do not understand?

THEOPHYL. After that our Lord had worked the miracle of the loaves, He immediately retires into another spot, lest on account of the miracle, the multitudes should take Him to make Him a king; wherefore it is said, And straightway He entered into a ship with his disciples, and came in to the parts of Dalmanutha.

AUG. Now in Matthew we read that He entered into the parts of Magdala. But we cannot doubt that it is the same place under another name; for several manuscripts even of St. Mark have only Magdala. It goes on, And the Pharisees came forth, and began to question to with him, seeking of him a sign from heaven, tempting him.

BEDE; The Pharisees, then, seek a sign from heaven, that He, Who had for the second time fed mammy thousands of men with a few loaves of bread, should now, after the example of Moses, refresh the whole nation in the last time with manna sent down from heaven, and dispensed amongst them all.

THEOPHYL. Or they seek for a sign from heaven, that is, they wish Him to make the sun and moon stand still, to bring down hail, and change the atmosphere; for they thought that He could not perform miracles from heaven, but could only in Beelzebub perform a sign on earth.

BEDE; When, as related above, He was about to refresh the believing multitude, He gave thanks, so now, on account of the foolish petition of the Pharisees, He groans; because, bearing about with Him the feelings of human nature, as He rejoices over the salvation of men, so He grieves over their errors. Wherefore it goes on, And he groaned in spirit, and said, Why does this generation seek after a sign? Verily I say unto you, If a sign shall be given to this generation. That is, no sign shall be given; as it is written in the Psalms, I have sworn once by my holiness, if I shall fail David, that is, I will not fail David.

AUG. Let no one, however, be perplexed that the answer which Mark says was given to them, when they sought a sign from heaven, is not the same as that which Matthew relates, namely, that concerning Jonah. He says that the Lord's answer was, that no sign should be given to it; by which we must understand such a one as they asked for, that is, one from heaven; but he has omitted to say, what Matthew has related.

THEOPHYL. Now the reason why the Lord did not listen to them was, that the time of signs from heaven had not arrived, that is, the time of the second Advent, when the powers of the heaven shall be shaken, and the moon shall not give her light. But in the time of the first Advent, all things are full of mercy, and such things do not take place.

BEDE; For a sign from heaven was not to be given to a generation of men, who tempted the Lord; but to a generation of men seeking the Lord, He shows a sign from heaven when in the sight of the Apostles He ascended into heaven. It goes on, And He left them, and entering into a ship again, he departed to the other side.

THEOPHYL. The Lord indeed quits the Pharisees, as men uncorrected; for where there is a hope of correction, there it is right to remain; but where the evil is incorrigible, we should go away. There follows: Now they had forgotten to take bread, neither had they in their ship with them more than one very loaf.

BEDE; Some may ask, how they had no bread, when they had filled seven baskets just before they embarked in the ship. But Scripture relates that they had forgotten to take them with them, which is a proof how little care they had for the flesh in other things, since in their eagerness to follow the Lord, even the necessity for refreshing their bodies had escaped from their mind.

THEOPHYL. By a special providence also the disciples forgot to take bread, that they might be blamed by Christ, and thus become better, and arrive at a knowledge of Christ's power. For it goes on, And be charged them, saying, Take heed, and beware of the leaven of the Pharisees and of the leaven of Herod.

PSEUD-CHRYS. Matthew says, of the leaven of the Pharisees and of the Sadducees; Luke, however, of the Pharisees only. All three, therefore, name the Pharisees, as being the most important of them, but Matthew and Mark have each mentioned one of the secondary sects; and fitly has Mark added of Herod, as a supplement to Matthew's narrative, in which they were left out. But in saying this, He by degrees brings the disciples to understanding and faith.

THEOPHYL. He means by leaven their hurtful and corrupt doctrine, full of the old malice, for the Herodians were the teachers, who said that Herod was the Christ.

BEDE; Or the leaven of the Pharisees is making the decrees of the divine law inferior to the traditions of men, preaching the law in word, attacking it in deed, tempting the Lord, and disbelieving His doctrine and His works; but the leaven of Herod is adultery, murder, rash swearing, a pretense of religion, hatred to Christ and His forerunner.

THEOPHYL. But the disciples themselves thought that the Lord spoke of the leaven of breath. Wherefore it goes on, And they reasoned amongst themselves, saying, it is because we have no bread; and this they said, as not understanding the power of

Christ, who could make bread out of nothing;

wherefore the Lord reproves them; for there follows, And when Jesus knew it, he said to them, Why reason you because you have no bread?

BEDE; Taking occasion then from the precept, which He had commanded, saying, Beware of the leaven of the Pharisees and of the leaven of Herod, our Savior teaches them what was the meaning of the five and the seven loaves, concerning which He adds,

And do you not remember when I broke the five loaves amongst five thousand, and how many baskets full of fragments ye look up? For if the leaven mentioned above means perverse traditions, of course the food, with which the people of God was nourished, means the true doctrine.

And when the seven among four thousand, how many baskets full of fragments took you up? And they said, Seven.

And he said unto them, how is it that you do not understand?

22. And he comes to Bethsaida; and they bring a blind man to him, and besought him to touch him.

23. And he took the blind man by the hand, and led him out of the town; and when he had spit on his eyes, and put his hands upon him, he asked him if he saw ought.

24. And he looked up, and said, I see men as trees, walking.

25. After that he put his hands again upon his eyes, and made him look up: and he was restored, and saw every man clearly.

26. And he sent him away to his house, saying, Neither go into the town, nor tell it to any in the town.

GLOSS. After the feeding of the multitude, the Evangelist proceeds to the giving sight to the blind, saying, And they come to Bethsaida, and they bring a blind man to him, and besought him to touch him.

BEDE; Knowing that the touch of the Lord could give sight to a blind man as well as cleanse a leper. It goes on, And he took the blind man by the hand, and led him out of the town.

THEOPHYL. For Bethsaida appears to have been infected with much infidelity, wherefore the Lord reproaches it, Woe to you, Bethsaida, for if the mighty works which were done in you had been done in Tyre and Sidon, they would have repented long ago in sackcloth and ashes. He then takes out of the town the blind man, who had been brought to Him, for the faith of those who brought him was not true faith. It goes on; And when he had spit in his eyes, and put his hands upon him, he asked him if he saw ought.

PSEUD-CHRYS. He spat indeed, and put His hand upon the blind man, because He wished to show that wonderful are the effects of the Divine word added to action; for the hand is the symbol of working, but the spittle, of the word proceeding out of the mouth. Again He asked him whether he could see any thing, which he had not done in the case of any whom He had healed, thus showing that by the weak faith of those who brought him, and of the blind man himself, his eyes could not altogether be opened.

Wherefore there follows: And he looked up, and said, I see men as trees walking; because he was still under the influence of unfaithfulness, he said that he saw men obscurely.

BEDE; Seeing indeed the shapes of bodies amongst the shadows, but unable to distinguish the outlines of the limbs, from the continued darkness of his sight; just as trees standing thick together are wont to appear to men who see them from afar, or by the dim light of the night, so that it cannot easily he known whether they be trees or men.

THEOPHYL. But the reason why he did not see at once perfectly, but in part, was, that he had not perfect faith; for healing is bestowed in proportion to faith.

PSEUDO-CHRYS. From the commencement, however, of the return of his senses, he leads him to apprehend things by faith, and thus makes him see perfectly; wherefore it goes on, After that, he put his hands again upon his eyes, and he began to see, and afterwards he adds, And he was restored, and saw all things clearly; that is, being perfectly healed in his senses and his intellect.

It goes on: And he sent him away to his house, saying, Go in to your home, and if you enter in to the town, tell it not to anyone.

Catena Aurea: Commentary on the Gospel of St. Mark

THEOPHYL. These precepts he gave him, because they were unfaithful, as has been said, lest perchance he should receive hurt in his soul from them, and they by their unbelief should run into a more grievous crime.

BEDE; Or else, he leaves an example to His disciples that they should not seek for popular favor by the miracles which they did. Mystically, however, Bethsaida is interpreted 'the house of time valley,' that is, the world, which is the vale of tears. Again, they bring to the Lord a blind man, that is, one who neither sees what he has been, what he is, nor what he is to be. They ask Him to touch him, for what is being touched, but feeling compunction?

BEDE; For the Lord touches us, when He enlightens our minds with the breath of His Spirit, and he stirs us up that we may recognize our own infirmity, and be diligent in good actions. He takes the hand of the blind man, that He may strengthen him to the practice of good works.

PSEUDO-JEROME; And He brings him out of the town, that is, out of the neighborhood of the wicked; and lie puts spittle into his eyes, that he may see the will of God, by the breath of the Holy Ghost; and putting His hands upon him, He asked him if he could see, because by the works of the Lord His majesty is seen.

BEDE; Or else, putting spittle into the eyes of the blind man, he hays His hands upon him that he may see, because He has wiped away the blindness of the human race both by invisible gifts, and by the Sacrament of His assumed humanity; for the spittle, proceeding from the Head, points out the grace of the Holy Ghost. But though by one word He could cure the man wholly and all at once, still He cures him by degrees, that He may show the greatness of the blindness of man, which can hardly, and only as it were step by step, be restored to light; and He exhibits to us His grace, by which He furthers each step towards perfection. Again, whoever is weighed down by a blindness of such long continuance, that he is unable to distinguish between good and evil, sees as it were men like trees walking, because he sees the deeds of the multitude without the light of discretion.

PSEUDO-JEROME; Or else, he sees men as trees, because he thinks all men higher than himself. But He put His hands again upon his eyes, that he might see all things clearly, that is, understand invisible things by visible, and with the eye of a pure mind contemplate, what the eye has not seen, the glorious state of his own soul after the rust of sin. He sent him to his home, that is, to his heart; that he might see in himself things which he had not seen before; for a man despairing of salvation does not think that he can do at all what, when enlightened, he can easily accomplish.

THEOPHYL. Or else, after He has healed him He sends him to his home; for the home of every one of us heaven, and the mansions which are there.

PSEUDO-JEROME. And He says to him, If thou enter into the town, tell it not to any one, that is, relate continually to your neighbors your blindness, but never tell them of your virtue.

27. And Jesus went out, arid his disciples, into the towns of Caesarea Philippi: and by the way he asked his disciples, saying to them, Whom do men say that I am?

28. And they answered, John the Baptist: but some say, Elias; and others, One of the prophets.

29. And he said to them, But whom say you that I am? And Peter answered and said to him, You are the Christ.

30. And he charged them that they should tell no man of him.

31. And he began to teach them, that the Son of man must suffer many things, and be rejected of the elders, and of the chief priests, and scribes, and be killed, and after three days rise again.

32. And he spoke that saying openly. And Peter took him, and began to rebuke him.

33. But when he had turned about and looked on his disciples, he rebuked Peter, saying, Get thee behind me, Satan: for you savor not the things that be of God, but the things that be of men.

THEOPHYL. After taking His disciples afar from the Jews He then asks them concerning himself, that they might speak the truth without fear of the Jews; wherefore it is said, And Jesus entered, and his disciples, into the towns of Caesarea Philippi.

BEDE; Philip was that brother of Herod, of whom we spoke above, who in honor of Tiberius Caesar called that town, which is now called Paneas, Caesarea Philippi. It goes on, And by the way he asked his disciples, saying to them, Whom do men say that I am?

PSEUDO-CHRYS. He asks the question with a purpose, for it was right that His disciples should praise Him better than the crowd.

BEDE; Wherefore He first asks what is the opinion of men, in order to try the faith of the disciples, lest their confession should appear to be founded on the common opinion. It goes on, And they answered, saying, Some say John the Baptist, some Elias, and others, One of the prophets.

THEOPHYL. For many thought that John had risen from the dead, as even Herod believed, and that he had performed miracles after his resurrection. After how ever having inquired into the opinion of others, He asks them what was the belief of their own minds on this point; wherefore it continues, And he said to them, But whom say you that I am?

CHRYS. From the manner, however, itself, of the question, He heads them to a higher feeling, and to higher thoughts, concerning Him, that they might not agree with the multitude. But the next words show what the head of the disciples, the mouth of the Apostles, answered; when all were asked, Peter answers and said to to him, You are the Christ.

THEOPHYL. He confesses indeed that He is the Christ announced by the Prophets; but the Evangelist Mark passes over what the Lord answered to his confession, and how He blessed him, lest by this way of relating it, he should seem, to be favoring his Master Peter; Matthew plainly goes through the whole of it.

Catena Aurea: Commentary on the Gospel of St. Mark

ORIGEN; Or else, Mark and Luke, as they wrote that Peter answered, You are the Christ, without adding what is put down in Matthew, the Son of the living God, so they omitted to relate the blessing which was conferred on this confession. It goes on, And he charged them that they should tell no man of him.

THEOPHYL. For He wished in the mean time to hide His glory, lest many should be offended because of Him, and so earn a worse punishment.

CHRYS. Or else, that He might wait to fix the pure faith in their minds, till the Crucifixion, which was an offense to them, was over for after it was once perfected, about the time of His ascension, He said unto the Apostles, Go you and teach all nations.

THEOPHYL. But after the Lord had accepted the confession of the disciples, who called Him the true God, He then reveals to them the mystery of the Cross. Wherefore it goes on, And he began to teach them that the Son of man must suffer many things, and be rejected of the elders and of the chief priests, and the scribes, and be killed, and after three days rise again;

and he spoke that saying openly, that is, concerning His future passion. But His disciples did not understand the order of the truth, neither could they comprehend His resurrection, but thought it better that He should not suffer.

CHRYS. The reason, however, why the Lord told them this, was to show, that after His cross and resurrection, Christ must be preached by His witnesses. Again, Peter alone, from the fervor of his disposition had the boldness to dispute about these things. Wherefore it goes on, And Peter took him up, and began to rebuke him.

BEDE; This, however, he speaks with the feelings of a man who loves and desires; as if he said, Thus cannot he, neither can my ears receive that the Son of God us to be slain.

CHRYS. But how is this, that Peter, gifted with a revelation from the Father, has so soon fallen, and become unstable? Surely, however, it was not wonderful that one who had received no revelation concerning the Passion should be ignorant of this. For that He was the Christ the Son of the living God, he had learnt by revelation, but the mystery of His cross and resurrection had not yet been revealed to him. He Himself, however, showing that He must come to His Passion, rebuked Peter; wherefore there follows, And when he had turned about and looked on his disciples, he rebuked Peter, &c.

THEOPHYL. For the Lord, wishing to show that His Passion was to take place on account of the salvation of men, and that Satan alone was unwilling that Christ should suffer, and the race of man be saved, called Peter Satan, because he savored the things that were of Satan, and, from unwillingness that Christ should suffer, became His adversary; for Satan is interpreted 'the adversary.'

PSEUDO-CHRYS. But He said not to the devil, when tempting Him, Get you behind me, but to Peter He said, Get you behind me, that is, follow Me, and resist not the design of My voluntary Passion. There follows, For you savour not the things which be of God, but which be of men.

THEOPHYL. He says that Peter savors the things which be of men, in that he in some way savored carnal affections, for Peter wished that Christ should spare Himself and riot be crucified.

34. And when he had called the people to him with his disciples also, he said unto them, Whoever will come after me, let him deny himself, and take up his cross, and follow me.

35. For whoever will save his life shall lose it; but whosoever shall lose his life for my sake and the Gospel's, the same shall save it.

36. For what shall it profit a man, if he shall gain the whole world, and lose his own soul?

37. Or what shall a man give in exchange for his soul?

38. Whoever therefore shall be ashamed of me and of my words in this adulterous and sinful generation; of him also shall the Son of man be ashamed, when he comes in the glory of his Father with the holy angels.

BEDE; After showing to His disciples the mystery of His passion and resurrection, He exhorts them, as well as the multitude, to follow the example of His passion. Wherefore it goes on; And when he had called the people to him with his disciples also, he said unto them, Whoever wishes to come after me, let him deny himself.

CHRYS. As if He would in say to Peter, You indeed do rebuke Me, who am willing to undergo My passion, but I tell you, that not only is it wrong to prevent Me from suffering, but neither can you be saved unless you yourself die. Again He says, Whoever wished to come after me; as if He said, I call you to those good things which a man should wish for, I do not force you to evil and burdensome things; for he who does violence to his hearer, often stands in his way; but he who leaves him free, rather draws him to himself. And a man denies himself when He cares not for his body, so that whether it be scourged, or whatever of like nature it may suffer, he bears it patiently.

THEOPHYL. For a man who denies another, be it brother or father, does not sympathize with him, nor grieve at his fate, though He be wounded and die; thus we ought to despise our body, so that if it should be wounded or hurt in any way, we should not mind its suffering.

CHRYS. But He says not, a man should not spare himself, but what is more, that He should deny himself, as if He had nothing in common with himself, but face danger, and look upon such things as if another were suffering; and this is really to spare himself; for parents then most truly act kindly to their children, when they give them up to their masters, with an injunction not to spare them. Again, He shows the degree to which a man should deny himself, when He says, And take up his cross, by which He means, even to the most shameful death.

THEOPHYL. For at that time the cross appeared shameful, because malefactors were fixed to it.

Catena Aurea: Commentary on the Gospel of St. Mark

PSEUDO-JEROME; Or else, as a skillful pilot, foreseeing a storm in a calm, wishes his sailors to be prepared; so also the Lord says, If any one will follow me, &c.

BEDE; For we deny r ourselves, when we avoid what we were of old, and strive to reach that point, whither we are newly called. And the cross is taken up by us, when either our body is pained by abstinence, or our soul afflicted by fellow-feeling for our neighbor.

THEOPHYL. But because after the cross we must have a new strength, He adds, and follow me.

CHRYS. And this He says, because it may happen that a man may suffer and yet not follow Christ, that is, when he does not suffer for Christ's sake; for he follows Christ who walks after Him, and conforms himself to His death, despising those principalities and powers under whose power before the coming of Christ, he committed sin. Then there follows For whosoever will save his life shall lose it, but whoever shall lose his life for my sake and the Gospel's, the same shall save it. I give you these commands, as it were to spare you; for whoever spares his son, brings him to destruction, but whoever does not spare him, saves him. It is therefore right to be always prepared for death; for if in the battles of this world, he who is prepared for death fights better than others, though none can restore him to life after death, much more is this the case in spiritual battle, when so great a hope of resurrection is set before him, since he who gives up his soul unto death saves it.

REMIG. And life is to he taken in this place for the present life, and not for the substance itself of the soul.

CHRYS. As therefore He had said, For whoever will save his life shall lose it, lest any one should suppose this loss to be equivalent to that salvation, He adds, For what shall it profit a man, if he shall gain the whole world, and lose his own soul, &c As if He said, Think not that he has saved his soul, who has shunned the perils of the cross; for when a man, at the cost of his soul, that is, His life, gains the whole world, what has He besides, now that his soul is perishing? Has no another soil to give for His soil? For a man can give the price of his house in exchange for the house, but in losing his soul he has not another soul to give.

And it is with a purpose that He says, Or what shall a man give in exchange for his soul? for God, in exchange for our salvation, has given the precious blood of Jesus Christ.

BEDE; Or else He says this, because in the of persecution, our life is to be laid aside, but in time of peace, our earthly desires are to be broken, which He implies when He says, For what shall it profit a man, &c. But we are often hindered by a habit of shamefacedness from expressing with our voice the rectitude which we preserve in our hearts; and therefore it is added, For whoever shall confess me and my words in this adulterous and sinful generation, him also shall the Son of man confess, when he comes in the glory of his Father with the holy angels.

THEOPHYL. For that faith which only remains in the mind is not sufficient, but the Lord requires also the confession of the mouth; for when the soul is sanctified by faith, the body ought also to be sanctified by confession.

PSEUDO-CHRYS. He then who has learned this, is bound zealously to confess Christ without shame. And this generation is called adulterous, because it has left God the true Bridegroom of the soul, and has refused to follow the doctrine of Christ, but has prostrated itself to the devil and taken up the seeds of impiety, for which reason also it is called sinful. Whoever therefore amongst them has denied the kingdom of Christ, and the words of God revealed in the Gospel, shall receive a reward befitting His impiety, when He hears in the second ,advent, I know you not.

THEOPHYL. Him then who shall have confessed that his God was crucified, Christ Himself also shall confess, not here, where He is esteemed poor and wretched, but in His glory and with a multitude of Angels.

GREG. There are however some, who confess Christ, because they see that all men are Christian; for if the name of Christ were not at this day in such great glory, the Holy Church would not have so many professors. The voice of profession therefore is not sufficient for a trial of faith whilst the profession of the generality defends it from shame. In the time of peace therefore there is another way, by which we may be known to ourselves. We are ever fearful of being despised by our neighbors, we think it shame to bear injurious words; if perchance we have quarreled with our neighbor, we blush to be the first to give satisfaction; for our carnal heart, in seeking the glory of this life, disdains humility.

THEOPHYL. But because He had spoken of His glory, in order to show that His promises were not vain, He subjoins, Verily I say to you, That there be some of them that stand here who shall not taste of death, till they have seen the kingdom of God come with power. As if He said, Some, that is, Peter, James, and John, shall not taste of death, until I show them, in my transfiguration, with what glory I am to come in my second advent; for the transfiguration was nothing else, but an announcement of the second coming of Christ, in which also Christ Himself and the Saints will shine.

BEDE; Truly it was done with a loving foresight, in order that they, having tasted for a brief moment the contemplation of everlasting joy, might with the greater strength bear up under adversity.

CHRYS. And He did not declare the names of those who were about to go up, lest the other disciples should feel some touch of human frailty, and He tells it to them beforehand, that they might come with minds better prepared to be taught all that concerned that vision.

BEDE; Or else the present Church is called the kingdom of God; and some of the disciples were to live in the body until they should see the Church built up, and raised against the glory of the world; for it was right to make some promises concerning this life to the disciples who were uninstructed, that they might be built up with greater strength for the time to come.

PSEUDO-CHRYS. But in a mystical sense, Christ is life, and the devil is death, and he tastes of death, who dwells in sin; even now every one, according as he has good or evil doctrines, tastes the bread either of life or of death. And indeed, it is a less evil to see death, a greater to taste of it, still worse to follow it, worst of all to be subject to it.

Mark 9

1. And he said to them, Verily I say unto you, that there be some of them that stand here, which shall not taste of death, till they have seen the kingdom of God come with power.

2. And after six days Jesus takes with him Peter, and James, and John, and leads them up into an high mountain apart by themselves: and he was transfigured before them.

3. And his raiment became shining, exceeding white as snow; so as no fuller on earth can white them.

4. And there appeared unto them Elias with Moses: and they were talking with Jesus.

5. And Peter answered and said to Jesus, Master, it is good for us to be here: and let us make three tabernacles; one for thee, and one for Moses, and one for Elias.

6. For he wist not what to say; for they were sore afraid.

7. And there was a cloud that overshadowed them; and a voice came out of the cloud, saying, This is my beloved Son: hear him.

8. And suddenly, when they had looked round about, they saw no man any more, save Jesus only with themselves.

PSEUDO-JEROME; After the consummation of the cross, the glory of the resurrection is shown, that they, who were to see with their own eyes the glory of the resurrection to come, might not fear the shame of the cross;

wherefore it is said, And after six days Jesus takes with him Peter, and James, and John, and led them up into an high mountain apart by themselves, and he was transfigured before them.

CHRYS. Luke in saying, After eight days, does not contradict this; for He reckoned in both the day on which Christ had spoken what goes before, and the day on which He took them up. And the reason that he took them up after six days, was that they, might be filled with a more eager desire during the space of these days, and with a watchful and anxious mind attend to what they saw.

THEOPHYL. And He takes with Him the three chiefs of the Apostles, Peter, as confessing and loving him, John, as the beloved one, James, as being sublime in speech and as a divine; for so displeasing was he to the Jews, that Herod wishing to please the Jews slew him.

PSEUDO-CHRYS. He does not however show His glory in a house, but He takes them up into a high mountain, for the loftiness of the mountain was adapted to showing forth the loftiness of His glory.

THEOPHYL. And He took them apart, because He was about to reveal mysteries to them. We must also understand by transfiguration not the change of His features, but that, whilst His features remained as before, there was added unto Him a certain ineffable brightness.

PSEUDO-CHRYS. It is not therefore fitting that in the kingdom of God any change of feature should take place, either in the Savior Himself, or in those who are to be made like to him, but only an addition of brightness.

BEDE; Our Savior then when transfigured did not lose the substance of real flesh, bit showed forth the glory of His own or of our future resurrection; for such as He then appeared to the Apostles, He will after the judgment appear to all His elect. It goes on, And his raiment became shining.

GREG. Because, in the height of the brightness of heaven above, they who shine in righteousness of life, will cling to Him; for by the name of garments, He means the just whom He joins to Himself. There follows And there appeared to them Elias with Moses, and they were talking with Jesus.

CHRYS. He brings Moses and Elias before them; first, indeed, because the multitudes said that Christ was Elias, and one of the Prophets, He shows Himself to the Apostles with them that they might see the difference between the Lord, and His servants. And again because the Jews accused Christ of transgressing the law, and thought Him a blasphemer, as if He arrogated to Himself the glory of His Father, He brought before them those who shone conspicuous in both ways; for Moses gave the Law, and Elias was zealous for the glory of God; for which reason neither would have stood near Him, if He had been opposed to God and to His law.

Catena Aurea: Commentary on the Gospel of St. Mark

And that they might know that He holds the power of life and of death, He brings before them both Moses who was dead, and Elias who had not yet suffered death. Furthermore He signified by this that the doctrine of the Prophets was the schoolmaster to the doctrine of Christ. He also signified the junction of the New and Old Testament, and that the Apostles shall be joined in the resurrection with the Prophets, and both together shall go forth to meet their common King. It goes on, And Peter answered and said to Jesus, Master, it is good for us to be here; and let us make three tabernacles, one for you, and one for Moses, and one for or Elias.

BEDE; If the transfigured humanity of Christ and the society of but two saints seen for a moment, could confer delight to such a degree that Peter would, even by serving them, stay their departure, how great a happiness will it be to enjoy the vision of Diety amidst choirs of Angels for ever? it goes on, For he wist not what to say; although, however, Peter from the stupor of human frailty knew not what to say, still He gives a proof of the feelings which were within him; for the cause of his not knowing what to say, was his forgetting that the kingdom was promised to the Saints by the Lord not in any earthly region, but in heaven; he did not remember that he and his fellow-Apostles were still hemmed in by mortal flesh and could not bear the state of immortal life, to which his soul had already carried him away, because in our Father's house in heaven, a house made with hands is not needed. But again even up to this time he is points at, as an ignorant man who wishes to make three tabernacles for the Law, the Prophets, and the Gospel, since they in no way can be separated from each other.

CHRYS. Again, Peter neither comprehended that the Lord worked His transfiguration for the showing forth of His true glory, nor that He did this in order to teach men, nor that it was impossible for them to leave the multitude and dwell in the mountain. It goes on, For they were sore afraid. But this fear of theirs was one by which they were raised from their usual state of mind to one higher, and they recognized that those who appeared to them were Moses and Elias. The soul also was drawn on to a state of heavenly feeling, as though carried away from human sense by the heavenly vision.

THEOPHYL. Or else, Peter, fearing to come down from the mount because he has now a presentiment that Christ must be crucified, said, It is good for us too be here, and not to go down there, that is, in the midst of the Jews; but if they who are furious against You come hither, we have Moses who beat down the Egyptians, we have also Elias, who brought fire down from heaven and destroyed the five hundred.

ORIGEN; Mark says his own person, For he wist not what to say. Where it is matter for consideration, whether perchance Peter spoke this in the confusion of his mind, by the motion of a spirit not his own; whether perchance that spirit himself who wished, as far as in him lay, to be a stumbling-block to Christ, so that He might shrink from that Passion, which was the saving of all men, did not here work as a seducer and wish under the color of good to prevent Christ from condescending to men, from coming to them, and taking death upon Himself for their sakes

BEDE; Now because Peter sought for a material tabernacle, he was covered with the shadow of the cloud, that he might learn that in the resurrection they are to be protected not by the covering of houses, but by the glory of the Holy Ghost; wherefore it goes on, There was a cloud that overshadowed them. And the reason why they obtained no answer from the Lord was, that they asked unadvisedly; but the Father answered for the Son, wherefore there follows And a voice came out of the cloud, saying, This is my beloved Son, in whom I am well pleased.

CHRYS. The voice proceeded from a cloud in which God is wont to appear, that they might believe that the voice was sent forth from God. But in that He says, This is my beloved Son, He declares that the will of the Father and the Son is one, and that, save that the is the Son, He is in all things One with Him who begot Him.

BEDE He then whose preaching, as Moses foretold, every soul that wished to he saved should hear when He came in the flesh, He now come in the flesh is proclaimed by God the Father to the disciples as the one whom they were to hear. There follows, And suddenly, when they had looked round about, they saw no man any more, save Jesus only with themselves; for as soon as the Son was proclaimed, at once the servants disappeared, lest the voice of the Father should seem to have been sent forth to them.

THEOPHYL. Again mystically; after the end of this world, which was made in six days, Jesus will take us up (if we be His disciples) into a high mountain, that is, into heaven, where we shall see His exceeding glory.

BEDE; And by the garments of the Lord are meant His saints,

who will shine with a new whiteness. By the fuller we must understand Him, to whom the Psalmist says, Wash me thoroughly from my wickedness, and cleanse me from my sin; for He cannot give to His faithful ones upon earth that glory which remains laid up for them in heaven.

REMIG. Or else, by the fuller are meant holy preachers and purifiers of the soul, none of whom in this life can so live as not to be stained with some spots of sin; but in the coming resurrection all the saints shall be purged from every stain of sin. Therefore the Lord will make them such as neither they themselves by taking vengeance on their own members, nor any preacher by his example and doctrine, can make.

CHRYS. Or else, white garments are the writings of Evangelists and Apostles, the like to which no interpreter can frame.

ORIGEN; Or else, fullers upon earth may by a moral interpretation be considered to be the wise of this world, who are thought to adorn even their foul understandings and doctrines with a false whitening drawn from their own minds. But their skill as fullers cannot produce any thing like a discourse which shows forth the brightness of spiritual conceptions in the unpolished words of Scripture, which by many are despised.

BEDE; Moses and Elias, of whom one, as we read, died, the other was carried away to heaven, signify the coming glory of all the Saints, that is, of all who in the judgment-time are either to be found alive in the flesh, or to be raised up from that death of which they tasted, and who are all equally to reign with Him.

THEOPHYL, Or else it means, that we are to see in glory both the Law and the Prophets speaking with Him, that is we shall then find that all those things which were spoken of Him by Moses and the other prophets agree with the reality; then too we shall hear the voice of the Father, revealing to us the Son of the Father, and saying, This is my beloved Son, and the cloud, that is, the Holy Ghost, the fount of truth, will overshadow us.

BEDE; And we must observe, that, as when the Lord was baptized in Jordan, so on the mountain, covered with brightness, the whole mystery of the Holy Trinity is declared, because we shall see in the resurrection that glory of the Trinity which we believers confess in baptism, and shall praise it all together. Nor is it without reason that the Holy Ghost appeared here in a bright cloud, there in the form of a dove; because he who now with a simple heart keeps the faith which He has embraced, shall then contemplate what he had believed with the brightness of open vision. But when the voice had been heard over the Son, He was found Himself alone, because when He shall have manifested Himself to His elect, God shall be all in all, yes Christ with His own, as the Head with the body, shall shine through all things.

9. And as they came down from the mountain, he charged them that they should tell no man what things they had seen, till the Son of man were risen from the dead.

10. And they kept that saying with themselves, questioning one with another what the rising from the dead should mean.

11. And they asked him, saying, Why say the Scribes that Elias must first come?

12. And he answered and told them, Elias verily comes first, and restores all things; and how it is written of the Son of man, that he must suffer many things, and be set at nought.

13. But I say to you, that Elias is indeed come, and they have done to him whatever they listed, as it is written of him.

ORIGEN; After the showing of the mystery on the mount, the Lord commanded His disciples, as they were coming down from the mount, not to reveal His transfiguration, before the glory of His Passion and Resurrection; wherefore it is said, And as they came down from the mountain, he charged them that they should tell no man what things they had seen, till the Son of man were risen from the dead.

CHRYS. Where He not only orders them to be silent, but mentioning His Passion, He implies the cause why they were to be silent.

THEOPHYL. Which He did lest men should be offended, hearing such glorious things of Him Whom they were about to see crucified. It was not therefore fitting to say such things of Christ before He suffered, but after His resurrection they were likely to be believed.

PSEUDO-CHRYS. But they, being ignorant of the mystery of the resurrection, took hold of that saying, and disputed one with another; wherefore there follows, And they kept that saying with themselves, questioning one with another what the rising from the dead should mean.

PSEUDO-JEROME; This which is peculiar to Mark, means, that when death shall have been swallowed up in victory, we shall have no memory for the former things. it goes on, And they asked him, saying, Why say the Scribes that Elias must first come.

CHRYS. The design of the disciples in asking this question seems to me to be this. We indeed have seen Elias with You, and have seen You before seeing Elias, but the Scribes say that Elias comes first; we therefore believe that they have lied.

BEDE; Or thus; the disciples thought that the change which they had seen in Him in the mount, was His transfiguration to glory; and they say, if You have already come in glory, wherefore does not Your forerunner appear? chiefly because they had seen Elias go away.

CHRYS. But what Christ answered to this, is seen by what follows, And he answered and told them, Elias verily comes first, and restores all things; in which He shows that Elias will come before His second advent. For the Scriptures declare two advents of Christ, namely, one which has taken place, and another which is to come; but the Lord asserts that Elias is the forerunner of the second advent.

BEDE; Again, He will restore all things, that is to say, those things which Malachi points out, saying, Behold, I will send you Elijah the prophet, and he shall turn the heart of the fathers to be children, and the heart of the children to their fathers; he will yield up also to death that debt, which to his prolonged life he has delayed too render.

THEOPHYL. Now the Lord puts this forward to oppose the notion of the Pharisees, who held that Elias was the forerunner of the first advent, showing that it led them to a false conclusion; wherefore he subjoins, And how it is written of the Son of man, that he must suffer many things, and be set at nought. As if He had said, When Elias the Tishbite comes, he will pacify the Jews, and will bring them to the faith, and thus be the forerunner of the second advent. If then Elias is the forerunner of the first advent, how is it written that the Son of man must suffer? One of these two things therefore will follow; either that Elias is not the forerunner of the first advent, and thus the Scriptures will be true; or that he is the forerunner of the first advent, and then the Scriptures will not be true, which sat that Christ must suffer; for Elias must restore all things, in which case there will not be an unbelieving Jew, but all, whoever hear him, must believe on his preaching.

BEDE; Or this, And how it is written: that is in the same say as the prophets have written many things in various places concerning the Passion of Christ, Elias also, when he comes, is to suffer many things, and to be despised by the wicked.

CHRYS. Now as the Lord asserted that Elias was to be the forerunner of the second advent, so consequently He asserted that John was the fore runner of the first; wherefore He subjoins, But I say to you, that Elias is indeed come.

GLOSS. He calls John Elias, not because he was Elias in person, but because he fulfilled the ministry of Elias; for as the latter will be the forerunner of the second advent, so the forerunner has been that of the first.

THEOPHYL. For again, John rebuked vice, and was a zealous man, and a hermit like Elias; but they heard him not as they will hear Elias, but killed him in wicked sport, and cut off his head; wherefore there follows, And they have done to him whatever they listed, as it is written of him.

PSEUDO-CHRYS. Or else, the disciples asked Jesus, how it was written that the Son of in man must suffer? Now in answer to this, He says, As John came in the likeness of Elias, and they evil entreated him, so according to the Scriptures must the Son of man suffer.

14. And when he came to his disciples, he saw a great multitude about them, and the Scribes questioning with them.

15. And straightway all the people, when they beheld him, were greatly amazed, and running to him saluted him.

16. And he asked the Scribes, What question you with them?

17. And one of the multitude answered and said, Master, I have brought to you my son, which has a dumb spirit;

18. And wherever he takes him, he tears him: and he foams, and gnashes with his teeth, and pines away: and I spoke to your disciples that they should cast him out; and they could not.

19. He answers him, and said, O faithless generation, how long

shall I be with you? how long shall I suffer you? bring him to me.

20. And they brought him to him: and when he saw him, straightway the spirit tore him; and he fell on the ground, and wallowed foaming.

21. And he asked his father, how long is it ago since this came to him? And he said, Of a child.

22. And oft times it has cast him into the fire, and into the waters, to destroy him: but if you can do any thing, have compassion on us, and help us.

23. Jesus said to him, If you can believe, all things are possible to him that believes.

24. And straightway the father of the child cried out, and said with tears, Lord, I believe; help you mine unbelief.

25. When Jesus saw that the people came running together, he rebuked the foul spirit, saying to him, You dumb and deaf spirit, I charge you, come out of him, and enter no more into him.

26. And the spirit cried, and rent him sore, and came out of him: and he was as one dead; insomuch that many said, He is dead.

27. But Jesus took him by the hand, and lifted him up; and he arose.

28. And when he was come into the house, his disciples asked

him privately, Why could not we cast him out?

29. And he said to them, This kind can come forth by nothing, but by prayer and fasting.

THEOPHYL. After He had shown His glory in the mount to the three disciples, He returns to the other disciples, who had not come up with Him into the mount; wherefore it is said, And when he came to his disciples, he saw a great multitude about them, and the Scribes questioning with them. For the Pharisees, catching the opportunity of the hour when Christ was not present, came up to them, to try to draw them over to themselves.

PSEUDO-JEROME; But there is no peace for man under the sun; envy is ever slaying the little ones, and lightning strike the tops of the great mountains. Of all those who run to the Church, some as the multitudes come in faith to learn, others, as the Scribes, with envy and pride. It goes on, And straightway all the people, when they beheld Jesus, were greatly amazed, and feared.

BEDE; In all cases, the difference between the mind of the Scribes and of the people ought to be observed; for the Scribes are never said to have shown any devotion, faith, humility, and reverence, but as soon as the Lord was come, the whole multitude was greatly amazed and feared, and ran up to Him, and saluted Him; wherefore there follows, And running to him, saluted him.

THEOPHYL. For the multitude was glad to see Him, so that they saluted Him from afar, as He was coming to them; but some suppose that His countenance had become more beautiful from His transfiguration, and that this induced the crowd to salute Him.

PSEUDO-JEROME; Now it was the people, and not the disciples, who on seeing Him were amazed and feared, for there is no fear in love; fear belongs to servants, amazement to fools. It goes on: And he asked them, What question you with them. Why does the Lord put this question? That confession may produce salvation, and the murmuring of our hearts may be appeased by religious words.

BEDE; The question, indeed, which was raised may, if I am not deceived, have been this, wherefore they, who were the disciples of the Savior, were unable to heal the demoniac, who was placed in the midst, which may be gathered from the following words; And one of the multitude answered and said, Master, I have brought to you my son, which has a dumb spirit;

and wherever he takes him, he tears him: and he foams, and gnashes with his teeth, and pines away.

CHRYS. The Scriptures declare that this man was weak in faith, for Christ says, O faithless generation: and He adds, If you can believe. But although his want of faith was the cause of their not casting out the devil, he nevertheless accuses the disciples; wherefore it is added, And I spoke to your disciples that they should cast him out; but they could not. Now observe his folly; in praying to Jesus in the midst of the crowd, he accuses the disciples, wherefore the Lord before the multitude so much the more accuses him, and not only aims the accusation at himself, but also extends it to all the Jews; for it is probable that many of those present had been offended, and had held wrong thoughts concerning His disciples.

Wherefore there follows, He answers them and says, O faithless generation, how long shall I be with you? how long shall I suffer you? By which He showed both that He desired death, and that it was a burden to Him to converse with them.

BEDE; So far, however, is He from being angry with the person, though He reproved the sin, that He immediately added, Bring him to me; and they brought him to him. And when He saw him, straightway the spirit tore him, and he fell on the ground and, wallowed foaming.

CHRYS. But this the Lord permitted for the sake of the father of the boy, that when he saw the devil vexing his child, he might be brought on to believe that the miracle was to be wrought.

THEOPHYL. He also permits the child to be vexed, that in this way we might know the devil's wickedness, who we would have killed him, he had not been assisted by the Lord. It goes on: And he asked his father, How long is it ago since this came to him? And he said, Of a child;

and oft times it has cast him into the fire and into to the waters to destroy him.

BEDE; Let Julian blush, who dares to say that all men are born in the flesh, without the infection of sin, as though they were innocent in all respects, just as Adam was when he was created.

For what was there in the boy, that he should be troubled from infancy with a cruel devil, if he were not held at all by the chain of original sin? since it is evident that he could not yet have had any sin of his own.

GLOSS. Now he expresses in the words of his petition his want of faith; for that is the reason why he adds, But if you can do anything, have compassion on us, and help us. For in this he says , If you can do anything, he shows that he doubts His power, because he had seen that the disciples of Christ had failed in curing him; but he says, have compassion on us, to show the misery of the son, who suffered, and the father, who suffered with him.

It goes on: Jesus said to him, If you can believe, all things are possible to him that believes.

PSEUDO-JEROME; This saying, you can, is a proof of the freedom of the will. Again, all things are possible to him that believes, which evidently means all those things which are prayed for with tears in the name of Jesus, that is, of salvation.

BEDE. The answer of the Lord was suited to the petition, for the man said, If you can do anything, help us; and to this the Lord answered, If you can believe on the other hand the leper whom cried out, with faith, Lord, if you will, you can make me clean, received an answer according to his faith, I will, be you clean.

CHRYS. His meaning is; such a plenitude of virtue is there in Me, that not only can I do this, but I will make others to have that power; wherefore if you can believe as you ought to do, you shall be able to cure not only him, but many more. In this way then, He endeavored to bring back to the faith, the man who as yet Speaks unfaithfully. There follows, And straightway the father of the child cried out, and said with tears, Lord, I believe; help you mine unbelief. But if he had already believed, saying, I believe, how is it that he adds, help you mine unbelief? We must say then that faith is manifold, that one sort of faith is elementary, another perfect; but this man, being but a beginner in believing, prayed the Savior to add to his virtue what was wanting.

BEDE; For no man at once reaches to the highest point, but in holy living a man begins with the least things that house may reach the great; for the beginning of virtue is different, from the progress and the perfection of it. Because then faith mounts up through the secret inspiration of grace, by the steps of its own merits, he who has not yet believed perfectly was at once a believer and an unbeliever.

PSEUDO-JEROME; By this also we are taught that our faith is tottering, if it lean not on the stay of the help of God. But faith by its tears receives the accomplishment of its wishes;

Wherefore it continues, When Jesus saw that the multitude came running together, he rebuked the foul spirit, saying to him, You dumb and deaf spirit, I charge you come out of him, and enter no more into him.

THEOPHYL. The reason that He rebuked the foul spirit, when He saw the crowd running together, was that he did not wish to cure him before the multitude, that He might give us a lesson to avoid ostentation.

PSEUDO-CHRYS. And His rebuking him, and saying, I charge thee, is a proof of Divine power. Again, in that He says not only, come out of him, but also enter no more into him, He shows that the evil spirit was ready to enter again, because the man was weak in faith, but was prevented by the command of the Lord.

It goes on, And the spirit cried, and rent him sore, and came out of him; and he was as one dead, inasmuch that many said, He is dead. For the devil was not able to inflict death upon him, because the true Life was come.

BEDE; But him, whom the unholy spirit made like to death, the holy Savior. Saved by the touch of His holy hand; wherefore it goes on, But Jesus took him by the hand, and lifted him up, and he arose. Thus as the Lord had shown Himself to be every God by the power of healing, so He showed that He had the very nature of our flesh, by the manner of His human touch. The Manichaean indeed madly denies that He was truly clothed in flesh; lie Himself; however, by raising, cleansing, enlightening so many afflicted persons by His touch, condemned his heresy before its birth.

It goes on: And when he was come into the house, his disciples asked him privately, Why could not we cast him out?

CHRYS. They feared that perchance they had lost the grace conferred upon them; for they had already received power over unclean spirits. It goes on: And he said to them, This kind can come forth by nothing but by prayer and fasting.

THEOPHYL. That is, the whole class of lunatics, or simply, of all persons possessed with devils. Both the man to be cured, and he who cures him, should fast; for a real prayer is offered up, when, fasting is joined with prayer, when he who prays is sober and not heavy with food.

BEDE; Again, in a mystical sense, on high the Lord. Bede unfolds the mysteries of the kingdom to His disciples, but below He rebukes the multitude for their Sins of unfaithfulness, and expels devils from those, who are vexed by then, Those who are still carnal and foolish, He strengthens, teaches, punishes, whilst He more freely instructs the perfect concerning the things of eternity.

THEOPHYL. Again, this devil is deaf and dumb; deaf; because he does not choose to hear the words of God; dumb, because he is unable to teach others their duty.

PSEUDO-JEROME; Again, a Sinner foams forth folly, gnashes with anger, pines away in sloth. But the evil spirit tears him, when coming to salvation, and in like manner those whom he would drag into his maw he tears asunder by terrors and losses, as he did Job.

BEDE, For often times when we try to turn to God after sin, our old enemy attacks us with new and greater snares, which he does, either to instill into us a hatred of virtue, or to avenge the injury of his expulsion.

GREG. But he who is freed from the power of the evil spirit is thought to be dead; for whoever has already subdued earthly desires, puts to death within himself his carnal mode of life, and appears to the world as a dead man, and many look upon him as dead; for they who know not how to live after the Spirit, think that he who does not follow after carnal pleasures is altogether dead.

PSEUDO-JEROME; Further, in his being vexed from his infancy, the Gentile people is signified, from the very birth of whom the vain worship of idols arose, so that they in their folly sacrificed their children to devils. And for this reason it is said that it cast him into the fire and into the water; for some of the Gentiles worshipped fire, others water.

BEDE; Or by this demoniac are signified those, who are bound by the guilt of original sin, and coming into the world as criminals, are to be saved by grace; and by fire is meant the heat of anger, by water, the pleasures of the flesh, which melt the soul by their sweetness. But He did not rebuke the boy, who suffered violence, but the devil, who inflicted it, because he who desires to amend a sinner, ought, whilst He exterminates his vice by rebuking and cursing it, to love and cherish the man.

PSEUDO-JEROME; Again, the Lord applies to the evil spirit what he had inflicted on the man, calling him deaf and dumb spirit, because he never will hear and speak what the penitent sinner can speak and hear. But the devil, quitting a man, never returns, if the man keep his heart with the keys of humility and charity, and hold possession of the gate of freedom. The man who was healed became as one dead, for it is said to those who are healed, You are dead, and your life is hid with Christ in God.

Catena Aurea: Commentary on the Gospel of St. Mark

THEOPHYL. Again, when Jesus, that is, the word of the Gospel, takes hold of the hand, that is, of our powers of action, then shall we be freed from the devil. And observe that God first helps us, then it is required of us that we do good; for which reason it is said that Jesus raised him, in which is shown the aid of God, and that he arose, in which is declared the zeal of man.

BEDE; Further, our Lord, while teaching the Apostles how the worst devil is to be expelled, gives all of us rules for our life; that is, He would have us know that all the more grievous attacks of evil spirits or of men are to be overcome by fastings and prayers; and again, that the anger of the Lord, when it is kindled for vengeance on our crimes, can be appeased by this remedy alone. But fasting in general is not only abstinence from food, but also from all carnal delights, yes, from all vicious passions. In like manner prayer taken generally, consists not only in the words by which we call upon the Divine mercy, but also in all those things which we do with the devotedness of faith in obedience to our Maker, as the Apostle testifies, when he says, Pray without ceasing.

PSEUDO-JEROME; Or else, the folly which is connected with the softness of the flesh, is healed by fasting; anger and laziness are healed by prayer. Each wound has its own medicine, which must be applied to it; that which is used for the heel will not cure the eye; by fasting, the passions of the body, by prayer, the plagues of the soul, are healed.

30. And they departed thence, and passed through Galilee; and

he would not that any man should know it.

31. For he taught his disciples, and said to them, The Son of man is delivered into the hands of men, and they shall kill him; and after that he is killed, he shall rise the third day.

32. But they understood not that saying, and were afraid to ask him.

33. And he came to Capernaum: and being in the house he asked them, What was it that you disputed among yourselves by the way?

34. But they held their peace: for by the way they had disputed among themselves, who should be the greatest.

35. And he sat down, and called the twelve, and said to them, If any man desire to be first, the same shall be last of all, and servant of all.

36. And he took a child, and set him in the midst of them: and when he had taken him in his arms, he said to them,

37. Whoever shall receive one of such children in my name, receives me: and whoever shall receive me, receives not me, but him that sent me.

THEOPHYL. It is after miracles that the Lord inserts a discourse concerning His Passion, lest it should be thought that He suffered because He could not help it; wherefore it is said, And they departed thence, and passed through Galilee: and he would not that any man should know it.

For he taught his disciples, and said to them, The Son of man is delivered into the hands of men, and they shall kill him.

BEDE; He always mingles together sorrowful and joyful things, that sorrow should not by its suddenness frighten the Apostles, but be borne by them with prepared minds.

THEOPHYL. After, however, saying what was sorrowful, He adds what ought to rejoice them; wherefore it goes on: And after that he is killed, he shall rise the third day; in order that we may learn that joys come on after struggles. There follows: But they understood not that saying, and were afraid to ask him.

BEDE; This ignorance of the disciples proceeds not so much from slowness of intellect, as from love for the Savior, for they were as yet carnal, and ignorant of the mystery of the cross, they could not therefore believe that He whom they had recognized as the true God, was about to die; being accustomed then to hear Him often talk in figures, and shrinking from the event of His death, they would have it, that something was conveyed figuratively in those things, which he spoke openly concerning His betrayal and passion. It goes on: And he came to Capernaum.

PSEUDO-JEROME; Capernaum means the city of consolation, and agrees with the former sentence, which He had spoken: And after that he is killed, he shall arise the third day. There follows: And being in the house he asked them, What was it that you disputed among yourselves by the way?

But they held their peace.

PSEUDO-CHRYS. Matthew however says, that the disciples came to Jesus, saying, Who is the greatest in the kingdom of heaven? The reason is, that he did not begin the narrative from its commencement, but omitted our Savior's knowledge of the thoughts and words of His disciples; unless we understand Him to mean, that even what they thought and said, when away from Christ, was said to Him, since it was as well known to Him as if it had been said to Him. It goes on: For by the way they had disputed among themselves, who should be the greatest. But Luke says, that "the thought entered into the disciples which of them should be the greatest"; for the Lord laid open their thought and intention from their private discourse, according to the Gospel narrative.

PSEUDO-JEROME; It was fit also that they should dispute concerning the chief place by the way the dispute is like the place where it is held; for lofty station is only entered upon to be quitted: as long as a man keeps it, it is slippery, and it is uncertain at what stage, that is, on what day it will end.

BEDE, The reason why the dispute concerning the chief place arose amongst the disciples seems to have been, that Peter, James, and John, were led apart from the rest into the mountain, and that something secret was there entrusted to them, also that the keys of the kingdom of heaven were promised to Peter, according to Matthew. Seeing however the thoughts of the disciples, the Lord takes care to heal the desire of glory by humility; for He first, by simply commanding humility, admonishes them that a high station was not to be aimed at.

Wherefore it goes on: And he sat down, and called the twelve, and said to them, If any man desire to be first, the same shall be last of all, and servant of all.

JEROME; Where it is to be observed, that the disciples disputed by the way concerning the chief place, but Christ Himself sat down to teach humility; for princes toil while the humble repose.

PSEUDO-CHRYS. The disciples indeed wished to receive honor at the hands of the Lord; they also had a desire to be made great by Christ, for the greater a man is, the more worthy of honor he becomes, for which reason He did not throw an obstacle in the way of that desire, but brought in humility.

THEOPHYL. For His wish is not that we should usurp for ourselves chief places, but that we should attain to lofty heights by lowliness. He next admonishes them by the example of a child's innocence; wherefore there follows: And he took a child, and set him inn the midst of them.

CHRYS. By this very sight, persuading them to humility and simplicity; for this little one was pure from envy and vain glory, and from a desire of superiority. But He does not only say, If you become such, you shall receive a great reward, but also, if you will honor others, who are such for my sake. Wherefore there follows: And when he had taken him in his arms, he said to them, Whoever shall receive one of such children in my name, receives me.

BEDE; By which, He either simply shows, that those who would become greater must receive the poor of Christ in honor of Him, or He would persuade them to be in malice children, to keep simplicity without arrogance, charity without envy, devotedness without anger. Again, by taking the child into His arms, He implies that the lowly are worthy of His embrace and love. He adds also, In my name, that they might, with the fixed purpose of reason, follow for His names sake that mold of virtue to which the child keeps, with nature for his guide. And because He taught that He Himself was received in children, lest it should be thought that there was nothing in Him but what was seen, he added, And whoever shall receive me, receive not me, but Him that sent me; thus wishing, that we should believe Him to be of the same nature and of equal greatness with His Father.

THEOPHYL. See, how great is humility, for it wins for itself the indwelling of the Father, and of the Son, and also of the Holy Ghost.

38. And John answered him, saying, Master, we saw one casting out devils in your name, and he follows not us: and we forbade him, because be follows not us.

39. But Jesus said, Forbid him not: for there is no man which shall do a miracle in my name, that can lightly speak evil of me.

40. For he that is not against us is on our part.

41. For whoever shall give you a cup of water to drink in my name, because you belong to Christ, verily I say to you, he shall not lose his reward.

42. And whoever shall offend one of these little ones that believe

in me, it is better for him that a millstone were hanged about his neck, and he were cast into the sea.

BEDE; John, loving the Lord with eminent devotion, thought that He who performed an office to which He had no right was to be excluded from the benefit of it. Wherefore it is said, And John answered him, saying, Master, we saw one casting out devils in your name, and he follows not us: and we forbade him, because he follows not us.

PSEUDO-CHRYS. For many believers received gifts, and yet were not with Christ, such was this man who cast out devils; for there were many of them deficient in some way; some were pure in life, but were not so perfect in faith; others again, contrariwise.

THEOPHYL. Or again, some unbelievers, seeing that the name of Jesus was full of virtue, themselves used it, and performed signs, though they were unworthy of Divine grace; for the Lord wished to extend His name even by those unworthy.

PSEUDO-CHRYS. It was not from jealousy or envy, however, that John wished to forbid him who cast out devils, but because he wished that all, who called on the name of the Lord, should follow Christ, and be one body with His disciples. But the Lord, however unworthy they who perform the miracles may be, incites others by their means to believe in Him, and induces themselves by this unspeakable grace to become better. Wherefore there follows: But Jesus said, Forbid him not.

BEDE; By which He shows that no one is fled to be driven away from that partial goodness which he possesses already, but rather to be stirred up to that which he has not as yet obtained

PSEUDO-CHRYS. In conformity to this, He shows that he is not to be forbidden, adding immediately after, For there is no man which shall do a miracle in my name, that can lightly speak evil of me. He says lightly, to meet the case of those who fell into heresy, such as were Simon and Menander, and Cerinthus; not that they did miracles in the name of Christ, but by their deceptions had the appearance of doing them. But these others, though they do not follow us, cannot however set themselves to say any thing against us, because they honor My name by working miracles.

THEOPHYL. For how can he speak evil of Me, who draws glory from My name, and works miracles by the invocation of this very name. There follows, For he that is not against you is on your part.

AUG. We must take care that this saying of the Lord appear not to be contrary to that, where He says, He who is not with me is against me. Or will any one say that the difference lies in that here He says to His disciples, For he that is not against you is on your part, but in the other He speaks of Himself, He who is not with me is against me? As if indeed it were possible that he who is joined to Christ's disciples, who ate as His members, should not be with Him. How if it were so, could it be true that he that receives you receives me? Or how is he not against Him, who is against His disciples? Where then will be that saying, He who despises you, despises me? But surely what is implied is, that a man is not with Him in as far as he is against Him, and is not against Him as far as he is with Him. For instance, he who worked miracles in the name of Christ, and yet did not join himself to the body of His disciples, in as far as he worked the miracles in His name, was with them, and was not against them: again, in that he did not join their society, he was not with them, and was against them. But because they forbade his doing that in which he was with them, the Lord said to them, Forbid him not; for they ought to have forbidden his being without their society, and thus to have persuaded him of the unity of the Church, but they should not have forbidden that in which he was with them, that is, his commendation of the name of their Lord and Master by the expulsion of devils. Thus the Church Catholic does not disapprove in heretics the sacraments, which are common, but she blames their division, or some opinion of theirs adverse to peace and to truth; for in this they are against us.

PSEUDO-CHRYS. Or else, this is said of those who believe on Him, but nevertheless do not follow Him from the looseness of their lives. Again, it is said of devils, who try to separate all from God, and to disperse His congregation. There follows, For whoever shall give you a cup of cold water to drink in my name, because you belong to Christ, verily I say to you, he shall not lose his reward.

THEOPHYL. Not only will I not forbid him who works miracles in My name, but also whosoever shall give you the smallest tithing for My name's sake, and shall receive you, not on account of human and worldly favor, but from love to Me, shall not lose his reward.

AUG. By which He shows, that he of whom John had spoken was not so far separated from the fellowship of the disciples, as to reject it, as a heretic, but as men are wont to hang back from receiving the Sacraments of Christ, and yet favor the Christian name, so as even to succor Christians, and do them service only because they are Christians. Of these He says they shall not lose their reward; not that they ought already to think themselves secure on account of this good will which they have towards Christians, without being washed with His baptism, and incorporated in His unity, but that they are already so guided by the mercy of God, as also to attain to these, and thus to go away from this life in security.

PSEUDO-CHRYS. And that no man may allege poverty, He mentions that of which none can be destitute, that is, a cup of cold water, for which also he will obtain a reward; for it is not the value of the gift, but the dignity of those who receive it, and the feelings of the giver, which makes a work worthy of reward. His words show that His disciples are to be received, not only on account of the reward, which he who receives them obtains, but also, because he thus saves himself from punishment.

There follows: And whoever shall offend one of these little ones that believe in me, it is better for him that a millstone were hanged about his neck, and he were cast into the sea: as though He would say, All who honor you for My sake have their reward, so also those who dishonor you, that is, offend you, shall receive the worst of vengeance. Further, from things which are palpable to us, He describes an intolerable torment, making mention of a millstone, and of being drowned; and He says not, let a millstone be hanged about his neck, but, it is better for him to suffer this, showing by this that some more heavy evil awaits him. But He means by little ones that believe in Me, not only those who follow Him, but those who call upon His name, those also who offer a cup of cold water, though they do not any greater works. Now He will have none of these offended or plucked away; for this is what is meant by forbidding them to call upon His name.

BEDE; And fitly the man who is offended is called a little one, for he who is great, whatever he may suffer, departs not from the faith; but he who is little and weak in mind looks out for occasions of stumbling. For this reason we must most of all look to those who are little ones in the faith, lest by our fault they should be offended, and go back from the faith, and fall away from salvation.

GREG. We must observe, however, that in our good works we must sometimes avoid the offense of our neighbor, sometimes look down upon it as of no moment. For in as far as we can do it without sin, we ought to avoid the offense of our neigh hour; but if a stumbling block is laid before men in what concerns the truth, it is better to allow the offense to arise, than that the truth should be abandoned.

GREG. Mystically by a millstone is expressed the tedious round and toil of a secular life, and by the depths of the sea, the worst damnation is pointed out. He who therefore, after having been brought to a profession of sanctity, destroys others, either by word or example, it had been indeed better for him that his worldly deeds should render him liable to death, under a secular garb, than that his holy office should hold him out as an example for others in his faults, because doubtless if he had fallen alone, his pain in hell would have been of a more endurable kind.

43. And if your hand offend you, cut it off: it is better for you to enter into life maimed, than having two hands to go into hell, into the fire that never shall be quenched:

44. Where their worm dies not, and the fire is not quenched.

45. And if your foot offend you, cut it off: it is better for you to enter halt into life, than having two feet to be cast into hell, into the fire that never shall be quenched:

46. Where their worm dies not, and the fire is not quenched.

47. And if your eye offend you, pluck it out: it is better for you to enter into the kingdom of God with one eye, than having two eyes to be cast into hell fire:

48. Where their worm dies not, and the fire is not quenched.

49. For every one shall be salted with fire, and every sacrifice shall be salted with salt.

50. Salt is good: but if the salt have lost his saltiness, wherewith will you season it? Have salt in yourselves, and have peace one with another.

BEDE; Because the Lord had taught us not to offend those who believe in Him, He now as next in order warns us how much we should beware of those who offend us, that is, who by their words or conduct strive to drag us into the perdition of sin; wherefore He says, And if your hand offend you, cut it off.

CHRYS. He says not this of our limbs, but of our intimate friends, whom as being necessary to us we look upon as our limbs; for nothing is so hurtful as mischievous society.

BEDE; That is, He calls by the name of hand, our intimate friend, of whose aid we daily stand in need, but if such a one should wish to do us a hurt in what concerns our soul, he is to be driven away from our society lest by choosing a portion in this life with one who is lost, we should perish together with him in that which is to come. Wherefore there follows, It is better for you to enter into life maimed, than having two hands to enter into hell.

GLOSS; By maimed He means, deprived of the help of some friend, for it is better to enter into life without a friend, than to go with him into hell.

PSEUDO-JEROME; Or else, It is better for you to enter into life maimed, that is, without the chief place, for which you have wished, than having two hands to go into eternal fire. The two hands for high station are humility and pride; cut off pride, keeping to the estate of lowliness.

PSEUDO-CHRYS. Then He introduces the witness of prophecy from the prophet Isaiah, saying, Where their worm dies not, and the fire is not quenched. He says not this of a visible worm, but He calls conscience, a worm, gnawing the soul for not having done any good thing; for each of us shall be made his own accuser, by calling to mind what he has done in this mortal life, and so their worm remains for ever.

BEDE; And as the worm is the pain which inwardly accuses, so the fire is a punishment which rages without us; or by the worm is meant the rottenness of hell, by the fire, its heat.

AUG. But those who hold that both of these, namely, the fire and the worm, belong to the pains of the soul, and not of the body, say also that those who are separated from the kingdom of God are tortured, as with fire, by the pangs of a soul, repenting too late, and hopelessly; and they not unfitly contend that fire may be put for that burning grief, as says the Apostle, Who is offended, and I burn not? They also think that by the worm must be understood the same grief, as is said: As a moth destroys a garment, and a worm wood, so grief tortures the heart of man.

All those who hesitate not to affirm that there will be pain both of body and soul in that punishment, affirm that the body is burnt by the fire. But although this is more credible, because it is absurd that there either the pains of body or of soul should be wanting, still I think that it is easier to say that both belong to the body than that neither; and therefore it seems to me that Holy Scripture in this place is silent about the pains of the soul, because it follows that the soul also is tortured in the pains of the body. Let each man therefore choose which he will, either to refer the fire to the body, the worm to the soul, the one properly, the other in a figure, or else both properly to the body; for living things may exist even in fire, in burnings without being wasted, in pain without death, by the wondrous power of the Almighty Creator.

It goes on: And if your foot offend thee, cut it off: it is better for you to enter halt into life, than having two feet to be cast into hell, into the fire that never shall be quenched;

where their worm dies not, and the fire is not quenched.

BEDE; A friend is called a foot, on account of its service in going about for us, since he is as it were ready for our use. It goes on: And if your eye offend thee, pluck it out: it is better for you to enter into the kingdom of God with one eye, than having two eyes to be cast into hell fire;

where their worm dies not, and the fire is not quenched. A friend who is useful, and anxious, and sharp in perception, is called an eye.

AUG. Here truly it appears that they who do acts of devotedness in the name of Christ, even before they have joined themselves to the company of Christians, and have been washed in the Christian Sacraments, are more useful than those who though already bearing the name of Christians, by their doctrine drag their followers with themselves into everlasting punishment; whom also under the name of members of the body, He orders, as an offending eye or hand, to be torn from the body, that is, from the fellowship itself of unity, that we may rather come to everlasting life without them, than with them go into hell.

But the separation of those who separate themselves from them consists in the very circumstance of their not yielding to them, when they would persuade them to evil, that is, offend them. If indeed their wickedness becomes known to all the good men, with whom they are connected, they are altogether cut off from all fellowship, and even from partaking in the heavenly

Sacraments. If however they are thus known only to the smaller number, whilst their wickedness is unknown to the generality, they are to be tolerated in such a way that we should not consent to join in their iniquity, and that the communion of the good should not be deserted on their account.

BEDE; But because the Lord had three times made mention of the worm and the fire, that we might be able to avoid this torment, He subjoins, For every one shall be salted with fire. For the stink of worms always arises from the corruption of flesh and blood, and therefore fresh meat is seasoned with salt, that the moisture of the blood may be dried off, and so it may not breed worms. And if, indeed, that which is salted with salt, keeps off the putrefying worm, that which is salted with fire, that is, seasoned again with flames, on which salt is sprinkled, not only casts off worms, but also consumes the flesh itself.

Flesh and blood therefore breed worms, that is, carnal pleasure, if unopposed by the seasoning of continence, produces everlasting punishment for the luxurious; the stink of which if any man would avoid, let him take care to chasten his body with the salt of continence, and his mind with the seasoning of wisdom, from the stain of error and vice. For salt means the sweetness of wisdom, and fire, the grace of the Holy Spirit. He says therefore, Every one shall be salted with fire, because all the elect ought to be purged by spiritual wisdom, from the corruption of carnal concupiscence. Or else, the fire is the fire of tribulation, by which the patience of the faithful is proved, that it may have its perfect work.

PSEUDO-CHRYS. Similar to this is that which the Apostle says,

And the fire shall try every man's work of what sort it is. Afterwards He brings in a witness from Leviticus: which says, And every oblation of your meat offering shall you season with salt.

PSEUDO-JEROME; The oblation of the Lord is the race of man, which is here salted by means of wisdom, whilst the corruption of blood, the nurse of rottenness, and the mother of worms, is being consumed, which there also shall be tried by the purgatorial fire.

BEDE; We may also understand the altar to be the heart of the elect, and the victims and sacrifices to be offered on the altar are good works. But in all sacrifices salt ought to be offered, for that is not a good work which is not purged by the salt of wisdom from all corruption of vain glory, and other evil and superfluous thoughts.

PSEUDO-CHRYS. Or else it is meant, that every gift of our victim, which is accompanied by prayer and the assisting of our neighbor, is salted with that divine fire, of which it is said, I am come to send fire on earth. Concerning which it is added: Salt is good; that is, the fire of love. But if the salt have lost his saltiness, that is, is deprived of itself, and that peculiar quality, by which it is called good, wherewith will you season it! For there is salt, which has saltiness, that is, which has the fullness of grace; and there is salt, which has no saltiness, for that which is not peaceful is salt unseasoned.

BEDE; Or the good salt is the frequent hearing of God's word, and the seasoning the hidden parts of the heart with the salt of spiritual wisdom.

THEOPHYL. For as salt preserves flesh, and suffers it not to breed worms, so also the discourse of the teacher, if it can dry up what is evil, constrains carnal men, and suffers not the undying worm to grow up in them. But if it be without saltiness, that is, if its virtue of drying up and preserving be gone, with what shall it be salted?

PSEUDO-CHRYS. Or, according to Matthew, the disciples of Christ are the salt, which preserves the whole world, resisting the rottenness which proceeds from idolatry and sinful fornication. For it may also be meant, that each of us has salt, in as far as he contains in himself the graces of God. Wherefore also the Apostle join together grace and salt, saying, Let your speech be always with grace, seasoned with salt. For salt is the Lord Jesus Christ, Who was able to preserve the whole earth, and made many to be salt in the earth, and if any of these be corrupted, (for it is possible for even the good to be changed into corruption,) they are worthy to be cast out.

PSEUDO-JEROME; Or otherwise; That salt is saltless which loves the chief place, and dares not rebuke others. Wherefore there follows, Have salt in yourselves, and have peace one with another. That is, let the love of your neighbor temper the saltiness of rebuke, and the salt of justice season the love of your neighbor.

GREG; Or this is said against those whom greater knowledge, while it raises above their neighbors, cuts off from the fellowship of others; thus the more their learning increases, the more they unlearn the virtue of concord.

GREG. He also who strives to speak with wisdom should be greatly afraid, lest by his eloquence the unity of his hearers be thrown into confusion, lest, while he would appear wise, he unwisely cut asunder the bonds of unity.

THEOPHYL. Or else, he who binds himself to his neighbor by the tie of love, has salt, and in this way peace with his neighbor.

AUG. Mark relates that the Lord said these things consecutively, and has put down some things omitted by every other Evangelist, some which Matthew has also related, others which both Matthew and Luke relate, but on other occasions, and in a different series of events. Wherefore it seems to me that our Lord repeated in this place discourses which He had used in other places, because they were pertinent enough to this saying of His, by which He prevented their forbidding miracles to be wrought in His name, even by him who followed Him not together with His disciples.

Mark 10

1. And he arose from thence, and comes into the coasts of Judea by the farther Side of Jordan: and the people resort to him again; and, as he was wont, he taught them again.

2. And the Pharisees came to him, and asked him, Is it lawful for a man to put away his wife? tempting him.

3. And he answered and said to them, What did Moses command you?

4. And they said, Moses suffered to write a bill of divorcement, and to put her away.

5. And Jesus answered and said to them, For the hardness of your heart he wrote you this precept.

6. But from the beginning of the creation God made them male and female.

7. For this cause shall a man leave his father and mother, and cleave to his wife.

8. And they two shall be one flesh: so then they are no more two, but one flesh.

9. What therefore God has joined together, let not man put asunder.

Catena Aurea: Commentary on the Gospel of St. Mark

10. And in the house his disciples asked him again of the same matter.

11. And he said to them, Whoever shall put away his wife, and marry another, commits adultery against her.

12. And if a woman shall put away her husband and be married to another, she commits adultery.

BEDE; Up to this time Mark had related what our Lord said and did in Galilee; here he begins to relate what He did, taught, or suffered in Judea, and first indeed across the Jordan on the east; and this is what is said in these words: And he arose from thence, and comes into the coasts of Judea, by the farther side of Jordan; then also on this side Jordan, when He came to Jericho, Bethany, and Jerusalem. And though all the province of the Jews is generally called Judea, to distinguish it from other nations, more especially, however, its southern portion was called Judea, to distinguish it from Samaria, Galilee, Decapolis, and the other regions in the same province.

THEOPHYL. But He enters the region of Judea, which the envy of the Jews had often caused Him to leave, because His Passion was to take place there. He did not, however, then go up to Jerusalem, but to the confines of Judea, that He might do good to the multitudes, who were not evil; for Jerusalem was, from the malice of the Jews, the worker of all the wickedness. Wherefore it goes on: And the people resort to him again, and, as he was wont, he taught them again.

BEDE; Mark the difference of temper in the multitude and in the

Pharisees. The former meet together, in order to be taught, and that their sick may be healed, as Matthew relates; the latter come to Him, to try to deceive their Savior by tempting Him. Wherefore there follows, And the Pharisees came to him, and asked him, Is it lawful for a man to put away his wife? tempting Him.

THEOPHYL. They come to Him indeed, and do not quit Him, lest the multitudes should believe on Him; and by continually coming to Him, they thought to bring Him into difficulty, and to confuse Him by their questions. For they proposed to Him a question, which had on either side a precipice, so that whether He said that it was lawful for a man to put away his wife, or that it was not lawful, they might accuse Him, and contradict what He said, out of the doctrines of Moses. Christ, therefore, being Very Wisdom, in answering their question, avoids their snares.

CHRYS. For being asked, whether it is lawful, he does not immediately reply, it is not lawful, lest they should raise an outcry, but He first wished them to answer Him as to the sentence of the law, that they by their answer might furnish Him with what it was right to say. Wherefore it goes on, And he answered and said to them, What did Moses command you?

And afterwards, And they said, Moses suffered to write a bill of divorcement, and to put her away. They put forward indeed this that Moses had said either on account of the question of our Savior, or wishing to excite against Him a multitude of men. For divorce was an indifferent thing among the Jews, and all practiced it, as though it were permitted by the law.

AUG. It makes nothing, however, to the truth of the fact, whether, as Matthew says, they themselves addressed to the Lord the question concerning the bill of divorcement, allowed to them by Moses, on our Lord's forbidding the separation, and confirming His sentence from the law, or whether it was in answer to a question of His, that they said this concerning the command of Moses, as Mark here says. For His wish was to give them no reason why Moses permitted it, before they themselves had mentioned the fact; since then the wish of the parties speaking, which is what the words ought to express, is in either way shown, there is no discrepancy, though there be a difference in the way of relating it. It may also be meant that, as Mark expresses it, the question put to them by the Lord, What did Moses command? was in answer to those who had previously asked His opinion concerning the putting away of a wife; and when they had replied that Moses permitted them to write a bill of divorcement, and to put her away, His answer was concerning that same law, given by Moses, how God instituted the marriage of a male, and a female, saying those things which Matthew relates; on hearing which they again rejoined what they had replied to Him when He first asked them, namely, Why then did Moses command?

AUG. Moses, however, was against a man's dismissing his wife, for he interposed this delay, that a person whose mind was bent on separation, might be deterred by the writing of the bill, and desist; particularly, since, as is related, among the Hebrews, no one was allowed to write Hebrew characters but the scribes. The law therefore wished to send him, whom it ordered to give a bill of divorcement, before he dismissed his wife, to them, who ought to be wise interpreters of the law, and just opponents of quarrel. For a bill could only be written for him by men, who by their good advice might overrule him, since his circumstances and necessity had put him into their bands, and so by treating between him and his wife they might persuade them to love and concord. But if a hatred so great had arisen that it could not be extinguished and corrected, then indeed a bill was to be written, that he might not lightly put away her who was the object of his hate, in such a way as to prevent his being recalled to the love, which he owed her by marriage, through the persuasion of the wise. For this reason it is added, For the hardness of your heart, he wrote this precept; for great was the hardness of heart which could not be melted or bent to the taking back and recalling the love of marriage, even by the interposition of a bill in a way which gave room for the just and wise to dissuade them.

PSEUDO-CHRYS. Or else, it is said, For the hardness of your hearts, because it is possible for a soul purged from desires and from anger to bear the worst of women; but if those passions have a redoubled force over the mind, many evils will arise from hatred in marriage. Thus then, He saves Moses, who had given the law, from their accusation, and turns the whole upon their head. But since what He had said was grievous to them, He at once brings back the discourse to the old law, saying, But from the beginning of the creation, God made them male and female.

BEDE; He says not male and females, which the sense would have required had it referred to the divorce of former wives, but male and female, so that they might be bound by the tie of one wife.

CHRYS. If however he had wished one wife to be put away and

another to be brought in, He would have created several women. Nor did God only join one woman to one man, but He also bade a man quit his parents and cleave to his wife. Wherefore it goes on: And he said, (that is, God said by Adam,) For this cause shall a man leave his father and mother, and cleave to his wife. From the very mode of speech, showing the impossibility of severing marriage, because He said, He shall cleave.

BEDE; And in like manner, because He says, he shall cleave to his wife, not wives. It goes on: And they two shall be one flesh.

CHRYS. Being framed out of one root, they will join into one body. It goes on: So then they are no more two, but one flesh.

BEDE; The reward then of marriage is of two to become one flesh. Virginity being joined to the Spirit, becomes of one spirit.

CHRYS. After this, bringing forward an awful argument, He said not, do not divide, but He concluded, What therefore God has joined together, let not man put asunder.

AUG. Behold the Jews are convinced out of the books of Moses, that a wife is not to be put away, while they fancied that in putting her away, they were doing the will of Moses. In like manner from this place, from the witness of Christ Himself, we know this, that God made and joined male and female, for denying which the Manichees are condemned, resisting now not the books of Moses, but the Gospel of Christ.

BEDE; What therefore God has conjoined by making one flesh of a man and a woman, that man cannot separate, but God alone.

Man separates, when we dismiss the first wife because we desire a second; but it is God who, separates, when by common consent, for the sake of serving God, we so have wives as though we had none.

CHRYS. But if two persons, whom God has joined together, are not to be separated; much more is it wrong to separate from Christ, the Church, which God has joined to Him.

THEOPHYL. But the disciples were offended, as not being fully satisfied with what had been said; for this reason they again question Him, wherefore there follows, And in the house, his disciples asked him again of the same matter.

PSEUDO-JEROME; This second question is said to be asked again by the Apostles, because it is on the subject of which the Pharisees had asked Him, that is, concerning the state of marriage; and this is said by Mark in his own person.

GLOSS. For a repetition of a saying of the Word, produces not weariness, but thirst and hunger; wherefore it is said, They that eat me shall yet be hungry, and they that drink me shall yet be thirsty; for the tasting of the honeyed words of wisdom yields all manner of savor to them who love her. Wherefore the Lord instructs His disciples over again; for it goes on, And he said to them, Whoever shall put away his wife and marry another, commits adultery upon her.

PSEUDO-CHRYS. The Lord calls by the name of adultery cohabitation with her who is not a man's wife; she is not, however, a wife, whom a man has taken to him, after quitting his first; and for this reason he commits adultery upon her, that is, upon the second, whom he brings in. And the same thing is true in the case of the woman; wherefore it goes on, And if a woman shall put away her husband, and marry another, she commits adultery; for she cannot be joined to another as her own husband, if she leave him who is really her own husband. The law indeed forbade what was plainly adultery; but the Savior forbids this, which was neither plain, nor known to all, though it was contrary to nature.

BEDE; In Matthew it is more fully expressed, Whoever shall put away his wife, except it be for fornication. The only carnal cause then is fornication; the only spiritual cause is the fear of God, that a man should put away his wife to enter into religion, as we read that many have done. But there is no cause allowed by the law of God for marrying another, during the lifetime of her who is quitted.

PSEUDO-CHRYS. There is no contrariety in Matthew's relating that He spoke these words to the Pharisees, though Mark says that they were spoken to the disciples; for it is possible that He may have spoken them to both.

13. And they brought young children to him, that he should touch them: and his disciples rebuked those that brought them.

14. But when Jesus saw it, he was much displeased, and said to them, Suffer the little children to come to me, and forbid them not: for of such is the kingdom of God.

15. Truly I say to you, Whoever shall not receive the kingdom of

God as a little child, he shall not enter therein.

16. And he took them up in his arms, put his hands upon them, and blessed them.

THEOPHYL. The wickedness of the Pharisees in tempting Christ, has been related above, and now is shown the great faith of the multitude, who believed that Christ conferred a blessing on the children whom they brought to Him, by the mere laying on of His hands. Wherefore it is said: And they brought young children to him, that he might touch them.

CHRYS. But the disciples, out of regard for the dignity of Christ, forbade those who brought them. And this is what is added: And his disciples rebuked those who brought them. But our Savior; in order to teach His disciples to be modest in their ideas, and to tread under foot worldly pride, takes the children to Him, and assigns to them the kingdom of God: wherefore it goes on: And he said to them, Suffer little children to come to me, and forbid them not

ORIGEN; If any of those who profess to hold the office of teaching in the Church should see a person bringing to them some of the foolish of this world, and low born, and weak, who for this reason are called children and infants, let him not forbid the man who offers such an one to the Savior, as though he were acting without judgment. After this He exhorts those of His disciples who are already grown to full stature to condescend to be useful to children, that they may become to children as children, that they may gain children; for He Himself, when He was in the form of God, humbled Himself, and became a child.

On which He adds: For of such is the kingdom of heaven.

CHRYS. For indeed the mind of a child is pure from all passions, for which reason, we ought by free choice to do those works, which children have by nature.

THEOPHYL. Wherefore He says not, for of these, but of such is the kingdom of God, that is, of persons who have both in their intention and their work the harmlessness and simplicity which children have by nature. For a child does not hate, does nothing of evil intent, nor though beaten does he quit his mother; and though she does him in vile garments, prefers them to kingly apparel; in like manner he, who lives according to the good ways of his mother the Church, honors nothing before her, nay, not pleasure, which is the queen of many; wherefore also the Lord subjoins, Truly I say to you, Whoever shall not receive the kingdom of God as a little child, he shall not enter therein.

BEDE; That is, if you have not innocence and purity of mind like that of children, you cannot enter into the kingdom of heaven. Or else, we are ordered to receive the kingdom of God, that is, the doctrine of the Gospel, a little child, because as a child, when he is taught, does not contradict his teachers, nor put together reasonings and words against them, but receives with faith what they teach, and obeys them with awe, so we also are to receive the word of the Lord with simple obedience, and without any gainsaying. It goes on: And he took them up in his arms, put his hands upon them, and blessed them.

PSEUDO-CHRYS. Fitly does He take them up into His arms to bless them, as it were, lifting into His own bosom, and reconciling Himself to His creation, which in the beginning fell from Him, and was separated from Him. Again, He puts His hands upon the children, to teach us the working of His divine power; and indeed, He puts His hands upon them, as others are wont to do, though His operation is not as that of others, for though He was God, He kept to human ways of acting, as being very man.

BEDE; Having embraced the children, He also blessed them, implying that the lowly in spirit are worthy of His blessing, grace, and love.

17. And when he was gone forth into the way, there came one running, and kneeled to him, and asked him, Good Master, what shall I do that I may inherit eternal life?

18. And Jesus said to him, Why call you me good? there is none good but one, that is, God.

19. You know the commandments, Do not commit adultery, Do not kill, Do not steal, Do not bear false witness, Defraud not, Honor your father and mother.

20. And he answered and said to him, Master, all these have I observed from my youth.

21. Then Jesus beholding him loved him, and said to him, One thing you lack: go your way, Sell whatsoever you have, and give to the poor, and you shall have treasure in heaven: and come, take up the cross, and follow me.

Catena Aurea: Commentary on the Gospel of St. Mark

22. And he was sad at that saying, and went away grieved: for he had great possessions.

23. And Jesus looked round about, and said to his disciples, How hardly shall they that have riches enter into the kingdom of God!

24. And the disciples were astonished at his words. But Jesus answered again, and said to them, Children, how hard is it for them that trust in riches to enter into the kingdom of God!

25. It is easier for a camel to go through the eye of a needle, than for a rich man to enter into the kingdom of God.

26. And they were astonished out of measure, saying among themselves, Who then can be saved?

27. And Jesus looking upon them said, With men it is impossible, but not with God: for with God all things are possible.

BEDE; A certain man had heard from the Lord that only they who are willing to be like little children are worthy to enter into the kingdom of heaven, and therefore he desires to have explained to him, not in parables, but openly, by the merits of what works a man may attain everlasting life. Wherefore it is said: And when he was gone forth into the way, there came one running, and kneeled to him, and asked him, Good Master, what shall I do that I may inherit eternal life?

THEOPHYL. I wonder at this young man, who when all others come to Christ to be healed of their infirmities, begs of Him the possession of everlasting life, notwithstanding his love of money, the malignant passion which afterwards caused his sorrow.

CHRYS. Because however he had come to Christ as he would to a man, and to one of the Jewish doctors, Christ answered him as Man. Wherefore it goes on: And Jesus said to him, Why call you me good? there is none good but the One God. In saying which He does not exclude men from goodness, but from a comparison with the goodness of God.

BEDE; But by this one God, who is good, we must not only understand the Father, but also the Son, whom says, I am the good Shepherd; and also the Holy Ghost, because it is said, The Father which is in heaven will give the good Spirit to them that ask him. For the One and Undivided Trinity itself, Father, Son amid Holy Ghost, is the Only and One good God. The Lord therefore does not deny Himself to be good, but implies that He is God; He does not deny that He is good Master, but He declares that no master is good but God.

THEOPHYL; Therefore the Lord intended by these words to raise the mind of the young man, so that he might know Him to be God. But He also implies another thing by these words, that when you have to converse with a man, you should not flatter him in your conversation, but look back upon God, the root and fount of goodness, and do honor to Him.

BEDE; But observe that the righteousness of the law, when kept in its own time, conferred not only earthly goods, but also eternal life on those who chose it. Wherefore the Lord's answer to one who inquires concerning everlasting life is, You know the commandments, Do not commit adultery, Do not kill; for this is the childlike blamelessness which is proposed to us, if we would enter the kingdom of heaven.

On which there follows, And he answered and said to him, Master, all these have I observed from my youth. We must not suppose that this man either asked the Lord, with a wish to tempt him, as some have fancied, or lied in his account of his life; but we must believe that he confessed with simplicity how he had lived; which is evident, from what is subjoined,

Then Jesus beholding him loved him, and said to him. If however he had been guilty of lying or of dissimulation, by no means would Jesus, after, looking on the secrets of his heart, have been said to love him.

ORIGEN; For in that He loved, or kissed him, He appears to affirm the truth of his profession, in saying that he had fulfilled all those things; for on applying His mind to him, He saw that the man answered with a good conscience.

PSEUDO-CHRYS. It is worthy of inquiry, however, how He loved a man, who, He knew, would not follow Him? But this is so much as to say, that since he was worthy of love in the first instance, because he observed the things of the law from his youth, so in the end, though he did not take upon himself perfection, he did not suffer a lessening of his former love. For although he did not pass the bounds of humanity, nor follow the perfection of Christ, still he was not guilty of any sin, since he kept the law according to the capability of a man, and in this mode of keeping it, Christ loved him.

BEDE; For God loves those who keep the commandments of the law, though they be inferior; nevertheless, He shows to those who would be perfect the deficiency of the law, for He came not to destroy the law, but to fulfill it. Wherefore there follows: And said to him, One thing you lacks: go your way, sell whatever you have, and give to the poor, and you shall have treasure in heaven: and come, follow me; for whoever would be perfect ought to sell all that he has, not a part, like Ananias and Sapphira, but the whole.

THEOPHYL. And when he has sold it, to give it to the poor, not to stage-players and luxurious persons.

CHRYS. Well too did He say, not eternal life, but treasure, saying, And you shall have treasure in heaven; for since the question was concerning wealth, and the renouncing of all things, He shows that He returns more things than He has bidden us leave, in proportion as heaven is greater than earth.

THEOPHYL. But because there are many poor who are not humble, but are drunkards or have some other vice, for this reason He says, And come, follow me.

BEDE; For he follows the Lord, who imitates Him, and walks in His footsteps. It goes on: And he was sad at that saying, and went away grieved.

CHRYS. And the Evangelist adds the cause of his grief, saying, For he had great possessions. The feelings of those who have little and those who have much are not the same, for the increase of acquired wealth lights up a greater flame of covetousness.

There follows: And Jesus looked round about, and said to his disciples, How hardly shall they that have riches enter into the kingdom of God.

THEOPHYL. He says not here, that riches are bad, but that those are bad who only have them to watch them carefully; for He teaches us not to have them, that is, not to keep or preserve them, but to use them in necessary things.

CHRYS. But the Lord said this to His disciples, who were poor and possessed nothing, in order to teach them not to blush at their poverty, and as it were to make an excuse to them, and give them a reason, why He had not allowed them to possess any thing. It goes on: And the disciples were astonished at his words; for it is plain, since they themselves were poor, that they were anxious for the salvation of others.

BEDE; But there is a great difference between having riches, and loving them; wherefore also Solomon says not, He that has silver, but, He that loves silver shall not be satisfied with silver. Therefore the Lord unfolds the words of His former saying to His astonished disciples, as follows: But Jesus answered again, and said to them, Children, how hard it is for them that trust in their riches to enter the kingdom of God. Where we must observe that He says not, how impossible, but how hard; for what is impossible cannot in any way come to pass, what is difficult can be compassed, though with labor.

CHRYS. Or else, after saying difficult, He then shows that it is impossible, and that not simply, but with a certain vehemence; and he shows this by an example, saying, It is easier for a camel to pass through the eye of a needle, than for a rich man to enter the kingdom of heaven.

THEOPHYL. It may be that by camel, we should understand the animal itself, or else that thick cable, which is used for large vessels.

BEDE; How then could either in the Gospel, Matthew and Joseph, or in the Old Testament, very many rich persons, enter into the kingdom of God, unless it be that they learned through the inspiration of God either to count their riches as nothing, or to quit them altogether. Or in a higher sense, it is easier for Christ to suffer for those who love Him, than for, the lovers of this world to turn to Christ; for under the name of camel, He wished Himself to he understood, because He bore the burden of our weakness; and by the needle, He understands the prickings, that is, the pains of His Passion. By the eye of a needle, therefore, He means the straits of His Passion, by which He, as it were, deigned to mend the torn garments of our nature. it goes on;

And they were astonished above measure, saying among themselves, Who then can be saved? Since the number of poor people is immeasurably the greater, and these might be saved, though tine rich perished, they must have understood Him to mean that all who love riches, although they cannot obtain them, are reckoned in the number of the rich. It goes on; And Jesus looking upon them said, With men it is impossible, but not with God; which we must not take to mean, that covetous and proud persons can enter into the kingdom of Heaven with their covetousness and pride, but that it is possible with God that they should be converted from covetousness arid pride to charity and lowliness.

CHRYS. And the reason why He says that this is the work of God is, that He may show that he who is put into this path by God, has much need of grace; from which it is proved, that great is the reward of those rich men, who are willing to follow the r discipline of Christ.

THEOPHYL. Or we must understand that by, with man it is impossible, but not with God, He means, that when we listen to God, it becomes possible, but as long as we keep our human notions, it is impossible. There follows, For all things are possible with God; when He says all things, you must understand, that have a being; which sin has not, for it is a thing without being and substance , Or else: sin does not come under the notion of strength, but of weakness, therefore sin, like weakness, is impossible with God But can God cause that not to have been done which has been done? To which we answer, that God is Truth, but to cause that which has been done should not have been done is falsehood. How then can truth do what is false? He must first therfore quit His own nature, so that they who speak thus really say, Can God cease to be God? which is absurd.

28. Then Peter began to say to him, Lo, we have left all, and have followed you.

29. And Jesus answered and said, Truly I say to you, there is no man that has left house, or brethren, or sisters, or father, or mother, or wife, or children, or lands, for my sake, and the Gospel's,

30. But he shall receive an hundredfold now in this time, houses, and brethren, and sisters, and mothers, and children, and lands, with persecutions; and in the world to come eternal life.

31. But many that are first shall be last; and the last first.

GLOSS. Because the youth, on hearing the advice of our Savior concerning the casting away of his goods, had gone away sorrowful, the disciples of Christ, who had already fulfilled the foregoing precept, began to question Him concerning their reward, thinking that they had done a great thing, since the young man, who had fulfilled the commandments of the law, had not been able to hear it without sadness. Wherefore Peter questions the Lord for himself and the others, in these words, Then Peter began to say to him, Lo, we have left all, and have followed you.

THEOPHYL. Although Peter had left but few things, still he calls these his all; for even a few things keep us by the bond of affection, so that he shall be beatified who leaves a few things.

BEDE; And because it is not sufficient to have left all, he adds that which makes up perfection, and have followed you. As if he said, We have done what You have commanded. What reward therefore will You give us? But while Peter asks only concerning the disciples, our Lord makes a general answer; wherefore it goes on: Jesus answered and said, Truly I say to you, There is no one that has left house, or brethren, on. sisters, or father, or mother, or children, or lands. But in saying this, He does not mean that we should leave our fathers, without helping them, or that we should separate ourselves from our wives; but He instructs us to prefer the glory of God to the things of this world.

CHRYS. But it seems to me that by these words He intended covertly to proclaim that there were to be persecutions, as it would come to pass that many fathers would allure their sons to impiety, and in many wives their husbands. Again He delays not to say, for my name's sake and the Gospel's, as Mark says, or for the kingdom of God, as Luke says; the name of Christ is the power of the Gospel, and of His kingdom; for the Gospel is received in the name of Jesus Christ, and the kingdom is made known, and comes by His name.

BEDE; Some, however, taking occasion from this saying, in which it is announced that he shall receive an hundredfold now in this time, teach that Jewish fable of a thousand years after the resurrection of the just, when all that we have left for the Lord's sake is to be restored with manifold usury, besides which we are to receive the crown of everlasting life. These persons do not perceive, that although the promise in other respects be honorable, yet in the hundred wives, which the other Evangelists mention, its foulness is made manifest: particularly when the Lord testifies that there shall be no marriage in the resurrection, and asserts that those things which are put away from us for His sake are to be received again in this life with persecutions, which, as they affirm, will not take place in their thousand years.

PSEUDO-CHRYS. This hundredfold reward therefore must be in participation, not in possession, for the Lord fulfilled this to them not carnally, but spiritually.

THEOPHYL. For a wife is busied in a house about her husband's food and raiment. See also how this is the case with the Apostles; for many women busied themselves about their food and their clothing, and ministered to them. In like manner the Apostles had many fathers and mothers, that is, persons who loved them; as Peter, for instance, leaving one house, had afterwards the houses of all the disciples. And what is more wonderful, they are to be persecuted and oppressed, for it is with persecutions that the Saints are to possess all things, for which reason there follows, But many that are first shall be last, and the last first. For the Pharisees who were first became the last; but those who left all and followed Christ were last in this world through tribulation and persecutions, but shall be first by the hope which is in God.

BEDE. This which is here said, shall receive a hundredfold, may be understood in a higher sense. For the number a hundred which is reckoned by changing from the left to the right hand, although it has the same appearance in the bending of the fingers as the ten had on the left, nevertheless is increased to a much greater quantity. This means, that all who have despised temporal things for the sake of the kingdom of heaven through undoubting faith, taste the joy of the same kingdom in this life which is full of persecutions, and in the expectation of the heavenly country, which is signified by the right hand, have a share in the happiness of all the elect.

But because all do not accomplish a virtuous course of life with the same ardor as they began it, it is presently added, But many that are first shall be last, and the last first; for we daily see many persons who, remaining in a lay habit, are eminent for their meritorious life; but others, who from their youth have been ardent in a spiritual profession, at last wither away in the sloth of ease, and with a hazy folly finish in the flesh, what they had begun in the Spirit.

32. And they were in the way going up to Jerusalem; and Jesus went before them: and they were amazed; and as they followed, they were afraid. And he took again the twelve, and began to tell them what things should happen to him,

33. Saying, Behold, we go up to Jerusalem; and the Son of man shall be delivered to the chief priests, and to the Scribes; and they shall condemn him to death, and shall deliver him to the Gentiles:

34. And they shall mock him, and shall scourge him, and shall spit upon him, and shall kill him: and the third day he shall rise again.

BEDE; The disciples remembered the discourse in which the Lord had foretold that He was about to suffer many things from the chief priests and scribes, and therefore in going up to Jerusalem, they were amazed. And this is what is meant, when it is Said, And they were in the way going up to Jerusalem, and Jesus went before them.

THEOPHYL. To show that He runs to meet His Passion, and that He does not refuse death, for the sake of our salvation; and they were amazed, and as they followed, they were afraid.

BEDE; Either lest they themselves should perish with Him, or at all events lest He, whose life and ministry was their joy, should fall under the hand of His enemies. But the Lord, foreseeing that the minds of His disciples would be troubled by His Passion, foretells to them both the pain of His Passion, and the glory of His resurrection; wherefore there follows, And he took again the twelve, and began to tell them what things should happen to him.

THEOPHYL. He did this to confirm the hearts of the disciples, that from hearing these things beforehand, they might the better bear them afterwards, and might not be alarmed at their suddenness, and also in order to show them that He suffered voluntarily; for he who fore-knows a danger, and flies not, though flight is in his power, evidently of his own will gives himself up to suffering. But He takes His disciples apart, because it was fitting that He should reveal the mystery of this Passion to those who were more closely connected with Him.

CHRYS. And He enumerates each thing that was to happen to Him; lest if He should pass any thing over, they should be troubled afterwards at suddenly seeing it; wherefore he adds, Behold, we go up to Jerusalem, and the Son of Man.

GLOSS. That is, He to whom suffering belongs; for the Godhead cannot suffer. Shall be delivered, that is, by Judas, to the Chief Priests, and to the Scribes, and they shall condemn him to death; judging Him to due guilty of death; and shall deliver him to the Gentiles, that is, to Pilate the Gentile; and his soldiers shall mock him, and shall spit upon him and scourge him, and put him to

Catena Aurea: Commentary on the Gospel of St. Mark

death.

CHRYS. But that when they were saddened on account of His passion and death, they should then also look for His resurrection, He adds, And the third day he shall rise again; for since He had not hid from them the sorrows and insults which happened, it was fitting that they should believe Him on other points.

35. And James and John, the sons of Zebedee, come to him, saying, Master, we would that you should do for us whatsoever we shall desire.

36. And he said to them, What would you that I should do for you?

37. They said to him, Grant to us that we may sit, one on your right hand, and the other on your left hand, in your glory.

38. But Jesus said to them, You know not what you ask: can you drink of the cup that I drink of? and be baptized with the baptism that I am baptized with?

39. And they said to him, We can. And Jesus said to them, You shall indeed drink of the cup that I drink of; and with the baptism that I am baptized withal shall you be baptized:

40. But to sit on my right hand and on my left hand is not mine to give; but it shall be given to them for whom it is prepared.

CHRYS. The disciples hearing Christ oftentimes speaking of His kingdom, thought that this kingdom was to be before His death, and therefore now that His death was foretold to them, they came to Him, that they might immediately be made worthy of the honors of the kingdom: wherefore it is said, And James and John, the sons of Zebedee, came to him, saying, Master, we would that you should do for us whatever we shall desire.

For ashamed of the human weakness which they felt, they came to Christ, taking Him apart from the disciples; but our Savior, not from ignorance of what they wanted to ask, but from a wish of making them answer Him, puts this question to them; And he said to them, What would you that I should do for you?

THEOPHYL. Now the above mentioned disciples thought that He was going up to Jerusalem, to reign there, and then to suffer what He had foretold. And with these thoughts, they desired to sit on the right and the left hand; wherefore there follows, They said to him, Grant to us that we may sit, one on your right hand, the other on your left hand, in the glory.

AUG. Matthew has expressed that this was said not by themselves, but by their mother, since she brought their wishes to the Lord; wherefore Mark briefly implies rather that they themselves, than that their mother, had used the words.

CHRYS. Or we may fitly say that both took place; for seeing themselves honored above the rest, they thought that they could easily obtain the foregoing petition; and that they might the more easily succeed in their request, they took their mother with them, that they might pray to Christ together with her.

AUG. Then the Lord both according to Mark, and too Matthew, answered them rather than their mother. For it goes on, But Jesus said to them, You know not what you ask.

THEOPHYL. It will not be as you think, that I am to reign as a temporal king in Jerusalem, but all these things, that is, these which belong to My kingdom, are beyond your understanding; for to sit on My right hand is so great a thing that it surpasses the Angelic orders.

BEDE; Or else, they know not what they ask, who seek from the Lord a seat of glory, which they do not yet merit.

CHRYS. Or else He says, You know not what you ask; as if He said, You speak of honors, but I am discoursing of wrestlings and toil; for this is not a time of rewards, but of blood, of battles, and dangers. Wherefore He adds, Can you drink of the cup that I drink of, and be baptized with the baptism that I am baptized withal? He draws them on by way of question, that by communication with Himself, their eagerness might increase.

THEOPHYL. But by the cup and baptism, He means the cross; the cup, that is, as being a potion by Him sweetly received, but baptism is the cause of the cleansing of our sins. And they answer Him, without understanding what He had said; wherefore it goes on: And they said to him, We can; for they thought that He spoke of a visible cup, and of the baptism of which the Jews made use, that is, the washings before their meals.

CHRYS. And they answered thus quickly, because they expected that what they had asked would he listened to; it goes on: And

Jesus said to them, You shall indeed drink of the cup that I drink of, and with the baptism that I am baptized withal shall you be baptized; that is, you shall be worthy of martyrdom, and suffer even as I.

BEDE; A question is raised, however, how James and John drank the cup of martyrdom, or how they were baptized with the baptism of the Lord, when the Scripture relates, that only James the Apostle was beheaded by Herod whilst John finished his life by a natural death. But if we read ecclesiastical histories, in which it is related, that he also on account of the witness which he bore was cast into a cauldron of burning oil, and was immediately sent away to the island of Patmos, we shall then see that the spirit of martyrdom was in him, and that John drank the cup of confession, which the Three Children also drank in the furnace of fire, though the persecutor did not spill their blood. It goes on: But to sit on my right hand and on my left hand is not mine to give, but it shall be given to them for whom it is prepared.

CHRYS. Where two questions are raised, one is, whether a seat on His right hand is prepared for any one; the other, whether the Lord of all has it not in His power to give it to those for whom it is prepared. To the first then we say, that no one sits on His right hand or on His left, for that throne is inaccessible to a creature. How then did He say, To sit on my right hand or on my left is not mine to give you, as though it belonged to some who were to sit there? He however answers the thoughts of those who asked Him, condescending to their meaning; for they did not know that lofty throne and seat, which is on the right hand of the Father, but sought one thing alone, that is, to possess the chief place, and to be set Over others. And since they had heard it said of the Apostles, that they were to sit on twelve thrones, they begged for a place higher than all the rest, not knowing what was said.

To the second question we must say, that such a gift does not transcend the power of the Son of God, but what is said by Matthew, it is prepared by My Father, is the same as if it were said, "by Me" wherefore also Mark did not say here, by My Father. What therefore Christ says here is this, you shall die, he says, for Me, but this is not enough to enable you to obtain the highest place, for if another person comes possessing besides martyrdom all other virtues, he will possess much more than you; for the chief place is prepared for those, who by works are enabled to become the first. Thus then the Lord instructed them not to trouble themselves vainly and absurdly for high places; at the same time He would not have Him made sad.

BEDE; Or else, it is not mine to give to you, that is, to proud persons, for such as yet they were. It is prepared for other persons, and be you other, that is, lowly, and it is prepared for you.

41. And when the ten heard it, they began to be much displeased with James and John.

42. But Jesus called them to him, and said to them, you know that they which are accounted to rule over the Gentiles exercise lordship over them; and their great ones exercise authority upon them.

43. But so shall it not be among you: hut whoever will be great

among you, shall be your minister:

44. And whoever of you will be the chiefest, shall be servant of all.

45. For even the Son of man came not to be ministered to, but to minister, and to give his life a ransom for many.

THEOPHYL. The other Apostles are indignant at seeing James and John seeking for honor; wherefore it is said, And when the ten heard it, they began to be much displeased with James and John. For being influenced by human feeling, they were moved with envy; and their first displeasure arose from their seeing that they were not taken up by the Lord; before that time they were not displeased, because they saw that they themselves were honored before other men. At this time the Apostles were thus imperfect, but afterwards they yielded the chief place one to another.

Christ however cures them; first indeed by drawing them to Himself in order to comfort them; and his is meant, when it is said, But Jesus called them to him; then by showing them that to usurp honor, and to desire the chief place, belongs to Gentiles. Wherefore there follows: And said to them, you know that they which are accounted to rule over the Gentiles exercise lordship; and their great ones exercise authority over them. The great ones of the Gentiles thrust themselves into the chief place tyrannically and as lords. It goes on: But so shall it not be among you.

BEDE; In which He teaches, that he is the greater, who is the less, and that he becomes the lord, who is servant of all: vain, therefore, was it both for the one party to seek for immoderate things, and the other to be annoyed at their desiring greater things, since we are to arrive at the height of virtue not by power but by humility. Then He proposes an example, that if they lightly regarded His words, His deeds might make them ashamed, saying, For even the Son of man came not to be ministered to, but to minister, and to give his life a ransom for many.

THEOPHYL. Which is a greater thing than to minister. For what can be greater or more wonderful than that a man should die for him to whom he ministers?

Nevertheless, this serving and condescension of humility was His glory, and that of all; for before He was made man, He was known only to the Angels; but now that lie has become man and has been crucified, He not only has glory Himself; but also has taken up others to a participation in His glory, and ruled by faith over the whole world.

BEDE; He did not say, however, that He gave His life as a ransom for all, but for many, that is, for those who would believe on Him.

46. And they came to Jericho: and as he went out of Jericho with his disciples and a great number of people, blind Bartimaeus, the son of Timaeus, sat by the highway side begging.

47. And when he heard that it was Jesus of Nazareth, he began to cry out, and say, Jesus, you Son of David, have mercy on me.

48. And many charged him that he should hold his peace: but he cried the more a great deal, You Son of David, have mercy on me.

49. And Jesus stood still, and commanded him to be called. And they call the blind man, saying to him, Be of good comfort, rise; he calls you.

50. And he, casting away his garment, rose, and came to Jesus.

51. And Jesus answered and said to him, What will you that I should do to you? The blind man said to him, Lord, that I might receive my sight.

52. And Jesus said to him, Go your way; your faith has made you whole. And immediately he received his sight, and followed Jesus in the way.

JEROME; The name of the city agrees with the approaching Passion of our Lord; for it is said, And they came to Jericho. Jericho means moon or anathema; but the failing of the flesh of Christ is the preparation of the heavenly Jerusalem. It goes on: And as he went out of Jericho with his disciples, and a great number of people, blind Bartimaeus, the son of Timaeus, sat by the wayside begging.

BEDE; Matthew says, that there were two blind men sitting by the wayside, who cried to the Lord, and received their sight; but Luke relates that one blind man was enlightened by Him, with a like order of circumstances, as He was going into Jericho; where no one, at least no wise human, will suppose that the Evangelists wrote things contrary to one another, but that one wrote more fully, what another has left out. We must therefore understand that one of them was the more important, which appears from this circumstance, that Mark has related the name and the name of his father.

AUG. It is for this reason that Mark wished to relate his case alone, because his receiving his sight had gained for the miracle a fame, illustrious in proportion to the extent of the knowledge of his affliction. But although Luke relates a miracle done entirely in the same way nevertheless we must understand that a similar miracle was wrought on another blind man, and a similar method of the same miracle. It goes on: And when he heard that it was Jesus of Nazareth, he began to cry out, and say, Jesus, you Son of David, have mercy upon me.

PSEUDO-CHRYS; The blind man calls the Lord, the Son of David, hearing the way in which the passing multitude praised Him, and feeling sure that the expectation of the prophets was fulfilled There follows And many charged him that he should hold his peace.

ORIGEN; As if he said, Those who were foremost in believing rebuked him when to He cried, You Son of David, that he might hold his peace, and cease to call Him by a contemptible name, when he ought to say, Son of God, have pity upon me. He however did not cease; wherefore it goes on: But he cried the more a great deal, You Son of David, have mercy upon me; and the Lord hearth his cry; wherefore there follows:

And Jesus stood still, and commanded him to be called. But

observe, that the blind man, of whom Luke speaks, is inferior to this one; for neither did Jesus call him, nor order him to be called, but He commanded him to be brought to Him, as though unable to come by himself; but this blind man by the command of our Lord is called to Him. Wherefore it goes on: And they call the blind man, saying to him, Be of good comfort, rise, he calls you; but he casting away his garment, comes to Him.

It goes on: And he casting away his garment, rose, and came to Jesus. Perchance, the garment of the blind man means the veil of blindness and poverty, with which he was surrounded, which he cast away and came to Jesus; and the Lord questions him, as he is approaching.

Wherefore there follows: And Jesus answered and said to him, What will you that I should do to thee.

BEDE; Could He who was able to restore sight be ignorant of what the blind man wanted? His reason then for asking is that prayer may be made to Him; He puts the question, to stir up the blind man's heart to pray.

CHRYS. Or He asks, lest men should think that what He granted the man was not what he wanted. For it was His practice to make the good disposition of those who were to be cured known to all men, and then to apply the remedy, in order to stir up others to emulation, and to show that He who was to be cured was worthy to obtain the grace. It goes on: The blind man said to him, Lord, that I may receive my sight.

BEDE; For the blind man looks down upon every gift except

light, because, whatever a blind man may possess, without light he cannot see what he possesses.

PSEUDO-JEROME; But Jesus, considering his ready will, rewards him with the fulfillment of his desire.

ORIGEN; Again, it is more worthy to say Rabboni, our, as it is in other places, Master, than to say Son of David; wherefore He gives him health, not on his saying, Son of David, but when he said Rabboni. Wherefore there follows: And Jesus said to him, Go your way; your faith has made you whole. And immediately he received his, sight, and followed him in the way.

THEOPHYL. The mind of the blind man is grateful, for when he was made whole, he did not leave Jesus, but followed Him.

BEDE; In a mystical sense, however, Jericho, which means the moon, points out the waning of our fleeting race. The Lord restored sight to the blind man, when drawing near to Jericho, because coming in the flesh, and drawing near to His Passion, He brought many to the faith; for it was not in the first years of His Incarnation, but in the few years before He suffered, that He showed the mystery of the Word to the world.

PSEUDO-JEROME; But the blindness in part, brought upon the Jews, will in the end be enlightened when He sends to them the Prophet Elias.

BEDE; Now in that on approaching Jericho, the restored sight to one man, and on quitting it to two, He intimated, that before His Passion He preached only to one nation, the Jews, but after His resurrection and ascension, through His Apostles He opened the mysteries both of His Divinity and His Humanity to Jews and Gentiles. Mark indeed, in writing that one receives his sight, refers to the saving of the Gentiles, that the figure might agree with the salvation of those, whom He instructed in the faith; but Matthew, who write His Gospel to the faithful among the Jews, because it was all so to reach the knowledge of the Gentiles, fitly says that two receive their sight, that He might teach us that the grace of faith belonged to each people.

Therefore, as the Lord was departing with His disciples and a great multitude from Jericho, the blind man was sitting, begging by the wayside; that is, when the Lord ascended into heaven, and many of the faithful followed Him, yes when all the elect from the beginning of the world entered together with Him the gate of heaven, presently the Gentile people began to have hope of its own illumination; for it now sits begging by the wayside, because it has not entered upon and reached the path of truth.

PSEUDO-JEROME; The people of the Jews also, because it kept the Scriptures and did not fulfill them, begs and starves by the wayside; but he cries out Son of David, have mercy upon me, because the Jewish people is enlightened by the merits of the Prophets. Many rebuke him that He may hold his peace that is sins and devils restrain the cry of the poor; and He cried out more because when the battle waxes great, hands are to be lofted up with crying to the Rock of help that is Jesus of Nazareth.

BEDE; Again, the people of the Gentiles having heard of the fame of the name of Christ, sought to be made a partaker of Him, but many spoke against Him, first the Jews, then also the

Gentiles, but the world which was to be enlightened should call upon Christ. The furry of those who attacked Him, however, could not deprive of salvation those who where fore-ordained to life.

And He heard the blind man's cry as He was passing, but stood when He restored his sight, because by His Humanity He pitied him, who by the power of His Divinity has driven away the darkness from our mind; for in that Jesus was born and suffered for our sakes, He as it were passed by, because this action is temporal; but when God is said to stand, it means, that, Himself without change, He sets in order all changeable things.

But the Lord calls the blind man, who cries to Him, which He sends the word of faith to the people of the Gentiles by preachers; and they call on the blind man to be of good cheer and to rise, and bid him come to the Lord, when by preaching to the simple, they bid him have hope of salvation, and rise from the sloth of vice, and gird themselves for a life or virtue. Again, he throws away his garment and heaps, who, throwing aside the bands of the world, with unencumbered pace hastens to the Giver of eternal light.

PSEUDO-JEROME; Again, time Jewish people comes leaping, stripped of the old man, as a hart leaping on the mountains, that is, laying aside sloth, it meditates on Patriarchs, Prophets, and Apostles on high, and raises itself to heights of holiness. How consistent also is the order of salvation. First we heard by the Prophets, then we cry aloud by faith, next we are called by Apostles, we rise u by penitence, we are stripped of our old garment by baptism, and of our choice we are questioned. Again, the blind man when asked requires, that he may see the will of the Lord.

BEDE; Therefore let us also imitate him, let us not seek for riches, earthly goods, or honors from the Lord, but for that Light, which we alone with the Angels can see, the way to which is faith; wherefore also Christ answers to the blind man, Your faith has saved you. But he sees and follows who works what his understanding tells him is good; for he follows Jesus, who understands and executes what is good, who imitates Him, who had no wish to prosper in this world, and bore reproach and derision. And because we have fallen from inward joy, by delight in the things of the body, He shows us what bitter feelings the return thither will cost us.

THEOPHYL. Further, it says that he followed the Lord in the way, that is, in this life, because after it all are excluded who follow Him not here, by working His commandments.

PSEUDO-JEROME; Or, this is the way of which He said, I am the Way, the Truth, and the Life. This is the narrow way, which leads to the heights of Jerusalem, and Bethany, to the mount of Olives, which is the mount of light and consolation.

Mark 11

1. And when they came nigh to Jerusalem, to Bethphage and Bethany, at the mount of Olives, he sends forth two of his disciples,

2. And said to them, Go your way into the village over against you: and as soon as you be entered into it, you shall find a colt tied, whereon never man sat; loose him, and bring him.

3. And if any man say to you, Why do you this? say you that the Lord has need of him; and straight-way he will send him hither.

4. And they went their way, and found the colt tied by the door without in a place where two ways met; and they loose him.

5. And certain of them that stood there said to them, What do you, loosing the colt?

6. And they said to them even as Jesus had commanded: and they let them go.

7. And they brought the colt to Jesus, and cast their garments on him; and he sat upon him.

8. And many spread their garments in the way: and others cut down branches off the trees, and strewed them in the way.

9. And they that went before, and they that followed, cried, saying, Hosanna; Blessed is he that comes in the name of the

Lord:

10. Blessed be the kingdom of our father David, that comes in the name of the Lord: Hosanna in the highest.

CHRYS. Now that the Lord had given sufficient proof of His virtue, and the cross was at hand, even at the door, He did those things which were about to excite them against Him with a greater openness; therefore although He had so often gone up to Jerusalem, He never however had done so in such a conspicuous manner as now.

THEOPHYL. That thus, if they were willing, they might recognize His glory, and by the prophecies, which were fulfilled concerning Him, know that He is very God; and that if they would not, they might receive a greater judgment, for not having believed so many wonderful miracles. Describing therefore this illustrious entrance, the Evangelist says, And when they came nigh to Jerusalem, and Bethany, at the mount of Olives, he sends forth two of his disciples.

BEDE; Bethany is a little village or town by the side of mount Olivet, where Lazarus was raised from the dead. But in what way He sent His disciples and for what purpose is shown in these words, And said to them, Go your way into the village over against you.

THEOPHYL. Now consider how many things the Lord foretold to His disciples, that they should find a colt; wherefore it goes on, And as soon as you be entered into it, you shall find a colt tied, whereon never man sat, loose him, and bring him; and that they should be impeded in taking it,

wherefore there follows, And if any man say to you, Why do you this? say you, The Lord has need of him; and that on saying this, they should be allowed to take him; wherefore it follows, And straightway he will send him hither; and as the Lord had said, it was fulfilled.

Thus it goes on; And they went their way, and found the colt tied by the door it without, in a place where two ways meet; and they loose him

AUG. Matthew says, an ass and a colt, the rest however do not mention the ass. Where then both may be the case, there is no disagreement, though one Evangelist mentions one thing, and a second mentions another; how much less should a question be raised, when one mentions one, and another mentions that same one and another. It goes on: And certain of them that stood there said to them, What do you, loosing, the colt?

And they said to them even as Jesus had commanded, and they let them take it, that is, the colt.

THEOPHYL. But they would not have allowed this, if the Divine power had not been upon them, to compel them, especially, as they were country people and farmers, and yet allowed them to take away the colt. It goes on: And they brought the colt to Jesus, and cast their garments out on him; and he sat upon him.

PSEUDO-CHRYS. Not indeed that He was compelled by

necessity to ride on a colt from the mount of Olives to Jerusalem, for He had gone over Judea and all Galilee on foot, but this action of His is typical. It goes on: And many spread their garments in the way: that is under the feet of the colt; and others cut down branches off the trees, and strewed them in the way. This, however, was rather done to honor Him, and is a Sacrament, than of necessity. It goes on:

And they that went before, and they that followed, cried, saying, Hosanna; blessed is he that comes in the name of the Lord. For the multitude, until it was corrupted, knew what was its duty, for which reason each honored Jesus according to his own strength. Wherefore they praised Him and took up the hymns of the Levites, saying, Hosanna, which according to some is the same as save me, but according to others means a layman, however suppose the former to be more probable, for there is in the 117th Psalm, Save now, I beseech you, O Lord, which in the Hebrew is Hosanna.

BEDE, But Hosanna is a Hebrew word, made out of two, one imperfect the other perfect. For save, or preserve, is in their language, hosy; but anna is a supplicatory interjection, as in Latin heu is an exclamation of grief.

PSEUDO-JEROME; They cry out Hosanna, that is save us, that man might be saved by Him who was blessed and was a conqueror and came in the name of the Lord, that is, of His Father, since the Father is so called because of the Son, and the Son, because of the Father.

PSEUDO-CHRYS. Thus then they give glory to God, saying,

Catena Aurea: Commentary on the Gospel of St. Mark

Blessed is he that comes in the name of the Lord. They also bless the kingdom of Christ, saying, Blessed be the kingdom of our father David, which comes.

THEOPHYL. But they called the kingdom of Christ, that of David, both because Christ was descended from the seed of David, and because David means man of a strong hand. For whose hand is stronger than the Lord's, by which so many and so great miracles were wrought.

PSEUDO-CHRYS. Wherefore also the prophets so often call Christ by the name of David, on account of the descent according to the flesh of Christ from David.

BEDE; Now we read in the Gospel of John that He fled into a mountain, lest they should make him their king. Now, however, when He comes to Jerusalem to suffer, He does not shun those who call Him king, that He might openly teach them that He was King over an empire not temporal and earthly, but everlasting in the heavens, and that the path to this kingdom was through contempt of death. Observe also the agreement of the multitude with the saying of Gabriel, The Lord God will give him the throne of his father David; that is, that He Himself may call by word and deed to a heavenly kingdom the nation to which David once furnished the government of a temporal rule.

PSEUDO-CHRYS. And further, they give glory to God, when they add Hosanna in the highest, that is, praise and glory be to the God of all, Who is in the highest.

PSEUDO-JEROME; Or Hosanna, that is, save in the highest as

well as in the lowest, that is, that the just be built on the ruin of Angels, and also that both those on the earth and those under the earth should be saved. In a mystical sense, also, the Lord approaches Jerusalem, which is 'the vision of peace,' which happiness remains fixed and unmoved, being, as the Apostle says, the mother of all believers.

BEDE; Bethany again means the house of obedience, because by teaching many before His Passion, he made for Himself a house of obedience; and it is said to be placed on the mount of Olives, because He cherishes His Church with the unction of spiritual gifts, and with the light of piety and knowledge. But He sent His disciples to a hold, which was over against them, that is, He appointed doctors to penetrate into the ignorant parts of the whole world, into, as it were, the walls of the hold placed against them.

PSEUDO-JEROME; The disciples of Christ are called two by two, and sent two by two, since charity implies more than one, as it is written, Woe to him that is alone. Two persons head the Israelites out of Egypt: two bring down the bunch of grapes from the Holy Land, that men in authority might ever join together activity and knowledge, and bring forward two commandments from the Two Tables, and he washed from two fountains, and carry the ark of the Lord on two poles, and know the Lord between the two Cherubim, and sing to Him with both mind and spirit.

THEOPHYL. The colt, however, was not necessary to Him, but He sent for it to show that He would transfer Himself to the Gentiles.

BEDE, For the colt of the ass, wanton and unshackled denotes the people of the nations, on whom no man had yet sat because no wise doctor had, by teaching them the things of salvation put upon them the bridle of correction, to oblige them to restrain their tongues from evil, or to compel them into the narrow path of life.

PSEUDO-JEROME. But they found the colt tied by the door with out , because the Gentile people were bound by the chain of their sins before the door of faith that is, without the Church.

AMBROSE; Or else they found it bound before the door, because whosoever is not in Christ is without, in the way; but he who is in Christ is not without. He has added in the way, or in a place where two ways meet, where there is no certain possession for any in man, nor stall, no food, nor stable; miserable is his service, whose rights are unfixed, for he who has not the one Master, has many. Strangers bind him that they may possess him, Christ looses him in order to keep him, for He knows that gifts are stronger ties than bonds.

BEDE; Or else, fitly did the colt stand in a place where two ways meet, because the Gentile people did not hold on in any certain road of life and faith, but followed in its error many doubtful paths of various sects.

PSEUDO-JEROME; Or, in a place where two roads meet, that is , in the freedom of which, hesitating between life and death.

THEOPHYL. Or else, in a place where two roads meet, that is, in this life, but it was loosed by the disciples, through faith and baptism.

PSEUDO-JEROME; But some said, What do you? as if they would say, Whom can remit sins?

THEOPHYL. Or else, those who prevent them are the devils who were weaker than the Apostles.

BEDE; Or else, the masters of terror, who resisted the teachers, when they came to save the Gentiles; but after that the power of the faith of the Lord appeared to believers, the faithful people were freed from the cavils of the adversaries, and were brought to the Lord, whom they bore in their hearts. But by the garments of the Apostles, which they put upon it, we may understand the teaching of virtues, or the interpretation of the Scriptures, or the various doctrines of the Church, by which they clothe the hearts, of men, once naked and cold and fit them to become the seats of Christ.

PSEUDO-JEROME; Or else, they put upon it their garments, that is, they bring to them the first robe of immortality by the Sacrament of Baptism. And Jesus sat upon it, that is, began to reign in them, so that sin should not reign in their own flesh, but righteousness, and peace, and joy in the Holy Ghost. Again, many spread their garments in the way, under the feet of the foal of the ass. What are feet, but those who carry, and the least esteemed, whom the Apostle has set to judge? And these too, though they are not the back on which the Lord sat, yet are instructed by John with the soldiers.

BEDE; Or else, many strew their garments in the way, because the Holy martyrs put off from themselves the garment of their own blood, and prepare a way for the more simple servants of God with their own blood. Many also strew their garments in the way, because they tame their bodies with abstinence, that they may prepare a way for God to the mount, or may give good examples to those who follow them. And they cut down branches from the trees, who in the teaching of the truth cull the sentences of the Fathers from their words, and by their lowly preaching scatter them in the patio of God, when He comes into the soul of the hearer.

THEOPHYL. Let us also strew the way of our life with branches which we cut from the trees, that is, imitate the saints, for these are holy trees, from which, he who imitates their virtues cuts down branches.

PSEUDO-JEROME; For the righteous shall flourish as a palm tree, straitened in their roots, but spreading out wide with flowers and fruits; for they are a good odor to Christ, and strew the way of the commandments of God with their good report. Those who went before are the prophets, and those who followed are the Apostles.

BEDE; And because all the elect, whether those who were able to become such in Judea, or those who now are such in time Church, believed and now believe in the Mediator between God and man, both those who go before and those who follow cried out Hosanna.

THEOPHYL; But both those of our deeds which go before and

those which follow after must be done to the glory of God; for some in their past life make a good beginning, hut their following life does not correspond with their former, neither does it end to the glory of God.

11. And Jesus entered into Jerusalem, and into the temple: and when he had looked round about upon all things, and now the eventide was come, he went out to Bethany with the twelve.

12. And on the morrow, when they were come from Bethany, he was hungry:

13. And seeing a fig tree afar off having leaves, be came, if haply he might find any thing thereon: and when he came to it, he found nothing but leaves; for the time of figs was not yet.

14. And Jesus answered and said to it, No man eat fruit of you hereafter for ever. And his disciples heard it.

BEDE; As the time of His Passion approached, the Lord wished to approach to the place of His Passion, in order to intimate that He underwent death of His own accord: wherefore it is said, And Jesus entered into Jerusalem, and into the temple. And by His going to the temple on first entering the city, He shows us beforehand a form of religion, which we are to follow, that if by chance we enter a place, where there is a house of prayer, we should first turn aside to it. We should also understand from this, that such was the poverty of the Lord, and so far was He from flattering man, that in so large a city, He found no one to be His host, no abiding place, but lived in a small country place with Lazarus and his sisters; for Bethany is a hamlet of the Jews.

Wherefore there follows: *And when, he had looked round about upon all things*, (that is, to see whether any one would take Him in,) *and now the eventide was come, he went out into Bethany with the twelve.* Nor did He do this once only, but during all the five days, from the time that He came to Jerusalem, to the day of His Passion, He moved always to do the same thing; during the day He taught in the temple, but at night, He went out and dwelt in the mount of Olives.

It goes on, *And on the morrow, when they were come from Bethany, he was hungry.*

CHRYS. How is it that He was hungry in the morning, as Matthew says, if it were not that by an economy He permitted it to His flesh? There follows *And seeing a fig tree afar off having leaves, he came, if haply he might find any thing thereon.* Now it is evident that this expresses a conjecture of the disciples, who thought that it was for this reason that Christ came to the fig tree, and that it was cursed, because He found no fruit upon it. For it goes on: *And when he came to it, he found nothing but leaves; for the time of figs was not yet.*

And Jesus answered and said to it, No man ear fruit of you hereafter forever. He therefore curses the fig tree for His disciples' sake, that they might have faith in Him. For He every where distributed blessings, and punished no one, yet at the same time, it was right to give them a proof of His chastising power, that they might learn that He could even cause the persecuting Jews to wither away; Ho was however unwilling to give this proof on men, wherefore He showed them on a plant a sign of His power of punishing. This proves that He came to the fig tree principally for this reason, and not on account of His hunger, for who is so silly as to suppose that in the morning He felt so greatly the pains of hunger, or what prevented the Lord from eating before He left Bethany? Nor can it be said that the sight of the figs excited His appetite to hunger, for it was not the season of figs; and if He were hungry, why did He not seek food elsewhere, rather than from a fig tree which could not yield fruit before its time? What punishment also did a fig tree deserve for not having fruit before its time? From all this then we may infer, that He wished to show His power, that their minds might not be broken by His Passion.

THEOPHYL. Wishing to show His disciples that if He chose He could in a moment exterminate those who were about to crucify Him; In a mystical sense, however, the Lord entered into the temple, but came out of it again, to show that He left it desolate, and open to the spoiler.

BEDE; Farther, He looks round about upon the hearts of all, and when in those who opposed the truth, He found no place to lay His head, He retires to the faithful, and takes up His abode with those who obey Him. For Bethany means the house of obedience.

PSEUDO-JEROME; He went in the morning to the Jews, and visits us in the eventide of the world.

BEDE; Just in the same way as He speaks parables, so also His deeds are parables; therefore He comes hungry to seek fruit off the fig tree, and though He knew the time of figs was not yet, He condemns it to perpetual barrenness, that He might show that the

Jewish people could not be saved through the leaves, that is, the words of righteousness which it had, without fruit, that is, good works, but should be cut down and cast into the fire. Hungering therefore, that is, desiring the salvation of mankind, He saw the fig tree, which is, the Jewish people, having leaves, or, the words of the Law and the Prophets, and He sought upon it the fruit of good works, by teaching them, by rebuking them, by working miracles, and He found it not, and therefore condemned it. Do you too, unless you would be condemned by Christ in the judgment, beware of being a barren tree, but rather offer to Christ the fruit of piety which He requires.

CHRYS. We may also say, in another sense, that the Lord sought for fruit on the fig tree before its time, and not finding it, cursed it, because all who fulfill the commandments of the Law, are said to bear fruit in their own time, as, for instance, that commandment, You shall not commit adultery; but he who not only abstains from adultery but remains a virgin, which is a greater thing, excels then in virtue. But the Lord exacts from the perfect not only the observance of virtue, but also that they bear fruit over and above the commandments.

15. And they come to Jerusalem: and Jesus went into the temple, and began to cast out them that sold and bought in the temple, and overthrew the tables of the moneychangers, and the seats of them that sold doves;

16. And would not suffer that any man should carry any vessel through the temple.

17. And he taught, saying to them, Is it not written, My house

shall be called of all nations the house of prayer? but you have made it a den of thieves.

18. And the Scribes and Chief Priests heard it, and sought how they might destroy him: for they feared him, because all the people was astonished at his doctrine.

BEDE; What the Lord had done in figure, when He cursed the barren fig tree, He now shows more openly, by casting out the wicked from the temple. For the fig tree was not at fault, in not having fruit before its time, but the priests were blamable; wherefore it is said, And they count to Jerusalem; and Jesus went in to the temple, and began to cast out them, that sold and bought in the temple. Nevertheless, it is probable that He found them buying and selling in the temple things which were necessary for its ministry. In them the Lord forbids men to carry on in the temple worldly matters, which they might freely do any where else, how much more do they deserve a greater portion of the anger of Heaven, who carry on in the temple consecrated to Him those things, which are unlawful wherever they may be done. It goes on: and overthrew the tables of the moneychangers.

THEOPHYL. He calls moneychangers, changers of a particular sort of money, for the word means a small brass coin. There follows, and the seats of them that sold doves.

BEDE; Because the Holy Spirit appeared over the Lord in the shape of a dove, the gifts of the Holy Spirit are fitly pointed out under the name of doves. The Dove therefore is sold, when the laying on of hands by which the Holy Spirit is received is sold for a price. Again, He overturns the seats of them who sell doves, because they who sell spiritual grace, are derived of their priesthood, either before men, or in the eyes of God.

THEOPHYL. But if a man by sinning gives up to the devil the grace and purity of baptism, he has sold his Dove, and for this reason is cast out of the temple. There follows, And would not suffer that any man should carry any vessel through the temple.

BEDE; He speaks of those vessels which were carried there for the purpose of merchandise. But God forbid that it should be taken to mean, that the Lord cast out of the temple, or forbade men to bring into it the vessels consecrated to God; for here He shows a type of the judgment to come, for He thrusts away the wicked from the Church, and restrains them by His everlasting word from ever again coming in to trouble the Church. Furthermore, sorrow, sent into time heart from above, takes away from the souls of the faithful those sins which were in them, and Divine grace assists them so that they should never again commit them. It goes on: And he taught, saying to them, My house shall be called of all nations the house of prayer.

PSEUDO-JEROME; According to Isaiah: But you have made it a den of thieves, according to Jeremiah.

BEDE; He says, to all nations, not to the Jewish nation alone, nor in the city of Jerusalem alone, but over the whole world; and he does not say a house of bulls, goats, and rams, but of prayer.

THEOPHYL. Further, He calls the temple, a den of thieves, on account of the money gained there; for thieves always troop together for gain. Since them they sold those animals which were offered in sacrifice for the sake of gain, He called them thieves.

BEDE; For they were in the temple for this purpose, either that they might persecute with corporal pains those who did not bring gifts, or spiritually kill those who did. The mind and conscience of the faithful is also the temple and the house of God, hut if it puts forth perverse thoughts, to the hurt of any one, it may be said that thieves haunt it as a den; therefore the mind of the faithful becomes the den of a thief, when leaving the simplicity of holiness, it plans that which may hurt others.

AUG. John, however, relates this in a very different order, wherefore it is manifest that not ounce only, but twice, this was done by the Lord, and that the first time was related by John, this last, by all the other three.

THEOPHYL. Which also turns to the greater condemnation of the Jews, because though the Lord did this so many times, nevertheless they did not correct their conduct.

AUG. In this again Mark does not keep the same order as Matthew, because how ever Matthew connects the facts together by this sentence And he left them, and went out of the city into Bethany, returning from whence in the morning, according to his relation, Christ cursed the tree, therefore it is supposed with greater probability that he rather has kept to the order of time, as to the ejection from the temple of the buyers and sellers. Mark therefore passed over what was done the first day when He entered into the temple, and on remembering it inserted it, when he had said that He found nothing on the fig tree but leaves, which was done on the second day, as both testify.

GLOSS. But the Evangelist sinews what effect the correction of the Lord had on the ministers of the temple, when He adds: And the Scribes and Chief Priests heard it, and sought how they might destroy him; according to that saying of Amos: They hate him that rebukes in the gate, and they abhor him that speaks uprightly. From this wicked design, however, they were kept back for a time solely by fear. Wherefore it is added, For they feared him, because all the people were astonished at his doctrine. For he taught them as one having authority, and not as the Scribes and Pharisees, as is said elsewhere.

19. And when even was come, he went out of the city.

20. And in the morning, as they passed by, they saw the fig tree dried up from the roots.

21. And Peter calling to remembrance said to him, Master, behold, the fig tree which you cursed is withered away.

22. And Jesus answering said to them, Have faith in God.

23. For verily I say to you, That whoever shall say to this mountain, Be you removed, and be you cast into the sea; and shall not doubt in his heart, but shall believe that those things which he said shall come to pass; he shall have whatever he said.

24. Therefore I say to you, What things ever you desire, when you pray, believe that you receive them, and you shall have them.

25. And when you stand praying, forgive, if you have ought against any: that your Father also which is in heaven may forgive you your trespasses.

26. But if you do not forgive, neither will your Father which is in heaven forgive your trespasses.

PSEUDO-JEROME; The Lord, leaving darkness behind Him in the hearts of the Jews, went out, as the sun, from that city to another which is well-disposed and obedient. And this is what is meant, when it is said, And when even was come, he went out of the city.

But the sun sets in one place, rises in another, for the light, taken from the Scribes, shines in the Apostles; wherefore He returns into the city; on which account there is added, And in the morning, as they passed by, (that is, going into the city,) they saw the fig tree dried up from the root.

THEOPHYL. The greatness of the miracle appears in the drying up so juicy and green a tree. But though Matthew says that the fig tree was at once dried up, and that the disciples on seeing it wondered, there is no reason for perplexity, though Mark now says, that the disciples saw the fig tree dried up on the morrow; for what Matthew says must be understood to mean that they did not see it at once, but on the next day.

AUG. The meaning is not that it dried up at the time, when they saw it, but immediately after the word of the Lord; for they saw it, not beginning to dry up, but completely dried up; and they thus understood that it had withered immediately after our Lord spoke.

PSEUDO-JEROME; Now the fig tree withered from the roots is the synagogue withered from Cain, and the rest, from whom all the blood from Abel up to Zechariah is required.

BEDE; Further, the fig tree was dried up from the roots to show that the nation was impious not only for a time and in part, and was to be smitten for ever, not merely to be afflicted by the attacks of nations from without and then to be freed, as had often been done; or else it was dried up from the roots, to show that it was stripped not only of the external favor of man, but altogether of the favor of heaven within it; for it lost both its life in heaven, and its country on earth.

PSEUDO-JEROME; Peter perceives the dry root, which is cut off, and has been replaced by the beautiful and fruitful olive, called by the Lord; wherefore it goes on: And Peter calling to remembrance said to him, Master, behold, the fig tree which you cursed is withered away.

CHRYS. The wonder of the disciples was the consequence of imperfect faith, for this was no great thing for God to do; since then they did not clearly know His power, their ignorance made them break out into wonder; and therefore it is added, And Jesus answering said to them, Have faith in God.

For verily I say it to you, That whosoever shall say to this mountain , &c. That is; You shall not only be able to dry up a tree, but also to change a mountain by your command and order.

THEOPHYL. Consider the Divine mercy, how it confers on us, if we approach Him in faith, the power of miracles, which He Himself possesses by nature, so that we should be able even to change mountains.

BEDE; The Gentiles, who have attacked the Church, are in the habit of objecting to us, that we have never had full faith in God, for we have never been able to change mountains. It could, however, be done, if necessity called for it, as once we read that it was done by the prayers of the blessed Father Gregory of Neocaesarea, Bishop of Pontus, by which a mountain left as much space of ground for the inhabitants of a city as they wanted.

CHRYS. Or else, as He did not dry up the fig tree for its own sake, but for a sign that Jerusalem should come to destruction, in order to show His power, in time same way we must also understand the promise concerning the mountain, though a removal of this sort is not impossible with God.

PSEUDO-JEROME; Christ then who is the mountain, which grew from the stone, cut out without hands, is taken up and cast into the sea, when the Apostles with justice say, Let us turn ourselves to other nations, Since you judged yourselves unworthy of hearing the word of God.

BEDE; Or else, because the devil is often on account of his pride called by the name of a mountain, this mountain, at the command of those who are strong in the faith, is taken up from the earth and cast into the sea, whenever, at the preaching of the word of God by the holy doctors, the unclean spirit is expelled from the hearts of those who are fore-ordained to life, and is allowed to exert the tyranny of his power over the troubled and embittered souls of the faithless. At which time, he rages the more fiercely, the more he grieves at being turned away from hurting the faithful. It goes On: Therefore I say run to you, What things soever you desire, when you pray, believe that you receive them, and you shall have them.

THEOPHYL. For whosoever sincerely believes evidently lifts up his heart to God, and is joined to Him, and his burning heart feels sure that he has received what he asked for, which he who has experienced will understand; and those persons appear to me to experience this, who attend to the measure and the manner of their prayers. For this reason the Lord says, You shall receive whatsoever you ask in faith; for he who believes that be is altogether in the hands of God, and interceding with tears, feels that he as it were has hold of the feet of the Lord in prayer, he shall receive what he has rightly asked for.

Again, would you in another way receive what you ask for? Forgive your brother, if he has in any way sinned against you; this is also what is added: And when you stand praying, forgive, if you have ought against any: that your Father also which is in heaven may forgive you your trespasses.

PSEUDO-JEROME; Mark has, as He is wont, expressed seven verses of the Lord's prayer in one prayer. But what can he, whose sins are all forgiven, require more, save that he may persevere in what has been granted to him.

BEDE; But we must observe that there is a difference in those who pray; he who has perfect faith, which works by love, can by his prayer or even his command remove spiritual mountains, as Paul did with Elymas the sorcerer. But let those who are unable to mount up to such a height of perfection pray that their sins should be forgiven them, and they shall obtain what they pray for, provided that they themselves first forgive those who have sinned against them. If however they disdain to do this, not only shall they be unable to perform miracles by their prayers, but they shall not even be able to obtain pardon for their sins, which is implied in what follows; But if you do not forgive, neither will your Father which is in heaven forgive your trespasses.

27. And they come again to Jerusalem: and as He was walking in the temple, there come to him the chief priests, and the Scribes, and the elders,

28. And say to him, By what authority do you these things? and who gave you this authority to do these things?

29. And Jesus answered and said to them, I will also ask of you one question, and answer me, and I will tell you by what authority I do these things.

30. The baptism of John, was it from heaven, or of men? Answer me.

31. And they reasoned with themselves, saying, If we shall say, From heaven; he will say, Why then did you not believe him?

32. But if we shall say, Of men; they feared the people; for all men committed John, that he was a prophet indeed.

33. And they answered and said to Jesus, we cannot tell. And Jesus answering said to them, Neither do I tell you by what authority I do these things.

THEOPHYL. They were angry with the Lord, for having cast out of the temple those who had made it a place of merchandise, and therefore they come up to Him, to question and tempt Him. Wherefore it is said: And they come again to Jerusalem: and as he was walking in the temple, there come to him the Chief Priests, and the Scribes, and the elders, and say to him, By what authority do you these things? and who gave you authority to do these things? As if they had said, Who are you that do these things? Do you make yourself a doctor, and ordain yourself Chief Priest?

BEDE; And indeed, when they say, By what authority do you these things, they doubt its being the power of God, and wish it to be understood that what He did was the devil's work. When they add also, Who gave you this authority, they evidently deny that He is the Son of God, since they believe that He works miracles, not by His own but by another's power.

THEOPHYL. Further, they said this, thinking to bring Him to judgment, so that if He said, by mine own power, they might lay hold upon Him; but if He said, by the power of another, they might make the people leave Him, for they believed Him to be God. But the Lord asks them concerning John, not without a reason, nor in a sophistical way, but because John had borne witness of Him. Wherefore there follows: And Jesus answered and said to them, I will also ask of you one question, and answer me, and I will tell you by what authority I do these things.

The baptism of John, was it from heaven, or of men answer me.

BEDE; The Lord might indeed have confuted the cavils of his tempters by a direct answer, but prudently puts them a question, that they might be condemned either by their silence or their speaking, which is evident from what is added, And they reasoned with themselves, saying, If we shall say, From heaven; he will say, Why then did you not believe him? As if He had said, he whom you confess to have had his prophecy from heaven bore testimony of Me, and you have heard from him, by what authority I do these things.

It goes on: But if we shall say, Of men; they feared the people. They saw then that whatever they answered, they should fall into a snare; fearing to be stoned, they feared still more the confession of the truth. Wherefore it goes on: And they answered and said to Jesus, We cannot tell.

PSEUDO-JEROME; They envied the Lamp, and were in the dark, wherefore it is said, I have ordained a lamp for my anointed; his enemies will I clothe with shame. There follows: And Jesus answering said to them, Neither do I tell you by what authority I do these things.

BEDE; As if He had said, I will not tell you what I know, since you will not confess what you know. Further, we must observe that knowledge is hidden from those who seek it, principally for two reasons, namely, when he who seeks for it either has not sufficient capacity to understand what he seeks for, or when through contempt for the truth, or some other reason, he is unworthy of having that for which he seeks opened to him.

Mark 12

1. And he began to speak to them by parables. A certain man planted a vineyard, and set a hedge about it, and dug a place for the winefat, and built a tower, and let it out to husbandmen, and went into a far country.

2. And at the season he sent to the husbandmen a servant, that he might receive from the husbandmen of the fruit of the vineyard.

3. And they caught him, and beat him, and sent him away empty.

4. And again he sent to them another servant; and at him they cast stones, and wounded him in the head, and sent him away shamefully handled.

5. And again he sent another; and him they killed, and many others; beating some, and killing some.

6. Having yet therefore one son, his well-beloved, he sent him also last to them, saying, They will reverence my son.

7. But those husbandmen said among themselves, This is the heir; come, let us kill him, and the inheritance shall be ours.

8. And they took him, and killed him, and cast him out of the vineyard.

9. What shall therefore the lord of the vineyard do? he will come and destroy the husbandmen, and will give the vineyard to

others.

10. And have you not read this Scripture; The stone which the builders rejected is become the head of the corner:

11. This was the Lord's doing, and it is marvelous in our eyes?

12. And they sought to lay hold on him, but feared the people: for they knew that he had spoken the parable against them: and they left him, and went their way.

GLOSS. After the Lord had closed the mouths of His tempters by a wise question, He next shows their wickedness in a parable; wherefore it is said: And he began to speak to them by parables. A certain man planted a vineyard.

PSEUDO-JEROME; God the Father is called a man by a human conception. The vineyard is the house of Israel; the hedge is the guardianship of Angels; the winefat is the law, the tower is the temple, and the husbandmen, the priests.

BEDE; Or else, the hedge is the wall of the city, the winefat is the altar, or those winefats, by which the psalms receive their name.

THEOPHYL. Or, the hedge is the law, which prohibited their mingling with strangers. There follows, And went into afar country.

BEDE; Not by any change of place, but He seemed to go away from the vineyard, that He might leave the husbandmen to act on their own freewill. It goes on: And at the season he sent to the husbandmen a servant, that he might receive from the husbandmen of the fruit of the vineyard.

PSEUDO-JEROME; The servants who were sent were the prophets, the fruit of the vineyard is obedience; some of the prophets were beaten, others wounded, others slain. Wherefore it goes on, And they caught him, and beat him, and sent him away empty.

BEDE; By the servant who was first sent, we must understand Moses, but they beat him, and sent him away empty, because they angered Moses in the tents.

There follows, And again he sent to them another servant, and they wounded him in the head, and sent him away shamefully handled. This other servant means David and the other Psalmists, but they wounded Him in time head and shamefully handled him, because they despised the songs of the Psalmists, and rejected David himself, saying, What portion have we in David?

It goes on, And he sent another; and him they killed, and many others; beating some, and killing some. By the third servant and his companions, understand the band of the prophets. But which of the prophets did they not persecute? In these three kinds of servants, as the Lord Himself elsewhere pronounces, may be included in a figure all the doctors under the law, when He says, that all things must be fulfilled which were written in the Law of Moses, and in the Prophets, and in the Psalms, concerning Me.

THEOPHYL. Or else, By the first servant, understand the

prophets who lived about the time of Elias, for Zedekiah the false prophet beat Micaiah; and by the second servant whom they wounded in the head, that is, evil entreated, We may understand the prophets who lived about the time of Hosea and Isaiah; but by the third servant understand the prophets who flourished about the time of Daniel and Ezekiel. It goes on, Having yet therefore one son, his well-beloved, he sent him also last to them, saying, Perchance they will reverence my son.

PSEUDO-JEROME; The well-beloved son and the last is the Only-begotten; and in that He Says, They will reverence my son, He speaks in irony.

BEDE; Or else, this is not said in ignorance, but God is said to doubt, that freedom of will may be left to man.

THEOPHYL. Or else, He said this not as though He were ignorant of what was to happen, but to show what it was right and fitting that they should do. But those husbandmen said amongst themselves, This is the heir, come, let us kill him, and the inheritance will be ours.

BEDE; The Lord proves most clearly that the chiefs of the Jews did not crucify the Son of God through ignorance, but through envy; for they understood that this was He to whom it was said, I will give you the heathen for your inheritance. But these evil husbandmen strove to seize upon it by slaying Him, when the Jews crucifying Him tried to extinguish the faith which is by Him, and rather to bring forward their own righteousness which is by the Law, and to thrust it on the nations, and to imbue them with it.

There follows: And they took him, and killed him, and cast him out of the vineyard.

THEOPHYL. That is, without Jerusalem, for the Lord was crucified out of the city.

PSEUDO-JEROME; Or else, they cast Him out of the vineyard, that is, out of the people, saying, You are a Samaritan, and have a devil. Or, as far as in them lay, they cast Him out of their own borders, and gave Him up to the Gentiles that they might receive Him.

There follows, What then will the Lord of the vineyard do? He will come and destroy those husbandmen, and give the vineyard to other.

AUG. Matthew indeed subjoins that they answered and said, He will miserably destroy those wicked men, which Mark here says was not their answer, but that the Lord after putting the question, as it were answered Himself. But we may easily understand either that their answer was, subjoined without the insertion of, they answered, or they said, which at the same time was implied; or else, that their answer, being the truth, was attributed to the Lord, since He also Himself gave this answer concerning them, being the Truth.

THEOPHYL. The Lord of the vineyard then is the Father of the Son who was slain, and the Son Himself is He who was slain, who will destroy those husbandmen, by giving them up to the Romans, and who will give the people to other husbandmen, that is, to the Apostles. Read the Acts of the Apostles, and you will find three thousand, and five thousand on a sudden believing and bearing fruit to God.

PSEUDO-JEROME; Or else, the vineyard is given to others, that is, to those who come from the east, and from the west, and from the south, and from the north, and who sit down with Abraham, Isaac, and Jacob in the kingdom of heaven.

BEDE; But that this was done by Divine interposition he affirms, by immediately afterwards adding, And have you not read this Scripture, The stone which the builders refused is become the head-stone in the corner? As if he had said, how is this prophecy to be fulfilled, save in that Christ, being rejected and slain by you, is to be preached to the Gentiles, who will believe on Him? Thus then as a corner stone, He will found the two people on Him self, and of the two people will build for Himself a city of the faithful, one temple. For the masters of the synagogue, whom He had just called husbandmen, He now calls builders, because the same persons, who seemed to cultivate His people, that they might bear the fruits of life, like a vineyard, were also commanded to construct and adorn this people, to be, as it were, a house worthy to have God for its inhabitant.

THEOPHYL. The stone then which the builders refused, the same has become the head-stone of the corner, that is, of the Church. For the Church is, as it were, the corner, joining together Jews and Gentiles; and this corner has been made by the Lord, and is wonderful in our eyes, that is, in the eyes of the faithful; for miracles meet with detraction from the faithless. The Church indeed is wonderful, as it were resting on wonders, for the Lord worked with the Apostles, and confirmed the word with signs. And this is what is meant, when it is said, This was the Lord's doing, and it is marvelous in our eyes.

PSEUDO-JEROME; This rejected stone, which is borne by that corner where the lamb and the bread met in the supper, ending the Old and beginning the New Testament, does things marvelous in our eyes as the topaz.

BEDE; But the Chief Priests showed that those things which the Lord had spoken were true; which is proved from what follows: And they sought to lay hold on him; for He Himself is the heir, whose unjust death He said was to be revenged by the Father. Again, in a moral sense, each of the faithful, when the Sacrament of Baptism is entrusted to him, receives on hire a vineyard, which he is to cultivate. But the servant sent to him is evil entreated, beaten, and cast out, when the word is heard by him and despised, or, what is worse, even blasphemed; further, he kills, as far as in him lies, the heir, who has trampled under foot time Son of God.

The evil husbandman is destroyed, and the vineyard given to another, when the humble shall be enriched with that gift of grace, which the proud man has scorned. And it happens daily in the Church, that the Chief Priests wishing to lay hands on Jesus, are held back by the multitude, when some one, who is a brother only in name, either blushes or fears to attack the unity of the faith of the Church, and of its peace, though he loves it not, on account of the number of good brethren who dwell together within it.

Catena Aurea: Commentary on the Gospel of St. Mark

13. And they send to him certain of the Pharisees and of the Herodians, to catch him in his words.

14. And when they were come, they say to him, Master, we know that you are true, and care for no man; for you regard not the person or men, but teach the way of God in truth; Is it lawful to give tribute to Caesar, or not?

15. Shall we give, or shall we not give? But he, knowing their hypocrisy, said to them, Why tempt you me? bring me a penny, that I may see it.

16. And they brought it. And he said to them, Whose is this image and superscription? And they said to him, Caesar's.

17. And Jesus answering said to them, Render to Caesar the things that are Caesar's, and to God the things that are God's. And they marveled at him.

BEDE; The Chief Priests though they sought to take Him, feared the multitude, and therefore they endeavored to effect what they could not do of themselves, by means of earthly powers, that they might themselves appear to be guiltless of His death; and therefore it is said, And they send to him certain of the Pharisees and of the Herodians, to catch him in his words.

THEOPHYL. We have said elsewhere of the Herodians, that they were a certain new heresy who said that Herod was the Christ, because the succession of the kingdom of Judah had failed. Others however say that the herodians, were the soldiers of Herod, whom the Pharisees brought as witnesses of the words of Christ, that they might take Him, and lead Him away. But observe how in their wickedness they wished to deceive Christ by flattery; for it goes on: Master, we know that you are true.

PSEUDO-JEROME For they questioned Him with honeyed words, and they surrounded Him as bees, who carry honey in the in mouth but a sting in their tail.

BEDE; But this bland and crafty question was intended to induce Him in His answer rather to fear God than Caesar, and to say that tribute should not he paid, so that the Herodians immediately on hearing it might hold Him to be an author of sedition against the Romans, and therefore they add, And care for no man: for you regard not the person of any.

THEOPHYL. So that you will not honor Caesar, that is, against the truth; therefore they add, But teach the way of God in truth. Is it lawful to give tribute to Caesar, or not? Shall we give, or shall we not give? For their whole plot was one which had a precipice on both sides, so that if He said that it was lawful to give tribute to Caesar, they might provoke the people against Him, as though He wished to reduce the nation itself to slavery; but if He said, that it was not lawful, they might accuse Him, as though He was stirring up the people against Caesar; but the Fountain of wisdom escaped their snares. Wherefore there follows: But he, knowing their hypocrisy, said to them, Why tempt you me? briny me a penny, that I may see it. And they brought it.

BEDE; A denarius was a piece of money, accounted equal to ten smaller coins, and bearing the image of Caesar; wherefore there follows: And he said to them, Whose is this image and superscription? And they said to him, Caesar's.

Let those who think that our Savior asked the question through ignorance and not by an economy, learn from this that He might have known whose image it was; but He puts the question, in order to return them a fitting answer; wherefore there follows: And Jesus answering said to them, Render to Caesar the things that are Caesar's, and to God the things that are God's.

THEOPHYL. As if He had said, Give what bears an image to him whose image it bears, that is, the penny to Caesar; for we can both pay Caesar his tribute, and offer to God what is His own.

BEDE; That is, tithes, first-fruits, oblations, and victims. In the same way as He gave tribute both for Himself and Peter, He also gave to God the things that are God's, doing the will of His Father.

PSEUDO-JEROME; Render to Caesar the money bearing his image, which is collected for him, and render yourselves willingly up to God, for the light of your countenance, O Lord, and not of Caesar's, is stamped upon us.

THEOPHYL. The inevitable wants of our bodies is as Caesar to each of us; the Lord therefore orders that there should be given to the body its own, that is, food and raiment, and to God the things that are God's. It goes on: And they marveled at him. They who ought to have believed, wondered at such great wisdom, because they had found no place for their craftiness.

18. Then come to him the Sadducees, which say there is no resurrection; and they asked him, saying,

19. Master, Moses wrote to us, If a man's brother die, and leave his wife behind him, and leave no children, that his brother should take his wife, and raise up seed to his brother.

20. Now there were seven brethren: and the first took a wife, and dying left no seed.

21. And the second took her, and died, neither left he any seed: and the third likewise.

22. And the seven had her, and left no seed: last of all the woman died also.

23. In the resurrection therefore, when they shall rise, whose wife shall she be of them? for the seven had her to wife.

24. And Jesus answering, said to them, Do you not therefore err, because you know not the Scriptures, neither the power of God?

25. For when they shall rise from the dead, they neither marry, nor are given in marriage; but are as the angels which are in heaven.

26. And as touching the dead, that they rise: have you not read in the book of Moses, how in the bush God spoke to him, saying, I am the God of Abraham, and the God of Isaac, and the God of Jacob?

27. He is not the God of the dead, but the God of the living: you therefore do greatly err.

GLOSS. After that our Lord has prudently escaped the crafty temptation of the Pharisees, it is shows how He also confounds the Sadducees, who tempt Him; wherefore it is Said: Then come to him the Sadducees, which say there is no resurrection.

THEOPHYL. A certain heretical sect of the Jews called Sadducees denied the resurrection, and said that there was neither angel nor spirit. These then coming to Jesus, craftily proposed to Him a certain tale, in order to show that no resurrection should take place, or had taken place; and therefore there is added, And they asked him, saying, Master.

And in this tale they lay down that seven men had married one woman, in order to make men draw back from belief in the resurrection.

BEDE; And fitly do they frame such a fable in order to prove the madness of those who assert the resurrection of the body. Such a thing however might really have happened at some time or other among them.

PSEUDO-JEROME; But in a mystical sense: what can this woman, leaving no seed of seven brothers, and last of all dying, mean except the Jewish synagogue, deserted by the seven-fold Spirit, which filled those seven patriarchs, who did not leave to her the seed of Abraham, that is, Jesus Christ? For although a Son was born to them, nevertheless He was given to us Gentiles.

This woman was dead to Christ, nor shall she be joined in the resurrection to any patriarch of the seven; for by the number seven is meant the whole company of the faithful. Thus it is said contrariwise by Isaiah, Seven women shall take hold of one man; that is, the seven Churches, which the Lord loves, reproves, and chastises, adore Him with one faith.

Wherefore it goes on: And Jesus answering, said to them, Do you not therefore err, not knowing the Scripture, neither the power of God!

THEOPHYL. As if He had said, you understand not what sort of a resurrection the Scriptures announce; for you believe that there will be a restoration of our bodies, such as they are now, but it shall not be so. Thus then you know not the Scriptures; neither again do you know the power of God; for you consider it as a difficult thing, saying, How can the limbs, which have been scattered, be united together and joined to the soul? But this in respect of the Divine power is as nothing.

There follows: For when they shall rise from the dead, they neither marry, nor are given in marriage; but are as the angels which are in heaven; as if He had said, There will be a certain heavenly and angelic restoration to life, when there shall be no more decay, and we shall remain unchanged; and for this reason marriage shall cease. For marriage now exists on account of our decay, that we may be carried on by succession of our race, and not fail; but then we shall be as the Angels, which need no succession by marriage, and never come to an end.

BEDE; We must here consider that the Latin custom does not answer to the Greek idiom. For properly different words are used for the marriage of men, and that of women; but here we may simply understand that, marry is meant of men, and given in marriage of women.

PSEUDO-JEROME; Thus then they do not understand the Scripture, in that in the resurrection, men shall be as the Angels of God, that is, no man there dies, no one is born, no infant is there, no old man.

THEOPHYL. In another way also they are deceived, not understanding the Scriptures; for if they had understood them, they should also have understood how by the Scriptures the resurrection of the dead may be proved; wherefore He adds, And as touching the dead, that they rise, have you not read in the took of Moses, how in the bush God spoke to him, saying, I am the God of Abraham, and the God of Isaac, and the God of Jacob?

PSEUDO-JEROME; But I say, in the bush, in which is an image of you; for in it the fire was kindled, but it did not consume its thorns; so my words set you on fire, but do not burn off your thorns, which have grown under the curse.

THEOPHYL. But I say, I am the God of Abraham, the God of Isaac, and the God of Jacob. As if He had said, The God of the living, wherefore He adds, He is not the God of the dead, but of the living; for He did not say, I have been, but I am, as if they had been present. But some one perhaps will say, that God spoke this only of the soul of Abraham, not of His body; to which I answer, that Abraham implies both, that is, soul and body, so that

He also is the God of the body, and the body lives with God, that is, in God's ordinance.

BEDE; Or else; because after proving that the soul remained after death, (for God could not be God of those who did not exist at all,) the resurrection of the body also might be inferred as a consequence, since it had done good and evil with the soul.

PSEUDO-JEROME; But when He says, The God of Abraham, the God of Isaac, and the God of Jacob; by naming God thrice, He implied the Trinity. But when He says, He is not the God of the dead, by naming again the One God, he implies One Substance. But they live who make good the portion, which they had chosen; and they are dead, who have lost what they had made good. You therefore do greatly err.

GLOSS. That is, because they contradicted the Scriptures, and derogated from the power of God.

28. And one of the scribes came, and having heard them reasoning together, and perceiving that he had answered them well, asked him, Which is the first commandment of all?

29. And Jesus answered him, The first of all the commandments is, Hear, O Israel; The Lord our God is one Lord:

30. And you shall love the Lord your God with all your heart, and with all your soul, and with all your mind, and with all your strength: this is the first commandment.

31. And the second is like, namely this, You shall love your

neighbor as yourself. There is none other commandment greater than these.

32. And the scribe said to him, Well, Master, you have said the truth: for there is one God; and there is none other but he:

33. And to love him with all the heart, and with all the understanding, and with all the soul, and with all the strength, and to hove his neighbor as himself, is more than all whole burnt offerings and sacrifices.

34. And when Jesus saw that he answered discreetly, he said to him, You are not far from the kingdom of God. And no man after that dare ask him any question.

GLOSS. After that the Lord confuted the Pharisees, and the Sadducees, who tempted Him, it is here shown how He satisfied the Scribe who questioned Him; wherefore it is said, And one of the scribes came, and having heard them reasoning together, and perceiving that he had answered them well, asked him, Which is the first commandment of all?

PSEUDO-JEROME; This question is only that which is a problem common to all skilled in the law, namely, that the commandments are differently set forth in Exodus, Leviticus, and Deuteronomy. Wherefore He brought forward not one but two commandments, by which, as by two paps rising on the breast of the bride, our infancy is nourished. And therefore there is added, And Jesus answered him, The first of all the commandments is, Hear, O Israel; the Lord your God is one God.

He mentions the first and greatest commandment of all; this is that to which each of us must give the first place in his heart, as the only foundation of piety, that is, the knowledge and confession of the Divine Unity, with the practice of good works, which is perfected in the love of God and our neighbor; wherefore there is added, You shall love the Lord your God with all your heart, and with all your mind, and with all your soul, and with all your strength: this is the first commandment.

THEOPHYL. See how He has enumerated all the powers of the soul; for there is a living power in tire soul, which He explains, when He says, With all your soul, and to this belong anger and desire, all of which He will have us give to Divine love. There is also another power, which is called natural, to which belong nutriment and growth, and this also is all to be given to God, for which reason He says, With all your heart. There is also another power, the rational which He calls the mind, and that too is to be given whole to God.

GLOSS. The words which are added, And with all your strength, may be referred to the bodily powers it goes on: And the second is like, namely this, You shall love your neighbor as yourself.

THEOPHYL. He says, that it is like because these two commandments are harmonious one with the other, and mutually contain the other. For he who loves God, loves also His creature; but the chief of His creatures is man, wherefore he who loves God ought to love all men. But he who loves his neighbor, who so often offends him, ought much more to hove Him, who is ever giving him benefits. And therefore on account of the connection between these commandments, He adds, There is none other commandment greater than these.

It goes on, And the Scribe said to him, Well, Master, you have said the truth: for there is one God, and there is none other but he:

and to love him with all the heart, and with all the soul, and with all the understanding, and with all the strength, cried to love his neighbor as himself, is more than all whole burnt offerings and sacrifices.

BEDE; He shows when He says, this is greater than all sacrifices, that a grave question was often debated between the scribes and Pharisees, which was the first commandment, or the greatest of the Divine law; that is, some praised offering and sacrifices, others preferred acts of faith and love, because many of the fathers before the law pleased God by that faith only, which works by love. This scribe shows that he was of the latter opinion. But it continues, And when Jesus saw that he answered discreetly, he said to him, You are not far from the kingdom of God.

THEOPHYL. By which He shows that he was not perfect, for He did not say, You are within the kingdom of heaven, but, You are not far from the kingdom of God.

BEDE; But the reason why He was not far from the kingdom of God was, that he proved himself to be a favorer of that opinion, which is proper to the New Testament and to Gospel perfection.

AUG. Nor let it trouble us that Matthew says, that He who

addressed this question to the Lord tempted Him; for it may be that though he came as a tempter, yet he was corrected by the answer of the Lord. Or at all events, We must not look upon the temptation as evil, and done with the intention of deceiving an enemy, but rather as the caution of a man who wished to try a thing unknown to him.

PSEUDO-JEROME; Or else, he is not far who comes with, knowledge; for ignorance is farther from the kingdom of God than knowledge; wherefore He says above to the Sadducees, you err, not knowing the Scriptures, or the power of God. it goes on: And no man after that dare ask him any questions.

BEDE; For since they were confuted in argument, they ask Him no farther questions, but take Him without any disguise, and give Him up to the Roman power. From which we understand that the venom of envy may be overcome, but can hardly lie quiet

35. And Jesus answered and said, while He taught in the temple, How say the Scribes that Christ is the Son of David?

36. For David himself said by the Holy Ghost, The Lord said to my Lord, Sit you on my right hand, till I make your enemies your footstool.

37. David therefore himself calls him Lord; and whence is he then his son? And the common people heard him gladly.

Catena Aurea: Commentary on the Gospel of St. Mark

THEOPHYL. Because Christ was coming to His Passion, He corrects a false opinion of the Jews, who said that Christ was the Son of David, not his Lord; wherefore it is said, And Jesus answered and said, while he taught in the temple.

PSEUDO-JEROME; That is, He openly speaks to them of Himself; that they may be inexcusable; for it goes on: How say the Scribes that Christ is the Son of David?

THEOPHYL. But Christ shows Himself to be the Lord, by the words of David. For it goes on: For David himself said by the Holy Ghost, The Lord said to my Lord, Sit you on my right hand; as if He had said, you cannot say that David said this without the grace of the Holy Spirit, but he called Him Lord in the Holy Spirit; and that He is Lord, he shows, by this that is added, Till I make your enemies your footstool; for they themselves were His enemies, whom God put under the footstool of Christ.

BEDE; But the putting down of His enemies by the Father, does not show the weakness of the Son, but the unity of nature, by which One works in the Other; for the Son also subjects the Father's enemies, because He glorifies His Father upon earth.

GLOSS. Thus then the Lord concludes from what has gone before the doubtful question. For from the foregoing words of David it is proved that Christ is the Lord of David, but according to the saying of the Scribes, it is proved that He is his son. And this is what is added, David himself then calls him Lord, how is he then his son?

BEDE; The question of Jesus is useful for He is even now against the Jews; for they, acknowledging that Christ is to come, assert that He is a mere man, a holy Person descended from David. Let us then ask them, as our Lord has taught us, if He be a mere man, and only the son of David, how David in the Holy Spirit calls Him Lord. They are not however reproved for calling Him David's son, but for not believing Him to be the Son of God. It goes on, And the common people heard him gladly.

GLOSS. Namely, because they saw that He answered and put questions wisely.

38. And he said to them in his doctrine, Beware of the Scribes, which love to go in long clothing, and love salutations in the marketplaces,

39. And the chief seats in the Synagogues, and the uppermost rooms at feasts:

40. Which devour widows' houses, and for a pretense make long prayers: these shall receive greater damnation.

PSEUDO-JEROME; After confuting the Scribes and Pharisees, He burns up as a fire their dry and withered examples; wherefore it is said, And he said to them in his doctrine, Beware of the Scribes, which love to go in long clothing.

BEDE; To walk in long clothing is to go forth into public clad in garments too much ornamented, in which amongst other things, that rich man, who fared sumptuously every day, is said to have sinned.

THEOPHYL. But they used to walk in honorable garments because they wished to be highly esteemed for it, and in like manner they desired other things, which lead to glory. For it goes on: And love salutations in the marketplaces, and the chief seats in the synagogues, and the uppermost rooms at feasts.

BEDE; We must observe that He does not forbid that those, to whom it falls by the rule of their office, should be saluted in the marketplace, or have chief seats and places at feasts, but He teaches that those who hove those things unduly, whether they have them or no, are to be avoided by the faithful as wicked men: that is, He blames the intention and not the office; although this too is culpable, that the very men who wish to be called masters of the synagogue in Moses' seat, should have to do with lawsuits in the marketplace. We are in two ways ordered to beware of those who are desirous of vain glory; first, we should not be seduced by their hypocrisy into thinking that what they do is good; nor secondly, should we be excited to imitate them, through a vain rejoicing in being praised for those virtues which they affect.

THEOPHYL. He also especially teaches the Apostles, not to have any communication with the scribes, but to imitate Christ Himself; and in ordaining them to be masters in the duties of life, He places others under them.

BEDE; But they do not only seek for praise from men, but also for gain. Wherefore there follows, Which devour widows' houses, under the pretense of long prayers. For there are men who pretending to be just hesitate not to receive money from persons who are troubled in conscience, as though they would be their advocates in the judgment. A hand stretched out to the poor is always an accompaniment to prayer, but these men pass the night in prayer, that they may take away money from the poor.

THEOPHYL. But the Scribes used to come to women, who were left without the protection of their husbands, as though they were their protectors; and by a pretense of prayer, a reverend exterior and hypocrisy, they used to deceive widows, and thus also devour the houses of the rich. it goes on, These shall receive a greater damnation, that is, than the other Jews, who sinned.

41. And Jesus sat over against the treasury, and beheld how the people cast money into the treasury: and many that were rich cast in much.

42. And there came a certain poor widow, and she threw in two mites, which make a farthing.

43. And he called to him his disciples, and said to them, Verily I say to you, That this poor widow has cast more in, than all they which have cast into the treasury:

44. For all they did cast in of their abundance; but she of her want did cast in all that she had, even all her living.

BEDE; The Lord, who had warned them to avoid the desire of high place and vain glory, now distinguishes by a sure test those who brought in gifts. Wherefore it is said, And Jesus sat over against the treasury, and beheld how the people cast money into the treasury. In the Greek language, phylassein means to keep, and gaza is a Persian word for treasure; wherefore the word gazophylacium which is here used means a place where riches are kept, which name also was applied to the chest in which the offerings of the people were collected, for the necessary uses of the temple, and to the porch in which they were kept. You have a notice of the porch in the Gospel, These words spoke Jesus in the treasury as He taught in the temple; and of the chest in the book of Kings, But Jehoida the priest took a chest.

THEOPHYL. Now there was a praiseworthy custom amongst the Jews, that those who were able and willing should put something into the treasury, for the maintenance of the priests, the poor, and the widows; wherefore there is added, And many that were rich cast in much. But whilst many people were so engaged, a poor widow came up, and showed her love by offering money according to her ability; wherefore it is said, And there came a certain poor widow, and she threw in two mites, which make a farthing

BEDE; Reckoners use the word 'quadrans' for the fourth part of anything, be it place, money, or time. Perhaps then in this place is meant the fourth part of a shekel, that is, five pence. It goes on, And he called to him his disciples, and said to them, Verily I say to you, That this poor widow has cast more in, than all they which have cast into the treasury: for God does not weigh the property but the conscience of those who offer; nor did He consider the smallness of the sum in her offering, but what was the store from which it came.

Wherefore He adds, For all they did cast in of their abundance, but she of her want did cast in all that she had, even all her living.

PSEUDO-JEROME; But in a mystical sense, they are rich, who bring forth from the treasure of their heart things new and old, which are the obscure and hidden things of Divine wisdom in both testaments; but who is the poor woman, if it be not I and those like me, who cast in what I can, and have the will to explain to you, where I have not the power. For God does not consider how much you hear, but what is the store from which it comes; but each at all events can bring his farthing, that is, a ready will, which is called a farthing, because it is accompanied by three things, that is, thought, word, and deed. And in that it is said that she cast in all her living, it is implied that all that the body wants is that by which it lives; wherefore it is said, All the labor of man is for his mouth.

THEOPHYL. Or else; That widow is the soul of man, which leaving Satan to which it had been joined, casts into the temple two mites, that is, the flesh and the mind, the flesh by abstinence, the mind by humility, that so it may be able to hear that it has cast away all its living, and has consecrated it, leaving nothing for the world of all that it possessed.

BEDE; Again, in an allegorical way, the rich men, who cast gifts into the treasury, point out the Jews puffed up with the righteousness of the law; the poor widow is the simplicity of the Church: poor indeed, because she has cast away the spirit of pride and of the desires of worldly things; and a widow, because Jesus her husband has suffered death for her. She casts two mites into the treasury, because she brings the love of God and of her neighbor, or the gifts of faith and prayer; which are looked upon as mites in their own insignificance, but measured by the merit of a devout intention are superior to all the proud works of the Jews. The Jew sends of his abundance into the treasury, because he presumes on his own righteousness; but the Church sends her whole living into God's treasury, because she understands that even her very living is not of her own desert, but of Divine grace.

Mark 13

1. And as he went out of the temple, one of his disciples said to him, Master, See what manner of stones and what buildings are here!

2. And Jesus answering said to him, See you these great buildings? there shall not be left one stone upon another, that shall not be thrown down.

BEDE; Because after the founding of the Church of Christ, Judea was to be punished for her treachery, the Lord fitly, after praising the devotedness of the Church in the person of the poor widow, goes out of the temple, and foretold its coming in, and the contempt in which the buildings now so wonderful were soon to be held, wherefore it is said, And as he went out of the temple, one of his disciples said to him, Master, see what manner of stones and what buildings are here!

THEOPHYL. For, since the Lord had spoken much concerning the destruction of Jerusalem, His disciples wondered, that such numerous and beautiful buildings were to be destroyed; and this is the reason why they point out the beauty of the temple, and He answers not only that they were to be destroyed, but also that one stone should not be heft upon another: wherefore it goes on: And Jesus answering said to him, See you these great buildings? there shall not be left one stone upon another, that shall not be thrown down. Now some may endeavor to prove that Christ's words were false, by saying that many ruins were left, but this is not at all the point; for though some ruins had been left, still at the consummation of all things one stone shall not be left upon another. Besides it is related, that Ælius Adrian overturned the city and the temple from the foundation, so that the word of the Lord here spoken was fulfilled.

BEDE; But it was ordered by Divine power that after that the grace of the faith of the Gospel was made known through the world, the temple itself with its ceremonies Should be taken away; lest perchance some one weak in the faith, if he saw that these things which had been instituted by God still remained, might by degrees drop from the sincerity of the faith, which is in Christ Jesus, into carnal Judaism.

PSEUDO-JEROME; Here also the Lord enumerates to His disciples the destruction of the last time, that is of the temple, with the people, and its letter; of which one stone shall not be left upon another, that is, no testimony of the Prophets upon those, to whom the Jews perversely applied them, that is, on Ezra, Zerubbabel, and the Maccabees.

BEDE; Again, when the Lord left the temple, all the edifice of the law and the frame work of the commandments were destroyed, so that nothing could be filled up by the Jews; and now that the head has been taken away, all the limbs fight one against the other.

3. And as he sat upon the mount of Olives over against the temple, Peter and James and John and Andrew asked him privately,

4. Tell us, when shall these things be? and what shall be the sign when all these things shall be fulfilled?

5. And Jesus answering them began to say, Take heed lest any man deceive you:

6. For many shall come in my name, saying, I am Christ; and shall deceive many.

7. And when you shall hear of wars and rumors of wars, be you not troubled: for such things must needs be; but the end shall not be yet.

8. For nation shall rise against nation, and kingdom against kingdom: and there shall be earthquakes in divers places, and there shall be famines and troubles: these are the beginnings of sorrows.

BEDE; Because the Lord, when some were praising the buildings of the temple, had plainly answered that all these were to be destroyed, the disciples privately inquired about the time and the signs of the destruction which was foretold; wherefore it is said: And as he sat upon the mount of Olives, over against the temple, Peter and James and John and Andrew asked him privately,

Tell us when shall these things be? and what shall be the sign when all these things shall be fulfilled. The Lord sits upon the mount of Olives, over against the temple, when He discourses upon the ruin and destruction of the temple, so that even His bodily position may be in accordance with the words which He speaks, pointing out mystically that, abiding in peace with the saints, He hates the madness of the proud. For the mount of Olives marks the fruitful sublimity of the Holy Church.

AUG. In answer to the disciples, the Lord tells them of things which were from that time forth to have their course; whether He meant the destruction of Jerusalem which occasioned their question, or His own coming through the Church, (in which He ever comes even to the end, for we know that He comes in His own, when His members are born day by day,) or the end itself, in which He will appear to judge the quick and the dead.

THEOPHYL. But before answering their question, He strengthens their minds that they may not be deceived, wherefore there follows: And Jesus answering them began to say, Take heed lest any man deceive you?

And this He says, because when the sufferings of the Jews began, some arose professing to be teachers, wherefore there follows: For many shall come in my name, saying, I am Christ; and shall deceive many.

BEDE; For many came forward, when destruction was hanging over Jerusalem, saying that they were Christs, and that the time of freedom was now approaching. Many teachers of heresy also arose in the Church even in the time of the Apostles; and many Antichrists came in the name of Christ, the first of whom was Simon Magus, to whom the Samaritans, as we read in the Acts of the Apostles, listened, saying, This man is the great power of God: wherefore also it is added here, And shall deceive many.

Now from the time of the Passion of our Lord there ceased not amongst the Jewish people, who chose the seditious robber and rejected Christ the Savior, either external wars or civil discord; wherefore it goes on: And when you shall bear of wars and rumors of wars, be you not troubled. And when these come, the Apostles are warned not to be afraid, or to leave Jerusalem and Judea, because the end was not to come at once, nay was to be put off for forty years. And this is what is added: for such things must needs be; but the end shall not be yet, that is, the desolation of the province, and the last destruction of the city and temple.

It goes on: For nation shall rise against nation, and kingdom against kingdom.

THEOPHYL. That is, the Romans against the Jews, which Josephus relates happened before the destruction of Jerusalem. For when the Jews refused to pay tribute, the Romans arose, in anger; but because at that time they were merciful, they took indeed their spoils, but did not destroy Jerusalem. What follows shows that God fought against the Jews, for it is said, And there shall be earthquakes in divers places, and there shall be famines.

BEDE; Now it is on record that this literally took place at the time of the Jewish rebellion. But kingdom against kingdom, the pestilence of those whose word spreads as a canker, dearth of the word of God, the commotion of the whole earth, and the separation from the true faith, may all rather be understood of heretics who, by fighting one against the other, bring about the triumph of the Church.

9. But take heed to yourselves: for they shall deliver you up to

councils; and in the synagogues you shall be beaten: and you shall be brought before rulers and kings for my sake, for a testimony against them.

10. And the Gospel must first be published among all nations.

11. But when they shall lead you, and deliver you up, take no thought beforehand what you shall speak, neither do you premeditate: but whatsoever shall be given you in that hour, that speak you: for it is not you that speak, but the Holy Ghost.

12. Now the brother shall betray the brother to death, and the father the son; and children shall rise up against their parents, and shall cause them to be put to death.

13. And you shall be hated of all men for my name's sake: but he that shall endure to the end, the same shall be saved.

BEDE; The Lord shows how Jerusalem and the province of Judea merited the infliction of such calamities, in the following words: But take heed to yourselves: for they shall deliver you up to councils; and in the synagogues you shall be beaten. For the greatest cause of destruction to the Jewish people was, that after slaying the Savior, they also tormented the heralds of His name and faith with wicked cruelty.

THEOPHYL. Fitly also did He premise a recital of those things which concerned the Apostles, that in their own tribulations they might find some consolation in the community of troubles and sufferings. There follows: And you shall be brought before rulers and kings for my sake, for a testimony against them. He says kings and rulers, as, for instance, Agrippa, Nero, and Herod. Again, His saying, for my sake, gave them no small consolation, in that they were about to suffer for His sake. For a testimony against them, means, as a judgment beforehand against them, that they might be inexcusable, in that though the Apostles were laboring for the truth, they would not join themselves to it.

Then, that they might not think that their preaching should be impeded by troubles and dangers, He adds: And the Gospel must first be published among all nations.

AUG. Matthew adds: And then shall the end come. Mark, however, by the word first means before the end come.

BEDE; Ecclesiastical historians testify that this was fulfilled, for they relate that all the Apostles long before the destruction of the province of Judea were dispersed to preach the Gospel over the whole world, except James the son of Zebedee and James the brother of our Lord, who had before shed their blood in Judea for the word of the Lord. Since then the Lord knew that the hearts of the disciples would be saddened by the fall and destruction of their nation, He relieves them by this consolation, to let them know that even after the casting away of the Jews, companions in their joy and heavenly kingdom should not be wanting, nay that many more were to be collected out of all mankind then perished in Judea.

GLOSS. Another anxiety might also arise in the breasts of the disciples. Lest therefore after hearing that they were to be brought before kings and rulers, they should fear that their want of science and eloquence should render them unable to answer, our Lord consoles them by saying, But when they shall lead you and deliver you up, take no thought beforehand what you shall speak, but whatsoever shall be given you in that hour, that speak you.

BEDE; For when we are led before judges for Christ's sake, all our duty is to offer up our will for Christ. As for the rest, Christ Himself who dwells in us speaks for us, and the grace of the Holy Ghost shall be given us, when we answer. Wherefore it goes on: For it is not you that shall speak, but the Holy Ghost.

THEOPHYL. He also foretells to them a worse evil, that they should suffer persecution from their relations. Wherefore there follows: Now the brother shall betray the brother to death, and the father the son; and children shall rise up against their parents, and shall cause them to be put to death; and you shall be hated of all men for my name's sake.

BEDE; This has often been seen in time of persecution, nor can there be any firm affection amongst men who differ in faith.

THEOPHYL. And this He says, that on hearing it, they might prepare themselves to bear persecutions and ills with greater patience. Then He brings them consolation, saying, And you shall be hated of all men for my name's sake; for the being hated for Christ's sake is a sufficient reason for suffering persecutions patiently, for it is not the punishment, but the cause, that makes the martyr. Again, that which follows is no small comfort amidst persecution: But he that shall endure to the end, the same shall be saved.

14. But when you shall see the abomination of desolation, spoken of by Daniel the prophet, standing where it ought not, (let him that reads understand,) then let them that be in Judea flee to the mountains:

15. And let him that is on the housetop not go down into the house, neither enter therein, to take any thing out of his house:

16. And let him that is in the field not turn back again for to take up his garment.

17. But woe to them that are with child, and to them that give suck in those days!

18. And pray you that your flight be not in the winter.

19. For in those days shall be affliction, such as was not from the beginning of the creation which God created to this time, neither shall be.

20. And except that the Lord had shortened those days, no flesh should be saved: but for the elect's sake, whom he has chosen, he has shortened the days.

GLOSS. After speaking of the things which were to happen before the destruction of the city, the Lord now foretells those which happened about the destruction itself of the city, saying, But when you shall see the abomination of desolation standing where it ought not, (let him that reads understand.)

AUG. Matthew says, standing in the holy place; but with this verbal difference Mark has expressed the same meaning; for He says where it ought not to stand, because it ought not to stand in the holy place.

BEDE; When we are challenged to understand what is said, we may conclude that it is mystical. But it may either be said simply of Antichrist, or of the statue of Caesar, which Pilate put into the temple, or of the equestrian statue of Adrian, which for a long time stood in the holy of holies itself. An idol is also called abomination according to the Old Testament, and he has added of desolation, because it was placed in the temple when desolate and deserted.

THEOPHYL. Or he means by the abomination of desolation, the entrance of enemies into the city by violence.

AUG. But Luke, in order to show that the abomination of desolation happened when Jerusalem was taken, in this same place gives the words of our Lord, And, when you shall see Jerusalem compassed with armies, then know that the desolation thereof is nigh. It goes on: Then let them that be in Judea flee to the mountains.

BEDE; It is on record that this was literally fulfilled, when on the approach of the war with Rome and the extermination of the Jewish people, all the Christians who were in that province, warned by the prophecy, fled far away, as Church history relates, and retiring beyond Jordan, remained for a time in the city of Pella under the protection of Agrippa, the king of the Jews, of whom mention is made in the Acts, and who with that part of the Jews, who chose to obey him, always continued subject to the

Roman empire.

THEOPHYL. And well does he say, Who are in Judea, for the Apostles were no longer in Judea, but before the battle had been driven from Jerusalem.

GLOSS. Or rather went out of their own accord, being led by the Holy Ghost. It goes on, And let him that is on the housetop not go down, into the house, neither enter therein, to take any thing out of his house; for it is a desirable thing to be saved even naked from such a destruction.

It goes on: But woe to them that are with child, and to them that give suck in those days.

BEDE; That is, they whose wombs or whose hands, overladen with the burden of children, in no small measure impede their forced flight.

THEOPHYL. But it seems to me, that in these words He foretells the eating of children, for when afflicted by famine and pestilence, they laid hands on their children.

GLOSS. Again, after having mentioned this double impediment to flight, which might arise either from the desire of taking away property, or from having children to carry, He touches upon the third obstacle, namely, that coming from the season; saying, And pray you that your flight be not in the winter.

THEOPHYL. That is, lest they who wish to fly should be impeded by the difficulties of the season. And He fitly gives the cause for so great a necessity for flight; saying, For in those days shall be affliction, such as was not from the beginning of the creation which God created to this time, neither shall be.

AUG. For Josephus, who has written the history of the Jews, relates that such things were suffered by this people, as are scarcely credible, wherefore it is said, not without cause, that there was not such tribulation from the beginning of the creation until now, nor shall ever be. But although in the time of Antichrist there shall be one similar or greater, we must understand that it is of that people, that it is said that there shall never happen such another. For if they are the first and foremost to receive Antichrist, that same people may rather be said to cause than to suffer tribulation.

BEDE; The only refuge in such evils is, that God who gives strength to suffer, should abridge the power of inflicting. Wherefore there follows: And except that the Lord had shortened those days.

THEOPHYL. That is, if the Roman war had not been soon finished, no flesh should be saved; that is, no Jew should have escaped; but for the elect's sake, whom he has chosen, that is, for the sake of the believing Jews, or who were hereafter to believe, He has shortened the days, that is, the war was soon finished, for God foresaw that many Jews would believe after the destruction of the city; for which reason He would not suffer the whole race to be utterly destroyed.

AUG. But some persons more fitly understand that the calamities themselves are signified by days, as evil days are spoken of in other parts of holy Scripture; for the days themselves are not evil, but what is done in them. The woes themselves therefore are said to be abridged, because through the patience which God gave they felt them less, and then what was great in itself was abridged.

BEDE; Or else; these words, In those days shall be affliction, properly agree with the times of Antichrist, when not only tortures more frequent, and more painful than before are to be heaped on the faithful, but also, what is more terrible, the working of miracles shall accompany those who inflict torments. But in proportion as this tribulation shall be greater then those which preceded, by so much shall it be shorter. For it is believed, that during three years and a half, as far as may be conjectured from the prophecy of Daniel and the Revelations of John, the Church is to be attacked. In a spiritual sense, however, when we see the abomination of desolation standing where it ought not, that is, heresies and climes reigning amongst them, who appear to be consecrated by the heavenly mysteries, then whosoever of us remain in Judea, that is, in the confession of the true faith, ought to mount the higher in virtue, the more men we see following the broad paths of vice.

PSEUDO-JEROME; For our flight is to the mountains, that he who has mounted to the heights of virtue may not go down to the depths of sin.

BEDE; Then let him who is on the house-top, that is, whose mind rises above carnal deeds, and who lives spiritually, as it were in the free air, not come down to the base acts of his former conversation, nor seek again those things which he had left, the desires of the world or the flesh. For our house either means this world, or that in which we live, our own flesh.

PSEUDO-JEROME; Pray that your flight may not be in the winter, or on the sabbath day, that is, that the fruit of our work may not be ended with the end of time; for fruit comes to an end in the winter and time in the sabbath.

BEDE; But if we are to understand it of the consummation of the world, He commands that our faith and love for Christ should not grow cold, and that we should not grow lazy and cold in the work of God, by taking a sabbath from virtue.

THEOPHYL. We must also avoid sin with fervor, and not coldly and quietly.

PSEUDO-JEROME; But the tribulation shall be great, and the days short, for the sake of the elect, lest the evil of this time should change their understanding.

21. And then if any man shall say to you, Lo, here is Christ; or, lo, he is there; believe him not:

22. For false Christs and false prophets shall rise, and shall show signs and wonders, to seduce, if it were possible, even the elect.

23. But take you heed: behold, I have foretold you all things.

24. But in those days, after that tribulation, the sun shall be darkened, and the moon shall not give her light,

25. And the stars of heaven shall fall, and the powers that are in heaven shall be shaken.

26. And then shall they see the Son of man coming in the clouds with great power and glory.

27. And then shall he send his angels, and shall gather together his elect from the four winds, from the uttermost part of the earth to the uttermost part of heaven.

THEOPHYL. After that the Lord had finished all that concerned Jerusalem, He now speaks of the coming of Antichrist, saying, Then if any man shall say to you, Lo, here is Christ; or, lo, he is there, believe him not. But when He says, then, think not that it means immediately after these things are fulfilled about Jerusalem; as Matthew also says after the birth of Christ, In those days came John the Baptist; does he mean immediately after the birth of Christ? No, but he speaks indefinitely and without precision. So also here, then may be taken to mean not when Jerusalem shall be made desolate, but about the time of the coming of Antichrist.

It goes on: For false Christs and false prophets shall arise, and shall show signs and wonders, to seduce, if it were possible, even the elect. For many shall take upon them the name of Christ, so as to seduce even the faithful.

AUG. For then shall Satan be unchained, and work through Antichrist in all his power, wonderfully indeed, but falsely. But a doubt is often raised whether the Apostle said Signs and lying wonders, because he is to deceive mortal senses, by phantoms, so as to appear to do what he does not, or because those wonders themselves, even though true, are to turn men aside to lies, because they will not believe that any power but a Divine power could do them, being ignorant of the power of Satan, especially when he shall have received such power as he never had before. But for whichever reason it is said, they shall be deceived by those signs and wonders who deserve to be deceived.

GREG. Why however is it said with a doubt if it were possible, when the Lord knows beforehand what is to be? One of two things is implied; that if they are elect, it is not possible; and if it is possible, they are not elect. This doubt therefore in our Lord s discourse expresses the trembling in the mind of the elect. And He calls them elect, because He sees that they will persevere in faith and good works; for those who are chosen to remain firm are to be tempted to fall by the signs of the preachers of Antichrist.

BEDE; Some however refer this to the time of the Jewish captivity, where many, declaring themselves to be Christs, drew after them crowds of deluded persons; but during the siege of the city there was no Christian to whom the Divine exhortation, not to follow false teachers, could apply. Wherefore it is better to understand it of heretics, who, coming to oppose the Church, pretended to be Christs; the first of whom was Simon Magus, but that last one, greater than the rest, is Antichrist.

It goes on: But take you heed: behold, I have foretold you all things.

AUG. For He did not only foretell to His disciples the good things which He would give to His saints and faithful ones, but also the woes in which this world was to abound, that we might look for our reward at the end of the world with more confidence, from feeling the woes in like manner announced as about to precede the end of the world.

THEOPHYL. But after the coming of Antichrist, the frame of the world shall be altered and changed, for the stars shall be obscured on account of the abundance of the brightness of Christ. Wherefore it goes on: But in those days, after that tribulation, the sun shall be darkened, and the moon shall not give her light;

and the stars of heaven shall fall.

BEDE; For the stars in the day of judgment shall appear obscure, not by any lessening of their own light, but because of the brightness of the true light, that is, of the most high Judge coming upon them; although there is nothing to prevent its being taken to mean, that the sun and moon with all the other heavenly bodies then for a time are really to lose their light, just as we are told was the case with the sun at the time of our Lord's Passion. But after the day of judgment, when there shall be a new sky and a new earth, then shall happen what Isaiah says: Moreover, the light of the moon shall be as the light of the sun, and the light of the sun shall be sevenfold. There follows, And the powers of heaven shall be shaken.

THEOPHYL. That is, the Angelic virtues shall be astonished, seeing that such great things are done, and that their fellow-servants are judged.

BEDE; What wonder is it that men should be troubled at this judgment, the sight of which makes the very Angelic powers to tremble? What will the stories of the house do when the pillars shake? What does the shrub of the wilderness undergo, when hen the cedar of paradise is moved?

PSEUDO-JEROME; Or else, the sun shall be darkened, at the coldness of their hearts, as in the winter time. And the moon shall not give her light with serenity, in this time of quarrel, and the stars of heaven shall fail in their light, when the seed of Abraham shall all but disappear, for to it they are likened. And the powers of heaven shall be stilled up to the wrath of vengeance, when they shall be sent by the Son of Man at His coming, of whose Advent it is said, And, then shall they see the Son of Man coming in the clouds with great power and glory, He, that is, who first came down like rain into the fleece of Gideon in all lowliness.

AUG. For since it was said by the Angels to the Apostles, He shall so come in like manner as you have seen him go into heaven, rightly do we believe that He will come not only in the same body, but on a cloud, since He is to come as He went away, and a cloud received Him as He was going.

THEOPHYL But they shall see the Lord as the Son of Man, that is, in the body, for that which is seen is body.

AUG. For the vision of the Son of Man is shown even to the bad, but the vision of the form of God to the pure in heart alone, for they shall see God. And because the wicked cannot see the Son of God, as He is in the form of God, equal to the Father, and at the same time both just and wicked are to see Him as Judge of the quick and dead, before Whom they shall be judged, it was necessary that the Son of Man should receive power to judge.

Concerning the execution of which power, there is immediately added And then shall he send his angels.

THEOPHYL. Observe that Christ sends the Angels as well as the Father; where then are they who say that He is not equal to the Father? For the Angels go forth to gather together the faithful, who are chosen, that they may be carried into the air to meet Jesus Christ. Wherefore it goes on: And gather together his elect from the four winds.

PSEUDO-JEROME; As corn winnowed from the threshing-floor of the whole earth.

BEDE; By the four winds, He means the four parts of the world, the east the west, the north, and the south. And lest any one should think that the elect are to be gathered together only from the four edges of the world, and not from the midland regions as well as the borders, He has fitly added, From the uttermost part of earth, to the uttermost part of heaven, that is from the extremities of the earth to its utmost bounds, where the circle of the heavens appears to those who look from afar to rest upon the boundaries of the earth. No one therefore shall be elect in that day who remains behind and does not meet the Lord in the air, when He comes to judgment. The reprobate also shall come to judgment, that when it is finished they may be scattered abroad and perish from before the face of God.

28. Now learn a parable of the fig tree; When her branch is yet tender, and puts forth leaves, you know that summer is near:

29. So you in like manner, when you shall see these things come to pass, know that it is nigh, even at the doors.

30. Verily I say to you, that this generation shall not pass, till all these things be done.

31. Heaven and earth shall pass away: but my words shall not pass away.

BEDE; Under the example of a tree the Lord gave a pattern of the end, saying, Now learn a parable of the fig tree, when her branch is yet tender, and puts forth leaves, you know that summer is near. So you in like manner, when you shall see these things come to pass, know that it is nigh, even at the doors.

THEOPHYL. As if He had said, As when the fig tree puts forth its leaves, summer follows at once, so also after the woes of Antichrist, at once, without an interval, shall be the coming of Christ, who will be to the just as summer after winter, but to sinners, winter after summer.

AUG. All that is said by the three Evangelists concerning the Advent of our Lord, if diligently compared together and examined, will perchance be found to belong to His daily coming in His body, that is, the Church, except those places where that last coming is so promised, as if it were approaching; for instance in the last part of the discourse according to Matthew, the coming itself is clearly expressed, where it is said, When the Son of Man shall come in his glory.

For what does he refer to in the words, when you shall see these things come to pass, but those things which He has mentioned above, amongst which it is said, And then you shall see the Son of Man coming in the clouds. The end therefore shall not be then, but then it shall be near at hand. Or are we to say, that not all those things which are mentioned above are to be taken in, but only some of them, that is, leaving out these words, Then shall you see the Son of man coming; for that shall be the end itself, and not its approach only. But Matthew has declared that it is to be received without exception, saying, When you shall see all these things, know that it is near, even at the doors. That which is said above must therefore be taken thus; And he shall send his angels, and gather together the elect from the four winds; that is, He shall collect His elect from the four winds of heaven, which He does in the whole of the last hour, coming in His members as in clouds.

BEDE; This fruit-bearing of the fig tree may also be understood to mean the state of the synagogue, which was condemned to everlasting barrenness, because when the Lord came, it had no fruits of righteousness in those who were then unfaithful. But the Apostle has said, that when the fullness of the Gentiles is come in, all Israel shall be saved. What means this, but that the tree, which has been long barren, shall then yield the fruit, which it had withheld? When this shall happen, doubt not that a summer of true peace is at hand.

PSEUDO-JEROME; Or else, the leaves which come forth are words now spoken, the summer at hand is the day of Judgment, in which every tree shall show what it had within it, deadness for burning, or greenness to be planted with the tree of life. There follows Verily I say to you, This generation shall not pass, till these things; be done.

BEDE; By generation He either means the whole race of mankind, or specially the Jews.

THEOPHYL. Or else, This generation shall not pass away, that is, the generation of Christians, until all things be fulfilled, which were spoken concerning Jerusalem and the coming of Antichrist; for He does not mean the generation of the Apostles, for the greater part of the Apostles did not live up to the destruction of Jerusalem.

But He says this of the generation of Christians, wishing to console His disciples, lest they should believe that the faith should fail at that time; for the immovable elements shall first fail, before the words of Christ fail; wherefore it is added, Heaven and earth shall pass away, but my words shall not pass away.

BEDE; The heaven which shall pass away is not the ethereal or starry heaven, but the heaven where is the air. For wherever the water of the judgment could reach, there also, according to the words of the blessed Peter, the fire of judgment shall reach. But the heaven and the earth shall pass away in that form which they now have, but in their essence they shall last without end.

32. But of that day and that hour knows no man, no, not the angels which are in heaven, neither the Son, but the Father.

33. Take you heed, watch and pray: for you know not when the time is.

34. For the Son of man is as a man taking a far journey, who left his house, and gave authority to his servants, and to every man his work, and commanded the porter to watch.

35. Watch you therefore: for you know not when the master of the house comes, at even, or at midnight, or at the cock crowing, or in the morning:

36. Lest coming suddenly he find you sleeping.

37. And what I say to you I say to all, Watch.

THEOPHYL. The Lord wishing to prevent His disciples from asking about that day and hour, says, But of that day and that hour knows no man, no, not the angels which are in heaven, neither the Son, but the Father. For if He had said, I know, but I will not reveal it to you, He would have saddened them not a little; but He acted more wisely, and prevents their asking such a question, lest they should importune Him, by saying, neither the Angels nor I.

HILARY; This ignorance of the day and hour is urged against the Only-Begotten God, as if, God born of God had not the same perfection of nature as God. But first, let common sense decide whether it is credible that He, who is the cause that all things are, and are to be, should be ignorant of any out of all these things. For how can it be beyond the knowledge of that nature, by which and in which that which is to be done is contained? And can He be ignorant of that day, which is the day of His own Advent? Human substances foreknow as far as they can what they intend to do, and the knowledge of what is to be done, follows upon the will to act. How then can the Lord of glory, from ignorance of the day of His coming, be believed to be of that imperfect nature, which has on it a necessity of coming, and has not attained to the knowledge of its own advent?

But again, how much more room for blasphemy will there be, if a feeling of envy is ascribed to God the Father, in that He has withheld the knowledge of His beatitude from Him to whom He gave a foreknowledge of His death. But if there are in Him all the treasures of knowledge, He is not ignorant of this day; rather we ought to remember that the treasures of wisdom in Him are hidden; His ignorance therefore must be connected with the hiding of the treasures of wisdom, which are in Him. For in all cases, in which God declares Himself ignorant, He is not under the power of ignorance, but either it is not a fit time for speaking, or it is an economy of not acting.

But if God is said then to have known that Abraham loved Him, when He did not hide that His knowledge from Abraham, it follows, that the Father is said to know the day, because He did not hide it from the Son. If therefore the Son knew not the day, it is a Sacrament of His being silent, as on the contrary the Father alone is said to know, because He is not silent. But God forbid that any new and bodily changes should be ascribed to the Father or the Son. Lastly, lest He should be said to be ignorant from weakness, He has immediately added, Take you heed, watch and pray, for you know not when the time is.

PSEUDO-JEROME; For we must needs watch with our souls before the death of the body.

THEOPHYL. But He teaches us two things, watching and prayer; for many of us watch, but watch only to pass the night in wickedness; He now follows this up with a parable, saying, For the Son of man is as a man taking a far journey, who left his house, and gave his servants power over every work, and commanded the porter to watch.

BEDE; The man who taking a far journey left his houses is Christ, who ascending as a conqueror to His Father after the resurrection, left His Church, as to His bodily presence, but has never deprived her of the safeguard of His Divine presence.

GREG. For the earth is properly the place for the flesh, which was as it were carried away to a far country, when it was placed by our Redeemer in the heavens. And he gave his servants power over every work, when, by giving to His faithful ones the grace of the Holy Ghost, He gave them the power of serving every good work. He has also ordered the porter to watch, because He commanded the order of pastors to have a care over the Church committed to them. Not only, however, those of us who rule over Churches, but all are required to watch the doors of their hearts, lest the evil suggestions of the devil enter into them, and lest our Lord find us sleeping.

Wherefore concluding this parable He adds, Watch you

therefore: for you know not when the master of the house comes, at even, or at midnight, or at cockcrow, or in the morning:

lest coming suddenly he find you sleeping.

PSEUDO-JEROME; For he who sleeps applies not his mind to real bodies, but to phantoms, and when he awakes, he possesses not what he had seen; so also are those, whom the love of this world seizes upon in this life; they quit after this life what they dreamed was real.

THEOPHYL. See again that He has not said, I know not when the time will be, but, you know not. For the reason why He concealed it was that it was better for us; for if, now that we know not the end, we are careless, what should we do if we knew it? We should keep on our wickednesses even to the end. Let us therefore attend to His words; for the end comes at even, when a man dies in old age; at midnight, when he dies in the midst of his youth; and at cockcrow, when our reason is perfect within us; for when a child begins to live according to his reason, then the cock cries loud within him, rousing him from the sleep of sense; but the age of childhood is the morning. Now all these ages must look out for the end; for even a child must be watched, lest he die unbaptized.

PSEUDO-JEROME; He thus concludes His discourse, that the last should hear from those who come first this precept which is common to all; wherefore He adds, But what I say to you I say to all, Watch.

AUG. For He not only speaks to those in whose hearing He then spoke, but even to all who came after them, before our time, and even to us, and to all after us, even to His last coming. But shall that day find all living, or will any man say that He speaks also to the dead, when He says, Watch, lest when he comes he find you, sleeping? Why then does He say to all, what only belongs to those who shall then be alive, if it be not that it belongs to all, as I have said? For that day comes to each man when his day comes for departing from this life such as he is to be, when judged in that day, and for this reason every Christian ought to watch, lest the Advent of the Lord find him unprepared; but that day shall find him unprepared, whom the last day of his life shall find unprepared.

Mark 14

1. After two days was the feast of the Passover, and of unleavened bread: and the Chief Priests and the Scribes sought how they might take him by craft, and put him to death.

2. But they said, Not on the feast day, lest there be an uproar of the people.

PSEUDO-JEROME; Let us now sprinkle our book, and our thresholds with blood, and put the scarlet thread around the house of our prayers, and bind scarlet on our hand, as was done to Zarah, that we may be able to say that the red heifer is slain in the valley. For the Evangelist, being about to speak of the slaying of Christ, premises, After two days was; the feast of the Passover, and of unleavened bread.

BEDE; Pascha which in Hebrew is phase, is not called from, Passion, as many think, but from passing over, because the destroyer, seeing the blood on the doors of the Israelites, passed by them, and did not smite them; or the Lord Himself, bringing aid to His people, walked above them.

PSEUDO-JEROME; Or else phase is interpreted a passing over, but Pascha means sacrifice. In the sacrifice of the lamb, and the passing of the people through the sea, or through Egypt, the Passion of Christ is prefigured, and the redemption of the people from hell, when He visits us after two days, that is, when the moon is most full, and the age of Christ is perfect, that when no part at all of it is dark, we may eat the flesh of the Lamb without spot, who takes away the sins of the world, in one house, that is, in the Catholic Church, shod with charity, and armed with virtue.

BEDE; The difference according to the Old Testament between the Passover and the feast of unleavened bread was, that the day alone on which the lamb was slain in the evening, that is, the fourteenth moon of the first month, was called Passover. But on the fifteenth moon, when they came out of Egypt, the feast of unleavened bread came on, which solemn time was appointed for seven days, that is, up to the twenty-first day of the same month in the evening. But the Evangelists indifferently use the day of unleavened bread for the Passover, and the Passover for the days of unleavened bread. Wherefore Mark also here says, After two days was the feast of the Passover, and of unleavened bread, because the day of the Passover was also ordered to be celebrated on the days of unleavened bread, and we also, as it were, keeping a continual passover, ought always to be passing out of this world.

PSEUDO-JEROME; But iniquity came forth in Babylon from the princes, who ought to have purified the temple and the vessels, and themselves according to the law, in order to eat the lamb. Wherefore there follows: And the Chief Priests and the Scribes sought how they might take him by craft, and put him to death. Now when the head is slain, the whole body is rendered powerless, wherefore these wretched men slay the Head.

But they avoid the feast day, which indeed befits them, for what feasting can there be for them, who have lost life and mercy? Wherefore it goes on: But they said, Not on the feast day, lest there be an uproar of the people.

BEDE; Not indeed, as the words seem to imply, that they feared the uproar, but they were afraid lest He should be taken out of their hands by the aid of the people.

THEOPHYL. Nevertheless, Christ Himself had determined for Himself the day of His Passion; for He wished to be crucified on the Passover, because He was the true Passover.

3. And being in Bethany in the house of Simon the leper, as he sat at meat, there came a woman having an alabaster box of ointment of spikenard very precious; and she broke the box, and poured it on his head.

4. And there were some that had indignation within themselves, and said, Why was this waste of the ointment made?

5. For it might have been sold for more than three hundred pence, and have been given to the poor. And they murmured against her.

6. And Jesus said, Let her alone; why trouble you her? she has wrought a good work on me.

7. For you have the poor with you always, and whenever you will you may do them good: but me you have not always.

8. She has done what she could: she is come aforehand to anoint my body to the burying.

9. Verily I say to you, Wherever this Gospel shall be preached

throughout the whole world, this also that she has done shall be spoken of for a memorial of her.

BEDE; The Lord when about to suffer for the whole world, and to redeem all nations with His blood, dwells in Bethany, that is, in the house of obedience; wherefore it is said, And being in Bethany in the house of Simon the leper, as he sat at meat, there came a woman.

PSEUDO-JEROME; For the fawn amongst the stags ever comes back to his couch, that is, the Son, obedient to the Father even to death, seeks for obedience from us.

BEDE; He says of Simon the leper, not because he remained still a leper at that time, but because having once been such, he was healed by our Savior; his former name is left, that the virtue of the Healer may be made manifest.

THEOPHYL. But although the four Evangelists record the anointing by a woman, there were two women and not one; one described by John, the sister of Lazarus; it was she who six days before the Passover anointed the feet of Jesus; another described by the other three Evangelists. Nay, if you examine, you will find three; for one is described by John, another by Luke, a third by the other two. For that one described by Luke is said to be a sinner and to have come to Jesus during the time of His preaching; but this other described by Matthew and Mark is said to have come at the time of the Passion, nor did she confess that she had been a sinner.

AUG. I however think that nothing else can be meant, but that the sinner who then came to the feet of Jesus was no other than the same Mary who did this twice; once, as Luke relates it, when coming for the first time with humility and tears she merited the remission of her sins. For John also relates this, when he began to speak of the raising of Lazarus before He came to Bethany, saying, It was that Mary which anointed the Lord with ointment, and wiped his feet with her hair, whose brother Lazarus was sick. But what she again did at Bethany is another act, unrecorded by Luke, but mentioned in the same way by the other three Evangelists. In that therefore Matthew and Mark say that the head of the Lord was anointed by the woman, whilst John says the feet, we must understand that both the head and the feet were anointed by the woman. Unless because Mark has said that she broke the box in order to anoint His head, any one is so fond of caviling as to deny that, because the box was broken, any could remain to anoint the feet of the Lord. But a man of a more pious spirit will contend that it was not broken so as to pour out the whole, or else that the feet were anointed before it was broken, so that there remained in the unbroken box enough to anoint the head.

BEDE; Alabaster is a sort of white marble, veined with various colors which is often hollowed out for boxes of ointment, because it keeps things of that nature most uncorrupt. Nard is an aromatic shrub of a large and thick root, but short, black, and brittle; though unctuous, it smells like cypress, and has a sharp taste, and small and dense leaves. Its tops spread themselves out like ears of corn, therefore, its gift being double, perfumers make much of the spikes and the leaves of the nard. And this is what is meant by Mark, when he says spikenard very precious, that is, the ointment which Mary brought for the Lord was not made of the root of nerd, but even, what made it more precious, by the addition of the spikes and the leaves, the gratefulness of its smell and virtue was augmented.

THEOPHYL. Or as is said in Greek, of pistic nard, that is, faithful, because the ointment of the nard was made faithfully and without counterfeit.

AUG. It may appear to be a contradiction, that Matthew and Mark after mentioning two days and the Passover, add afterwards that Jesus was in Bethany, where that precious ointment is mentioned; whilst John, just before he speaks a of the anointing, says, that Jesus came into Bethany six days before the feast. But those persons who are troubled by this, are not aware that Matthew and Mark do not place that anointing in Bethany immediately after that two days of which he foretold, but by way of recapitulation at the time when there were yet six days to the Passover.

PSEUDO-JEROME; Again in a mystic sense, Simon the leper means the world, first infidel, and afterwards converted, and the woman with the alabaster box, means the faith of the Church, who says, My spikenard sends forth its smell. It is called pistic nard, that is, faithful, and precious. The house filled with the smell of it is heaven and earth; the broken alabaster box is carnal desire, which is broken at the Head, from which the whole body is framed together, whilst He was reclining, that is, humbling Himself, that the faith of the sinner might be able to reach Him, for she went up from the feet to the head, and down from the head to the feet by faith, that is, to Christ and to His members.

It goes on: And there were some that had indignation within themselves, and said, Why was this loss of the ointment? By the figure synecdoche, one is put for many, and many for one; for it is the lost Judas who finds loss in salvation; thus in the fruitful vine rises the snare of death. Under the cover of his avarice, however, the mystery of faith speaks; for our faith is bought for three hundred pence, in our ten senses, that is, our inward and outward senses which are again trebled by our body, soul, and spirit.

BEDE; And in that he says, And they murmured against her, we must not understand this to be spoken of the faithful Apostles, but rather of Judas mentioned in the plural.

THEOPHYL. Or else, it appears to be aptly implied that many disciples murmured against the woman, because they had often heard our Lord talking of alms. Judas, however, was indignant, but not with the same feeling, but on account of his love of money, and filthy gain; wherefore John also records him alone, as accusing the woman with a fraudulent intent. But he says, They murmured against her, meaning that they troubled her with reproaches, and hard words. Then our Lord reproves His disciples, for throwing obstacles against the wish of the woman.

Wherefore it goes on: And Jesus said, Let her alone, why trouble you her? For after she had brought her gift, they wished to prevent her purpose by their reproaches.

ORIGEN; For they were grieved at the waste of the ointment, which might be sold for a large sum and given to the poor. This however ought not to have been, for it was right that it should be poured over the head of Christ, with a holy and fitting stream; wherefore it goes on, She has wrought a good work on me. And so effectual is the praise of this good work, that it ought to excite all of us to fill the head of the Lord with sweet-smelling and rich offerings, that of us it may be said that we have done a good work over the head of the Lord. For we always have with us, as long as we remain in this life, the poor who have need of the care of those who have made progress in the word, and are enriched in the wisdom of God; they are not however able always day and night to have with them the Son of God, that is, the Word and Wisdom of God.

For it goes on: For you have the poor always with you, and whenever you will you may do them good; but me you have not always.

BEDE; To me, indeed, He seems to speak of His bodily presence, that He should by no means be with them after His resurrection, as He then was living with them in all familiarity.

PSEUDO-JEROME. He says also, She has wrought a good work on me, for whosoever believes on the Lord, it is counted to Him for righteousness. For it is one thing to believe Him, and to believe on Him, that is, to cast ourselves entirely upon Him.

It goes on: She has done what she could, she is come aforehand to anoint my body to the burying.

BEDE; As if the Lord said, What you think is a waste of ointment is the service of my burial.

THEOPHYL. For she is come aforehand as though led by God to anoint my body, as a sign of my approaching burial; by which He confounds the traitor, as if He said, With what conscience can you confound the woman, who anoints my body to the burial, and cost not confound yourself, who will deliver me to death? But the Lord makes a double prophecy; one that the Gospel shall be preached over the whole world, another that the deed of the woman shall be praised.

Wherefore it goes on: Verily I say to you, Wherever this gospel shall he preached throughout the whole world, this also that she has done shall be spoken of for a memorial of her.

BEDE; Observe also, that as Mary won glory throughout the whole world for the service which she rendered to the Lord, so, on the contrary, he who was bold enough to reprove her service, is held in infamy far and wide; but the Lord in rewarding the good with due praise has passed over in silence the future shame of the impious.

10. And Judas Iscariot, one of the twelve, went to the Chief Priests, to betray him to them.

11. And when they heard it, they were glad, and promised to give him money. And he sought how he might conveniently betray him.

BEDE; The unhappy Judas wishes to compensate with the price of his Master for the loss which he thought he had made by the pouring out of the ointment; wherefore it is said, And Judas

Iscariot, one of the twelve, went to the Chief Priests to betray him to them.

CHRYS. Why do you tell me of his country? would that I could also have been ignorant of his existence. But there was another disciple called Judas the zealot, the brother of James, and lest by calling him by this name there should arise a confusion between the two, he separates the one from the other. But he says not Judas the traitor, that he may teach us to be guiltless of detraction, and to avoid accusing others. In that however he says, one of the twelve, he enhanced the detestable guilt of the traitor; for there were seventy other disciples, these however were not so intimate with Him, nor admitted to such familiar intercourse. But these twelve were approved by Him, these were the regal band, out of which the wicked traitor came forth.

PSEUDO-JEROME; But he was one of the twelve in number, not in merit, one in body, not in soul. But he went to the Chief Priests after he went out and Satan entered into him. Every living thing unites with what is like itself.

BEDE; But by the words, he went out, it is shown that he was not invited by the Chief Priests, nor bound by any necessity, but entered upon this design from the spontaneous wickedness of his own mind.

THEOPHYL. It is said, to betray him to them, that is, to announce to them when He should be alone. But they feared to rush upon Him when He was teaching, for fear of the people.

PSEUDO-JEROME; And he promises to betray Him, as his

master the devil said before, All this power I will give you. It goes on, And when they heard it they were glad, and promised to give him money. They promise him money, and they lose their life, which he also loses on receiving the money.

CHRYS. Oh! the madness, yea, the avarice of the traitor, for his covetousness brought forth all the evil. For covetousness retains the souls which it has taken, and confines them in every way when it has bound them, and makes them forget all things, maddening their minds. Judas, taken captive by this madness of avarice, forgets the conversation, the table of Christ, his own discipleship, Christ's warnings and persuasion. For there follows, And he sought how he might conveniently betray him.

PSEUDO-JEROME; No opportunity for treachery can be found, such that it can escape vengeance here or there.

BEDE; Many in this day shudder at the crime of Judas in selling his Master, his Lord and his God, for money, as monstrous and horrible wickedness; they however do not take heed, for when for the sake of gain they trample on the rights of charity and truth, they are traitors to God, who is Charity and Truth.

12. And the first day of unleavened bread, when they killed the Passover, his disciples said to him Where will you that we go and prepare that you may eat the Passover?

13. And he sent forth two of his disciples, and said to them, Go you into the city, and there shall meet you a man bearing a pitcher of water: follow him.

14. And wherever he shall go in, say you to the good man of the house, The Master said; Where is the guest chamber, where I shall eat the Passover with my disciples?

15. And he will show you a large upper room furnished and prepared: there make ready for us.

16. And his disciples went forth, and came into the city, and found as he had said to them: and they made ready the Passover.

CHRYS. Whilst Judas was plotting how to betray Him, the rest of the disciples were taking care of the preparation of the Passover: wherefore it is said, And the first day of unleavened bread, when they killed the Passover, his disciples said to him, Where will you that we go and prepare where you may eat the Passover.

BEDE; He means by the first day of the Passover the fourteenth day of the first month, when they threw aside leaven, and were wont to sacrifice, that is, to kill the lamb at even. The Apostle explaining this says, Christ our Passover is sacrificed for us. For although He was crucified on the next day, that is, on the fifteenth moon, yet on the night when the lamb was offered up, He committed to His disciples the mysteries of His Body and Blood, which they were to celebrate, and was seized upon and bound by the Jews; thus He consecrated the beginning of His sacrifice, that is, of His Passion.

PSEUDO-JEROME; But the unleavened bread which was eaten with bitterness, that is with bitter herbs, is our redemption, and the bitterness is the Passion of our Lord.

Catena Aurea: Commentary on the Gospel of St. Mark

THEOPHYL. From the words of the disciples, Where will you that we go? it seems evident that Christ had no dwelling-place, and that the disciples had no houses of their own; for if so, they would have taken Him thither.

PSEUDO-JEROME; For they say, Where will you that we go? to show us that we should direct our steps according to the will of God. But the Lord points out with whom He would eat the Passover, and after 1 His custom He sends two disciples, which we have explained above; wherefore it goes on, And he sent forth two of his disciples, and he said to them, Go you into the city.

THEOPHYL. He sends two of His disciples, that is, Peter and John, as Luke says, to a man unknown to Him, implying by this that He might, if He had pleased, have avoided His Passion. For what could not He work in other men, who influenced the mind of a person unknown to Him, so that he received them? He also gives them a sign how they were to know the house, when He adds, And there shall meet you a man bearing a pitcher of water.

AUG. Mark says a pitcher, Luke a two-handled vessel; one points out the kind of vessel, the other the mode of carrying it; both however mean the same truth.

BEDE; And it is a proof of the presence of His divinity, that in speaking with His disciples,

He knows what is to take place elsewhere; wherefore it follows, And his disciples went forth, and came into the city, and found as he had said to them; and they made ready the Passover.

CHRYS. Not our Passover, but in the meanwhile that of the Jews; but He did not only appoint ours, but Himself became our Passover. Why too did He eat it? Because He was made under the Law, to redeem them that were under the Law, and Himself give rest to the Law. And lest any one should say that He did away with it, because He could not fulfill its hard and difficult obedience, He first Himself fulfilled it, and then set it to rest.

PSEUDO-JEROME. And in a mystical sense the city is the Church, surrounded by the wall of faith, the man who meets them is the primitive people, the pitcher of water is the law of the letter.

BEDE; Or else, the water is the layer of grace, the pitcher points out the weakness of those who were to show that grace to the world.

THEOPHYL. He who is baptized carries the pitcher of water, and he who bears baptism upon him comes to his rest, if he lives according to his reason; and he obtains rest, as being in the house. Wherefore it is added, Follow him.

PSEUDO-JEROME; That is, him who leads to the lofty place, where is the refreshment prepared by Christ. The lord of the house is the Apostle Peter, to whom the Lord has entrusted His house; that there may be one faith under one Shepherd. The large upper-room is the wide-spread Church, in which the name of the Lord is spoken of, prepared by a variety of powers and tongues.

BEDE; Or else, the large upper-room is spiritually the Law, which comes forth from the narrowness of the letter, and in a lofty place, that is, in the lofty chamber of the soul, receives the Savior. But it is designedly that the names both of the bearer of the water, and of the lord of the house, are omitted, to imply that power is given to all who wish to celebrate the true Passover, that is, to be embued with the sacraments of Christ, and to receive Him in the dwelling-place of their mind.

THEOPHYL. Or else, the lord of the house is the intellect, which points out the large upper room, that is, the loftiness of intelligences, and which, though it be high, yet has nothing of vain glory, or of pride, but is prepared and made level by humility. But there, that is, in such a mind Christ's Passover is prepared by Peter and John, that is by action and contemplation.

17. And in the evening he comes with the twelve.

18. And as they sat and did eat, Jesus said, Verily I say to you, One of you which eats with me shall betray me.

19. And they began to be sorrowful, and to say to him one by one, Is it I? and another said, Is it I?

20. And he answered and said to them, It is one of the twelve, that dips with me in the dish.

21. The Son of man indeed goes, as it is written of him: but woe to that man by whom the Son of man is betrayed! good were it for that man if he had never been born.

BEDE; The Lord who had foretold His Passion, prophesied also of the traitor, in order to give him room for repentance, that understanding that his thoughts were known, he might repent. Wherefore it is said, And in the evening he comes with the twelve.

And as they sat and did eat, Jesus said, Verily I say to you, One of you which eats with me shall betray me.

CHRYS. Where it is evident that He did not proclaim him openly to all, lest He should make him the more shameless; at the same time He did not altogether keep it silent, lest thinking that he was not discovered, he should boldly hasten to betray Him.

THEOPHYL. But how could they eat reclining, when the law ordered that standing and upright they should eat the Passover? It is probable that they had first fulfilled the legal Passover, and had reclined, when He began to give them His own Passover.

PSEUDO-JEROME; The evening of the day points out the evening of the world; for the last, who are the first to receive the penny of eternal life, come about the eleventh hour. All the disciples then are touched by the Lord; so that there is amongst them the harmony of the harp, all the well attuned strings answer with accordant tone; for it goes on: And they began to be sorrowful, and to say to him one by one, Is it I? One of them however, unstrung, and steeped in the love of money, said, Is it I, Lord? as Matthew testifies.

THEOPHYL. But the other disciples began to be saddened on account of the word of the Lord; for although they were free from this passion, yet they trust Him who knows all hearts, rather than themselves. It goes on: And he answered and said to them, It is one of the twelve, that dips with me in the dish.

BEDE; That is, Judas, who when the others were sad and held back their hands, puts forth his hand with his Master into the dish. And because He had before said, One of you shall betray me, and yet the traitor perseveres in his evil, He accuses him more openly, without however pointing out his name.

PSEUDO-JEROME; Again, He says, One out of the twelve, as it were separate from them, for the wolf carries away from the flock the sheep which he has taken, and the sheep which quits the fold lies open to the bite of the wolf.

But Judas does not withdraw his foot from his traitorous design though once and again pointed at, wherefore his punishment is foretold, that the death denounced upon him might correct him, whom shame could not overcame; wherefore it goes on: The Son of man indeed goes, as it is written of him.

THEOPHYL. The word here used, goes, shows that the death of Christ was not forced but voluntary.

PSEUDO-JEROME; But because many do good, in the way that Judas did, without its profiting them, there follows: Woe to that man by whom the Son of man is betrayed! good were it for that man if he had never been born.

BEDE; Woe too to that man, today and for ever, who comes to the Lord's table with an evil intent. For he, after the example of

Judas, betrays the Lord, not indeed to Jewish sinners, but to his own sinning members. It goes on: Good were it for that man if he had never been born.

PSEUDO-JEROME; That is, hidden in his mother's inmost womb, for it is better for a man not to exist than to exist for torments.

THEOPHYL. For as respects the end for which he was designed, it would have been better for him to have been born, if he had not been the betrayer, for God created him for good works; but after he had fallen into such dreadful wickedness, it would have been better for him never to have been born.

22. And as they did eat, Jesus took bread, and blessed, and broke it, and gave to them, and said, Take, eat: this is my body.

23. And he took the cup, and when he had given thanks, he gave it to them: and they all drank of it.

24. And he said to them, This is my blood of the new testament, which is shed for many.

25. Verily I say to you, I will drink no more of the fruit of the vine, until that day that I drink it new in the kingdom of God.

BEDE; When the rites of the old Passover were finished, He passed to the new, in order, that is, to substitute the Sacrament of His own Body and Blood, for the flesh and blood of the lamb. Wherefore there follows: And as they did eat, Jesus took bread;

that is, in order to show that He Himself is that person to whom the Lord swore, You are a Priest for ever after the order of Melchizedec. There follows: And blessed, and broke it.

THEOPHYL. That is, giving thanks, He broke it, which we also do, with the addition of some prayers.

BEDE; He Himself also breaks the bread, which He gives to His disciples, to show that the breaking of His Body was to take place, not against His will, nor without His intervention; He also blessed it, because He with the Father and the Holy Spirit filled His human nature, which He took upon Him in order to suffer, with the grace of Divine power. He blessed bread and brake it, because He deigned to subject to death His manhood, which He had taken upon Him, in such a way as to show that there was within it the power of Divine immortality, and to teach them that therefore He would the more quickly raise it from the dead. There follows: And gave to them, and said, Take, eat: this is my body.

THEOPHYL. That, namely, which I now give and which you take. But the bread is not a mere figure of the Body of Christ, but is changed into the very Body of Christ. For the Lord said, The bread which I give you is my flesh. But the flesh of Christ is veiled from our eyes on account of our weakness, for bread and wine are things to which we are accustomed, if however we saw flesh and blood we could not bear to take them. For this reason the Lord bending Himself to our weakness keeps the forms of bread and wine, but changes the bread and wine into the reality of His Body and Blood.

CHRYS. Even now also that Christ is close to us; He who prepared that table, Himself also consecrates it. For it is not man who makes the offerings to be the Body and Blood of Christ, but Christ who was crucified for us. The words are spoken by the mouth of the Priest, and are consecrated by the power and the grace of God. By this word which He spoke, This is my body, the offerings are consecrated; and as that word which says, Increase and multiply, and fill the earth, was sent forth but once, yet has its effect throughout all time, when nature does the work of generation; so also that voice was spoken once, yet gives confirmation to the sacrifice through all the tables of the Church even to this day, even to His advent.

PSEUDO-JEROME; But in a mystical sense, the Lord transfigures into bread His body, which is the present Church, which is received in faith, is blessed in its number, is broken in its sufferings, is given in its examples, is taken in its doctrines; and He forms His Blood in the chalice of water and wine mingled together, that by one we may be purged from our sins, by the other redeemed from their punishment. For by the blood of the lamb our houses are preserved from the smiting of the Angel, and our enemies perish in the waters of the Red sea, which are the sacraments of the Church of Christ. Wherefore it goes on: And he took the cup, and when he had given thanks, he gave it to them. For we are saved by the grace of the Lord, not by our own deserts.

GREG. When His Passion was approaching, He is said to have taken bread and given thanks. He therefore gave thanks, who took upon Him the stripes of other men's wickedness; He who did nothing worthy of smiting, humbly gives a blessing in His

Passion, to show us, what each should do when beaten for his own sins, since He Himself bore calmly the stripes due to the sin of others; furthermore to show us, what we who are the subjects of the Father should do under correction, when He who is His equal gave thanks under the lash.

BEDE; The wine of the Lord's cup is mixed with water, because we should remain in Christ and Christ in us. For on the testimony of John, the waters are the people, and it is not lawful for any one to offer either wine alone, or water alone, lest such an oblation should mean that the head may be severed from the members, and either that Christ could suffer without love for our redemption, and that we can be saved or be offered to the Father without His Passion. It goes on: And they all drank of it.

PSEUDO-JEROME; Happy intoxication, saving fullness, which the more we drink gives the greater sobriety of mind!

THEOPHYL. Some say that Judas did not partake in these mysteries, but that he went out before the Lord gave the Sacrament. Some again say that He gave him also of that Sacrament.

CHRYS. For Christ offered His blood to him who betrayed Him, that he might have remission of his' sins, if he had chosen to cease to be wicked.

PSEUDO-JEROME; Judas therefore drinks and is not satisfied, nor can he quench the thirst of the everlasting fire, because he unworthily partakes of the mysteries of Christ. There are some in the Church whom the sacrifice does not cleanse, but their foolish thought draws them on to sin, for they have plunged themselves in the stinking slough of cruelty.

CHRYS. Let there not be therefore a Judas at the table of the Lord; this sacrifice is spiritual food, for as bodily food, working on a belly filled with humors which are opposed to it, is hurtful, so this spiritual food if taken by one polluted with wickedness, rather brings him to perdition, not by its own nature, but through the fault of the recipient. Let therefore our mind be pure in all things, and our thought pure, for that sacrifice is pure. There follows: And he said to them, This is my blood of the New Testament, which is shed for many.

BEDE; This refers to the different circumstances of the Old Testament, which was consecrated by the blood of calves and of goats; and the lawgiver said in sprinkling it, This is the blood of the Testament which God has enjoined to you. It goes on: Which is shed for many.

PSEUDO-JEROME; For it does not cleanse all. It goes on: Verily I say to you, I will drink no more of the fruit of the vine, until that day that I drink it new in the kingdom of God.

THEOPHYL. As if He had said, I will not drink wine until the resurrection; for He calls His resurrection the kingdom, as He then reigned over death. But after His resurrection He ate and drank with His disciples, showing that it was He Himself who had suffered. But He drank it new, that is, in a new and strange manner, for He had not a body subject to suffering, and requiring food, but immortal and incorruptible. We may also understand it in this way. The vine is the Lord Himself, by the offspring of the vine is meant mysteries, and the secret understanding, which He Himself begets, who teaches man knowledge. But in the kingdom of God, that is, in the world to come, He will drink with His disciples mysteries and knowledge, teaching us new things, and revealing what He now hides.

BEDE; Or else, Isaiah testifies that the synagogue is called the vine or the vineyard of the Lord, saying, The vineyard of the Lord of hosts is the house of Israel. The Lord therefore when about to go to His Passion, says, I will drink no more of the fruit of the vine, as if He had said openly, I will no longer delight in the carnal rites of the synagogue, in which also these rites of the Paschal Lamb have held the chief place. For the time of my resurrection shall come, that day shall come, when in the kingdom of heaven, that is, raised on high with the glory of immortal life, I will be filled with a new joy, together with you, for the salvation of the same people born again of the fountain of spiritual grace.

PSEUDO-JEROME; But we must consider that here the Lord changes the sacrifice without changing the time; so that we never celebrate the Caena Domini before the fourteenth moon. He who celebrates the resurrection on the fourteenth moon, will celebrate the Caena Domini on the eleventh moon, which was never done in either Old or New Testament.

26. And when they had sung an hymn, they went out into the mount of Olives.

27. And Jesus said to them, All you shall be offended because of

me this night: for it is written, I will smite the shepherd, and the sheep shall be scattered.

28. But after that I am risen, I will go before you into Galilee.

29. But Peter said to him, Although all shall be offended, yet will not I.

30. And Jesus said to him, Verily I say to you, That this day, even in this night, before the cock crow twice, you shall deny me thrice.

31. But he spoke the more vehemently, If I should die with you, I will not deny you in any wise. Likewise also said they all.

THEOPHYL. As they returned thanks, before they drank, so they return thanks after drinking; wherefore it is said, And when they had sung a hymn, they went out into the mount of Olives, to teach us to return thanks both before and after our food.

PSEUDO-JEROME; For by a hymn he means the praise of the Lord, as is said in the Psalms, The poor shall eat and be satisfied; they that seek after the Lord shall praise him. And again, All such as be fat upon earth have eaten and worshipped.

THEOPHYL. He also shows by this that He was glad to die for us, because when about to be betrayed, He deigned to praise God. He also teaches us when we fall into troubles for the sake of the salvation of many, not to be sad, but to give thanks to God, who through our distress works the salvation of many.

BEDE; That hymn in the Gospel of John may also be meant, which the Lord sang, returning thanks to the Father, in which also He prayed, raising His eyes to heaven, for Himself and His disciples, and those who were to believe, through their word.

THEOPHYL. Again, He went out into a mountain, that they might come to Him in a lonely place, and take Him without tumult. For if they had come to Him, whilst He was abiding in the city, the multitude of the people would have been in an uproar, and then His enemies, who took occasion against Him, should seem to have slain Him justly, because He stirred up the people.

BEDE; Beautifully also does the Lord lead out His disciples, when they had tasted His Sacraments, into the mount of Olives, to show typically that we ought through the reception of the Sacraments to rise up to higher gifts of virtue, and graces of the Holy Ghost, that we may be anointed in heart.

PSEUDO-JEROME; Jesus also is held captive on the mount of Olives, whence He ascended to heaven, that we may know, that we ascend into heaven from that place in which we watch and pray; there we are bound and do not tend back again to earth.

BEDE; But the Lord foretells to His disciples what is about to happen to them, that when they have gone through it, they may not despair of salvation, but work out their repentance, and be freed; wherefore there follows: And Jesus said to them, All you shall be offended because of me this night.

PSEUDO-JEROME; All indeed fall, but all do not remain fallen.

For shall not he who sleeps also rise up again? It is a camel thing to fall, but devilish to remain lying when fallen.

THEOPHYL. The Lord allowed them to fall that they might not trust in themselves, and lest He should seem to have prophesied, what He had said, as an open accusation of them, He brings forward the witness of Zechariah the Prophet; wherefore it goes on: For it is written, I will smite the shepherd, and the sheep shall be scattered.

BEDE; This is written in different words in Zacharias, and in the person of the Prophet it is said to the Lord; Smite the shepherd, and the sheep shall be scattered.

PSEUDO-JEROME; For the Prophet prays for the Passion of the Lord, and the Father answers, I will smite the shepherd according to the prayers of those below. The Son is sent and smitten by the Father, that is, He is made incarnate and suffers.

THEOPHYL. But the Father says, I will smite the shepherd, because He permitted him to be smitten. He calls the disciples sheep, as being innocent and without guile. At last He consoles them, by saying, But after that I am risen I will go before you into Galilee.

PSEUDO-JEROME; In which the true resurrection is promised, that their hope may not be extinguished. There follows: But Peter said to him, Although all shall be offended, yet will not I. Lo, a bird unfledged strives to raise itself on high; but the body weighs down the soul, so that the fear of the Lord is overcome by the fear of human death.

BEDE; Peter then promised in the ardor of his faith, and the Savior as God knew what was to happen. Wherefore it goes on: And Jesus said to him, Verily I say to you, that this day, even in this night, before the cock crow twice, you shall deny me thrice.

AUG. Though all the Evangelists say that the Lord foretold that Peter was to deny before the cock crew, Mark alone has related it more minutely, wherefore some from inattention suppose that he does not agree with the others. For the whole of Peter's denial is threefold; if it had begun altogether after the cock crew, the other three Evangelists would seem to have spoken falsely, in saying, that before the cock crew, he would deny him thrice. Again, if he had finished the entire threefold denial before the cock began to crow, Mark would in the person of the Lord seem to have said needlessly, Before the cock crow twice, you shall deny me thrice. But because that threefold denial began before the first cock-crowing, the other three did not notice when Peter was to finish it, but how great it was to be, that is, threefold, and when it was to begin, that is, before the cock crew, although the whole was conceived in his mind, even before the first cock crew; but Mark has related more plainly the interval between his words themselves.

THEOPHYL. We are to understand that it happened thus; Peter denied once, then the cock crew, but after he had made two more denials, then the cock crew for the second time.

PSEUDO-JEROME; Who is the cock, the harbinger of day, but the Holy Ghost? by whose voice in prophecy, and in the Apostles, we are roused from our threefold denial, to most bitter tears after our fall, for we have thought evil of God, spoken evil of our neighbors, and done evil to ourselves.

BEDE; The faith of the Apostle Peter, and his burning love for our Lord, is shown in what follows. For it goes on: But he spoke the more vehemently, If I should die with you, I will not deny you in any wise.

THEOPHYL. The other disciples also showed a fearless zeal. For there follows, Likewise also said they all, but nevertheless they acted against the truth, which Christ had prophesied.

32. And they came to a place which was named Gethsemane: and he said to his disciples, Sit you here, while I shall pray.

33. And he takes with him Peter and James and John, and began to be sore amazed, and to be very heavy;

34. And said to them, My soul is exceeding sorrowful to death: tarry you here, and watch.

35. And he went forward a little, and fell on the ground, and prayed that if it were possible, the hour might pass from him.

36. And he said, Abba, Father, all things are possible to you; take away this cup from me: nevertheless not what I will, but what you will.

37. And he comes, and finds them sleeping, and said to Peter, Simon, sleep you? could not you watch one hour?

38. Watch you and pray, lest you enter into temptation. The spirit truly is ready, but the flesh is weak.

39. And again he went away, and prayed, and spoke the same words.

40. And when he returned, he found them asleep again, (for their eyes were heavy,) neither wist they what to answer him.

41. And he comes the third time, and said to them, Sleep on now, and take your rest: it is enough, the hour is come; behold, the Son of man is betrayed into the hands of sinners.

42. Rise up, let us go; lo, he that betrays me is at hand.

GLOSS. After that the Lord, had foretold the offense of His disciples, the Evangelist gives an account of His prayer, in which He is supposed to have prayed for His disciples; and first describing the place of prayer, he says, And they came to a place which was named Gethsemane.

BEDE; The place Gethsemane, in which the Lord prayed, is shown up to this day at the foot of the Mount of Olives. The meaning of Gethsemane is, the valley of the fat, or of fatness. Now when our Lord prays on a mountain, He teaches us that we should when we pray ask for lofty things; but by praying in the valley of fatness, He implies that in our prayer humility and the fatness of interior love must be kept. He also by the valley of humility and the fatness of charity underwent death for us.

PSEUDO-JEROME; In the valley of fatness also, the fat bulls beset Him. There follows, And he said to his disciples, Sit you here, while I shall pray; they are separated from Him in prayer, who are separated in His Passion; for He prays, they sleep, overcome by the sloth of their heart.

THEOPHYL. It was also His custom always to pray by Himself, in order to give us an example, to seek for silence and solitude in our prayers. There follows: And he takes with him Peter, and James, and John. He takes only those who had been witnesses of His glory on Mount Tabor, that they who had seen His glory might also see His sufferings, and learn that He is really man, in that He is sorrowful. Wherefore there follows: And began to be sore amazed, and very heavy. For since He had taken on Himself the whole of human nature, He took also those natural things which belong to man, amazement, heaviness, and sorrow; for men are naturally unwilling to die.

Wherefore it goes on: And he said to then, My soul is exceeding sorrowful to death.

BEDE; As being God, dwelling in the body, He shows the frailty of flesh, that the blasphemy of those who deny the mystery of His Incarnation might find no place; for having taken up a body, He must needs also take up all that belongs to the body, hunger, thirst, pain, grief; for the Godhead cannot suffer the changes of these affections.

THEOPHYL. But some have understood this, as if He had said, I am sorrowful, not because I am to die, but because the Jews, my countrymen, are about to crucify me, and by these means to be shut out from the kingdom of God.

PSEUDO-JEROME; By this also we are taught to fear and to be sorrowful before the judgment of death, for not by ourselves, but by Him only, can we say, The prince of this world comes, and has nothing in Me. There follows: Tarry you here, and watch.

BEDE; He does not mean natural sleep by the sleep which He forbids, for the time of approaching danger did not allow of it, but the sleep of unfaithfulness, and the torpor of the mind. But going forward a little, He falls on His face, and shows his lowliness of mind, by the posture of His body. Wherefore there follows: And he went forward a little, and fell on the ground, and prayed that, if it were possible, the hour might pass from him.

AUG. He said not, if He could do it, but if it could be done; for whatever He wills is possible. We must therefore understand, if it be possible, as if it were; if He is willing.

And lest any one should suppose that He lessened His Father's power, he shows in what sense the words are to be understood; for there follows, And he said, Abba, Father, all things are possible to you. By which He sufficiently shows, that the words, if it be possible, must be understood not of any impossibility, but of the will of His Father. As to what Mark relates, that he said not only Father, but Abba, Father, Abba is the Hebrew for Father. And perhaps the Lord said both words, on account of some Sacrament contained in them; wishing to show that He had taken upon Himself that sorrow in the person of His body, the Church, to which He was made the chief corner stone, and which came to Him, partly from the Hebrews, who are represented by the word Abba, partly from the Gentiles, to whom Father belongs.

BEDE; But He prays, that the cup may pass away, to show that He is very man, wherefore He adds: Take away this cup from me. But remembering why He was sent, He accomplishes the dispensation for which He was sent, and cries out, But not what I will, but what you will. As if He had said, If death can die, without my dying according to the flesh, let this cup pass away; but since this cannot be otherwise, not what I will, but what you will. Many still are sad at the prospect of death, but let them keep their heart right, and avoid death as much as they can; but if they cannot, then let them say what the Lord said for us.

PSEUDO-JEROME; By which also He ceases not up to the end to teach us to obey our fathers, and to prefer their will to ours. There follows: And he comes, and finds them sleeping. For as they are asleep in mind, so also in body. But after His prayer, the Lord coming, and seeing His disciples sleeping, rebukes Peter alone. Wherefore it goes on: And said to Peter, Simon, sleep you? could not you watch with me one hour? As if He had said, If you could not watch one hour with me, how wilt thou be able to despise death, thou who promises to die with me?

It goes on: Watch and pray, that you enter not into temptation, that is, the temptation of denying me.

BEDE; He does not say, Pray that you may not be tempted, because it is impossible for the human mind not to be tempted, but that you enter not into temptation, that is, that temptation may not vanquish you.

PSEUDO-JEROME; But he is said to enter into temptation, who neglects to pray. There follows: The spirit indeed is willing, but the flesh is weak.

THEOPHYL. As if He had said, Your spirit indeed is ready not to deny me, and for this reason you promise; but your flesh is weak, in that unless God give power to your flesh through prayer, you shall enter into temptation.

BEDE; He here represses the rash, who think that they can compass whatever they are confident about. But in proportion as we are confident from the ardor of our mind, so let us fear from the weakness of our flesh. For this place makes against those, who say that there was but one operation in the Lord and one will. For He shows two wills, one human, which from the weakness of the flesh shrinks from suffering; one divine, which is most ready.

It goes on: And again he went away and prayed, and spoke the same words.

THEOPHYL. That by His second prayer He might show Himself to be very man. It goes on: And when he returned, he found them asleep again; He however did not rebuke them severely. For their eyes were heavy, (that is, with sleep,) neither wist they what to answer him. By this learn the weakness of men, and let us not, whom even sleep can overcome, promise things which are impossible to us. Therefore He goes away the third time to pray the prayer mentioned above.

Wherefore it goes on: And he comes the third time and said to them, Sleep on now, and take your rest. He is not vehement against them, though after His rebuke they had done worse, but He tells them ironically, Sleep on now, and take your rest, because He knew that the betrayer was now close at hand. And that He spoke ironically is evident, by what is added: It is enough, the hour is come; behold, the Son of man is betrayed into the hands of sinners. He speaks this, as deriding their sleep, as if He had said, Now indeed is a time for sleep, when the traitor is approaching.

Then He says; Arise, let us go; lo, he that betrays me is at hand; he did not say this to bid them fly, but that they might meet their enemies.

AUG. Or else; In that it is said, that after He had spoken these words, Sleep on now, and take your rest, He added, It is enough, and then, the hour is come; behold, the Son of man is betrayed, we must understand that after saying, Sleep on now, and take your rest, our Lord remained silent for a short time, to give space for that to happen, which He had permitted; and then that He added, the hour is come; and therefore He puts in between, it is enough, that is, your rest has been long enough.

PSEUDO-JEROME; The threefold sleep of the disciples points out the three dead, whom our Lord raised up; the first, in a house; the second, at the tomb; the third, from the tomb. And the threefold watch of the Lord teaches us in our prayers, to beg for the pardon of past, future, and present sins.

43. And immediately, while he yet spoke, comes Judas, one of

the twelve, and with him a great multitude with swords and staves, from the Chief Priests and the Scribes and the elders.

44. And he that betrayed him had given them a token, saying, Whomever I shall kiss, that same is he; take him, and lead him away safely.

45. And as soon as he was come, he goes straight way to him, and said, Master, Master, and kissed him.

46. And they laid their hands on him, and took him.

47. And one of them that stood by drew a sword, and smote a servant of the High Priest, and cut off his ear.

48. And Jesus answered and said to them, Are you come out, as against a thief, with swords and with staves to take me?

49. I was daily with you in the temple teaching, and you took me not: but the Scriptures must be fulfilled.

50. And they all forsook him, and fled.

51. And there followed him a certain young man, having a linen cloth cast about his naked body; and the young men laid hold on him:

52. And he left the linen cloth, and fled from them naked.

BEDE; After that our Lord had prayed three times, and had obtained by His prayers that the fear of the Apostles should be amended by future repentance, He, being tranquil as to His Passion, goes to His persecutors, concerning the coming of whom the Evangelist says, And immediately, while he yet spoke, comes Judas Iscariot, one of the twelve.

THEOPHYL. This is not put without reason, but to the greater conviction of the traitor, since though he was of the chief company amongst the disciples, he turned himself to furious enmity against our Lord. There follows: And with him a great multitude with swords and staves from the Chief Priests and the Scribes and the elders.

PSEUDO-JEROME; For he who despairs of help from God, has recourse to the power of the world.

BEDE; But Judas had still something of the shame of a disciple, for he did not openly betray Him to his persecutors, but by the token of a kiss. Wherefore it goes on: And he that betrayed him had given them a token, saying, Whomever I shall kiss, that same is he; take him, and lead him away safely.

THEOPHYL. See how in his blindness he thought to deceive Christ by the kiss, so as to be looked upon by Him as His friend. But if you were a friend, Judas, how did you come with His enemies? But wickedness is ever without foresight. It goes on: And as soon as he was come, he goes straightway to him, and said, Master, master; and kissed him.

PSEUDO-JEROME; Judas gives the kiss as a token, with poisonous guile, just as Cain offered a crafty, reprobate sacrifice.

BEDE; With envy and with a wicked confidence, he calls Him master, and gives Him a kiss, in betraying Him. But the Lord receives the kiss of the traitor, not to teach us to deceive, but lest he should seem to avoid betrayal, and at the same time to fulfill that Psalm, Among them that are enemies to peace I labor for peace.

It goes on: And they laid hands on him, and took him.

PSEUDO-JEROME; This is the Joseph who was sold by his brethren, and into whose soul the iron entered. There follows: And one of them that stood by drew a sword, and, smote a servant of the High Priest, and cut off his ear.

BEDE; Peter did this, as John declares, with the same ardent mind with which he did all things; for he knew how Phineas had by punishing sacrilegious persons received the reward of righteousness and of perpetual priesthood.

THEOPHYL. Mark conceals his name, lest he should seem to be praising his master for his zeal for Christ Again, the action of Peter points out that they were disobedient and unbelieving, despising the Scriptures; for if they had had ears to hear the Scriptures, they would not have crucified the Lord of glory. But he cut off the ear of a servant of the High Priest, for the Chief Priests especially passed over the Scriptures, like disobedient servants.

It goes on; And Jesus answered and said to them, Are you come out as against a thief, with swords and with staves to take me?

BEDE; As if He had said, it is foolish to seek with swords and staves Him, who offers Himself to you of His own accord and to search, as for one who hides Himself, by night and by means of a traitor, for Him who taught daily in the temple.

THEOPHYL. This, however, is a proof of His divinity, for when He taught in the temple they were unable to take Him, although He was in their power, because the time of His Passion had not yet come; but when He Himself was willing, then He gave Himself up, that the Scriptures might be fulfilled, for he was led as a lamb to the slaughter, not crying nor raising His voice, but suffering willingly.

It goes on: And they all forsook him and fled.

BEDE; In this is fulfilled the word, which the Lord had spoken, that all His disciples should be offended in Him that same night. There follows: And there followed him a certain young man, having a linen cloth cast about his naked body, that is, he had no other clothing but this linen cloth.

It goes on: And they laid hold on him, and he left the linen cloth, and fled from them naked. That is, he fled from them, whose presence and whose deeds he abhorred, not from the Lord, for whom his love remained fixed in his mind, when absent from Him in body.

PSEUDO-JEROME; Just as Joseph left his mantle behind him, and fled naked from the wanton woman; so also let him, who would escape the hands of the evil ones, quit in mind all that is of the world, and fly after Jesus.

THEOPH. It appears probable that this young man was of that house, where they had eaten the Passover. But some say that this young man was James, the brother of our Lord, who was called Just; who after the ascension of Christ received from the Apostles the throne of the bishopric of Jerusalem.

GREG. Or, he says this of John, who, although he afterwards returned to the cross to hear the words of the Redeemer, at first was frightened and fled.

BEDE; For that he was a young man at that time, is evident from his long sojourn in the flesh. Perhaps he escaped from the hands of those who held him for the time, and afterwards got back his garment and returned, mingling under cover of the darkness with those who were leading Jesus, as though he was one of them, until he arrived at the door of the High Priest, to whom he was known, as he himself testifies in the Gospel. But as Peter, who washed away the sin of his denial with the tears of penitence, shows the recovery of those who fall away in time of martyrdom, so the other disciples who prevented their actual seizure, teach the prudence of flight to those who feel themselves unequal to undergo tortures.

53. And they led Jesus away to the High Priest: and with him were assembled all the Chief Priests and the elders and the Scribes.

54. And Peter followed him afar off, even into the palace of the High Priest: and he sat with the servants, and warmed himself at

the fire.

55. And the Chief Priests and all the council sought for witness against Jesus to put him to death; and found none.

56. For many bare false witness against him, but their witness agreed not together.

57. And there arose certain, and bare false witness against him, saying,

58. We heard him say, I will destroy this temple that is made with hands, and within three days I will build another made without hands.

59. But neither so did their witness agree together.

GLOSS. The Evangelist had related above how our Lord had been taken by the servants of the Priests, now he begins to relate how He was condemned to death in the house of the High Priest: wherefore it is said, And they led Jesus away to the High Priest.

BEDE; He means by the High Priest Caiaphas, who (as John writes) was High Priest that year, of whom Josephus relates that he bought his priesthood of the Roman Emperor. There follows: And with him were assembled all the Chief Priests and the elders and the scribes.

PSEUDO-JEROME; Then took place the gathering together of the bulls among the heifers of the people. It goes on: And Peter followed him afar off, even into the palace of the High Priest.

For though fear holds him back, love draws him on.

BEDE; But rightly does he follow afar off, who is just about to betray Him; for he could not have denied Christ, if he had remained close to Him. There follows, And he sat with the servants, and warmed himself at the fire.

PSEUDO-JEROME; He warms himself at the fire in the hall, with the servants. The hall of the High Priest is the enclosure of the world, the servants are the devils, with whom whoever remains cannot weep for his sins; the fire is the desire of the flesh.

BEDE; For charity is the fire of which it is said, I am come to send fire on the earth, which flame coming down on the believers, taught them to speak with various tongues the praise of the Lord. There is also a fire of covetousness, of which it is said, They are all adulterers as an oven; this fire, raised up in the hall of Caiaphas by the suggestion of an evil spirit, was arming the tongues of the traitors to deny and blaspheme the Lord. For the fire lit up in the hall amidst the cold of the night was a figure of what the wicked assembly was doing within; for because of the abounding of iniquity the love of many waxes cold. Peter, who for a time was benumbed by this cold, wished as it were to be warmed by the coals of the servants of Caiaphas, because He sought in the society of traitors the consolation of worldly comfort.

It goes on, And the Chief Priests and all the council sought for witness against Jesus to put him to death.

THEOPHYL. Though the law commanded that there should be but one High Priest, there were then many put into the office, and stripped of it, year by year, by the Roman emperor. He therefore calls chief priests those who had finished the time allotted to them, and had been stripped of their priesthood. But their actions are a sign of their judgment, which they carried on as they had prejudged, for they sought for a witness, that they might seem to condemn and destroy Jesus with justice.

PSEUDO-JEROME; But iniquity lied as the queen did against Joseph, and the priests against Susannah, but a flame goes out, if it has no fuel; wherefore it goes on, And found none. For many bare false witness against him, but their witness agreed not together. For whatever is not consistent is held to be doubtful.

There follows, And there arose certain, and bare false witness against him, saying, We heard him say,

I will destroy this temple that is made with hands, and within three days I will build another made without hands. It is usual with heretics out of the truth to extract the shadow; He did not say what they said, but something like it, of the temple of His body, which He raised again after two days.

THEOPHYL. For the Lord had not said, I will destroy, but, Destroy, nor did He say, made with hands, but, this temple.

BEDE; He had said also, I will raise up, meaning a thing with life and soul, and a breathing temple. He is a false witness, who understands words in a sense, in which they are not spoken.

60. And the High Priest stood up in the midst, and asked Jesus, saying, Answer you nothing? what is it which these witness against you?

61. But he held his peace, and answered nothing. Again the High Priest asked him, and said to him, Are you the Christ, the Son of the Blessed?

62. And Jesus said, I am: and you shall see the Son of man sitting on the right hand of power, and coming in the clouds of heaven.

63. Then the High Priest rent his clothes, and said, What need we any further witnesses?

64. You have heard the blasphemy: what think you? And they all condemned him to be guilty of death.

65. And some began to spit on him, and to cover his face, and to buffet him, and to say to him Prophesy: and the servants did strike him with the palms of their hands.

BEDE; The more Jesus remained silent before the false witnesses who were unworthy of His answer, and the impious priests, the more the High Priest, overcome with anger, endeavored to provoke Him to answer, that he might find room for accusing Him, from any thing whatever which He might say. Wherefore it is said, And the High Priest stood up in the midst, and asked Jesus, saying, Answer you nothing? what is it which these witness against you? The High Priest, angry and impatient at finding no room for accusation against Him, rises from his seat, thus showing by the motion of his body the madness of his mind.

PSEUDO-JEROME; But our God and Savior Himself, Who brought salvation to the world, and assisted mankind by His love, is led as a sheep to the slaughter, without crying, and remained mute and kept silence yes even from good words. Wherefore it goes on, But he held his peace, and answered nothing. The silence of Christ is the pardon for the defense or excuse of Adam.

THEOPHYL. But He remained silent because He knew that they would not attend to his words; wherefore He answered according to Luke, If I tell you, you will not believe. Wherefore there follows, Again the High Priest asked him, and said to him, Are you the Christ, the Son of the Blessed? The High Priest indeed puts this question, not that he might learn of Him and believe, but in order to seek occasion against Him. But he asks, Art thou the Christ, the Son of the Blessed, because there were many Christs, that is, anointed persons, as Kings and High Priests, but none of these was called the Son of the Blessed God, that is, the Ever-praised.

PSEUDO-JEROME; But they looked from afar off for Him, whom though near they cannot see, as Isaac from the blindness of his eyes does not know Jacob who was under his hands, but prophesies long before things which were to come to him. It goes on, Jesus said, I am; namely, that they might be inexcusable.

THEOPHYL. For He knew that they would not believe, nevertheless He answered them, lest they should afterwards say, If we had heard any thing from Him, we would have believed on

Him; but this is their condemnation, that they heard and did not believe.

AUG. Matthew, however, does not say that Jesus answered I am, but, You have said. But Mark shows, that the words I am were equivalent to You have said. There follows, And you shall see the Son of Man sitting on the right hand of power, and coming in the clouds of heaven.

THEOPHYL. As if He had said, you shall see Me as the Son of Man sitting on the right hand of the Father, for He here calls the Father power. He will not however come without a body, but as He appeared to those who crucified Him, so will He appear in the judgment.

BEDE; If therefore to you, O Jew, O Pagan, and heretic, the contempt, weakness, and cross in Christ are a subject of scorn, see how by this the Son of Man is to sit at the right hand of the Father, and to come in His majesty on the clouds of heaven.

PSEUDO-JEROME; The High Priest indeed asks the Son of God, but Jesus in His answer speaks of the Son of Man, that we may by this understand that the Son of God is also the Son of Man; and let us not make a quaternity in the Trinity, but let man be in God and God in man. And He said, Sitting on the right hand of power, that is, reigning in life everlasting, and in the Divine power. He says, And coming with the clouds of heaven. He ascended in a cloud, He will come with a cloud; that is, He ascended in that body alone, which He took of the Virgin, and He will come to judgment with the whole Church, which is His body and His fullness.

LEO; But Caiaphas, to increase the odiousness of what they had heard, rent his clothes, and without knowing what his frantic action meant, by his madness, deprived himself of the honor of the priesthood, forgetting that command, by which it is said of the High Priest, He shall not uncover his head or rend his clothes. For there follows: Then the High Priest rent his clothes, and said, What need, we any further witnesses? you have heard, the blasphemy: what think you?

THEOPHYL. The High Priest does after the manner of the Jews; for whenever any thing intolerable or sad occurred to them, they used to rend their clothes. In order then to show that Christ had spoken great and intolerable blasphemy, he rent his clothes.

BEDE; But it was also with a higher mystery, that in the Passion of our Lord the Jewish priest rent his own clothes, that is, his ephod, whilst the garment of the Lord could not be rent, even by the soldiers, who crucified Him. For it was a figure that the Jewish priesthood was to be rent on account of the wickedness of the priests themselves. But the solid strength of the Church, which is often called the garment of her Redeemer, can never be torn asunder.

THEOPHYL. The Jewish priesthood was to be rent from the time that they condemned Christ as guilty of death; wherefore there follows, And they all condemned him to be guilty of death.

PSEUDO-JEROME; They condemned Him to be guilty of death, that by His guiltiness He might absolve our guilt. It goes on: And some began to spit on him, and to cover his face, and to buffet him, and to say to him, Prophesy: and the servants did strike him with the palms of their hands; that is, that by being spit upon He might wash the face of our soul, and by the covering of His face, might take away the veil from our hearts, and by the buffets, which were dealt upon His head, might heal the head of mankind, that is, Adam, and by the blows, by which He was smitten with the hands, His great praise might be testified by the clapping of our hands and by our lips, as it is said, O clap your hands: together, all you people.

BEDE; By saying, Prophesy, who is he that smote you, they mean to insult Him, because He wished to be looked upon as a prophet by the people.

AUG. We must understand by this, that the Lord suffered these things till morning, in the house of the High Priest, whither He had first been brought.

66. And as Peter was beneath in the palace, there comes one of the maids of the High Priest:

67. And when she saw Peter warming himself, she looked upon him, and said, And you also were with Jesus of Nazareth.

68. But he denied, saying, I know not, neither understand I what you say. And he went out into the porch; and the cock crew.

69. And a maid saw him again, and began to say to them that stood by, This is one of them.

70. And he denied it again. And a little after, they that stood by said again to Peter, Surely you are one of them: for you are a Galilaean, and your speech agrees thereto.

71. But he began to curse and to swear, saying, I know not this man of whom you speak.

72. And the second time the cock crew. And Peter called to mind the word that Jesus said to him, Before the cock crow twice, you shall deny me thrice. And when he thought thereon, he wept.

AUG. Concerning the temptation of Peter, which happened during the injuries before mentioned, all the Evangelists do not speak in the same order. For Luke first relates the temptation of Peter, then these injuries of the Lord; but John begins to speak of the temptation of Peter, and then puts in some things concerning our Lord's ill-treatment, and adds, that He was sent from there to Caiaphas the High Priest, and then he goes back to unfold the temptation of Peter, which he had begun. Matthew and Mark on the other hand first notice the injuries done to Christ, then the temptation of Peter. Concerning which it is said, And as Peter was beneath in the palace, there comes one of the maids of the High Priest.

BEDE; But what can be meant by his being first recognized by a woman, when men were more able to know him, if it be not that that sex might be seen to sin in the death of our lord, and that sex be redeemed by His Passion?

It goes on: But he denied, saying, I know not, neither understanding I what you say.

PSEUDO-JEROME, Peter when he had not the Spirit yielded and lost courage at the voice of a girl, though with the Spirit he was not afraid before princes and kings.

THEOPHYL. The Lord allowed this to happen to him by His providence, that is, lest he should be too much elated, and at the same time, that he might prove himself merciful to sinners, as knowing from himself the result of human weakness. There follows: And he went out into the porch; and the cock crew.

BEDE; The other Evangelists do not mention this crowing of the cock; they do not however deny the fact, as also some pass over many other things in silence, which others relate. There follows: And a maid saw him again, and began to say to them that stood by, This is one of them.

AUG. This maid is not the same, but another, as Matthew says. Indeed we must also understand, that in this second denial he was addressed by two persons, that is, by the maid whom Matthew and Mark mention, and by another person, of whom Luke takes notice. It goes on: And he denied it again. Peter had now returned, for John says that he denied Him again standing at the fire; wherefore the maid said what has been mentioned above, not to him, that is, Peter, but to those who, when he went out, had remained, in such a way however that he heard it; wherefore coming back and standing again at the fire, he contradicted them, and denied their words. For it is evident, if we compare the accounts of all the Evangelists on this matter, that Peter did not the second time deny him before the porch, but within the palace at the fire, whilst Matthew, and Mark who mention his having gone out are silent, for the sake of brevity, as to his return.

BEDE; By this denial of Peter we learn, that not only he denies Christ, who says that He is not the Christ, but he also, who although he is a Christian, denies himself to be such. For the Lord did not say to Peter, You shall deny thyself to be my disciple, but, You shall deny me; he therefore denied Christ, when he said that he was not His disciple. There follows: And a little after, they that stood by said again to Peter, Surely you are one of them, for you are a Galilaean, and your speech agrees thereto. Not that the Galileans spoke a different tongue from the inhabitants of Jerusalem, for they were both Hebrews, but that each province and region has its own peculiarities, and cannot avoid a vernacular pronunciation.

THEOPHYL. Therefore Peter was seized with fear, and forgetting the word of the Lord, which said, Whoever shall confess me before men, him will I confess before my Father, he denied our Lord; wherefore there follows: But he began to curse and to swear, saying, I know not this man of whom you speak.

BEDE; How hurtful is it to speak with the wicked. He denies before infidels that he knows the man, whom, amongst the disciples, he had confessed to be God. But the Scripture is wont to point out a Sacrament of the causes of things, by the state of the time; thus Peter, who denied at midnight, repented at cock crow; wherefore it is added: And the second time the cock crew. And Peter called to mind the word which Jesus said to him, Before the cock crow twice, you shall deny me thrice. And he began to weep.

THEOPHYL. For tears brought Peter by penitence to Christ. Confounded then be the Novatians, who he say that he who sins after receiving baptism, is not received to the remission of his sin. For behold Peter, who had also received the Body and Blood of the Lord, is received by penitence; for the failings of saints are written, that if we fall by want of caution, we also may be able to run back through their example, and hope to be relieved by penitence.

PSEUDO-JEROME; But in a mystical sense, the first maid means the wavering, the second, the assent, the third man is the act. This is the threefold denial which the remembrance of the word of the Lord washes away through tears. The cock then crows for us when some preacher stirs up our hearts by repentance to compunction. We then begin to weep, when we are set on fire within by the spark of knowledge, and we go forth, when we cast out what we were within.

Mark 15

1. And straightway in the morning the Chief Priests held a consultation with the elders and Scribes and the whole council, and bound Jesus, and carried him away, and delivered him to Pilate.

2. And Pilate asked him, Art thou the King of the Jews? And he answering said to him, You say it.

3. And the Chief Priests accused him of many things: but he answered nothing.

4. And Pilate asked him again, saying, Answer you nothing? Behold how many things they witness against you.

5. But Jesus yet answered nothing; so that Pilate marveled.

BEDE; The Jews had a custom of delivering him whom they had condemned to death, bound to the judge. Wherefore after the condemnation of Christ, the Evangelist adds: And straightway in the morning the Chief Priests held a consultation with the elders and Scribes and the whole council, and bound Jesus, and carried him away, and delivered him to Pilate. But it must be observed, that they did not then first bind Him, but they bound Him on first taking Him in the garden by night, as John declares.

THEOPHYL. They then gave Jesus up to the Romans, but were themselves given up by God into the hands of the Romans, that the Scriptures might be fulfilled, which say, Recompense them after the work of their hands.

It goes on: And Pilate asked him, Are you the King of the Jews?

BEDE; By Pilate's asking Him about no other accusation, except whether He was King of the Jews, they are convicted of impiety, for they could not even find a false accusation against our Savior. It goes on: And he answering said to him, You say. He answers in this way so as both to speak the truth, and yet not to be open to cavil.

THEOPHYL. For His answer is doubtful, since it may mean, You say, but I do say not so. And observe that He does somewhere answer Pilate, who condemned Him unwillingly, but does not choose to answer the priests and great men, and judges them unworthy of a reply. It goes on: And the Chief Priests accused him of many things.

AUG. Luke has also laid open the false charges which they brought against Him; for he thus relates it: And they began to accuse him, saying, We found this fellow perverting the nation, and forbidding to give tribute to Caesar, saying that he himself is Christ a King.

There follows: And Pilate asked him, saying, Answer you nothing? Behold how many things they witness against you.

BEDE; He indeed who condemns Jesus is a heathen, but he refers it to the people of the Jews as the cause. There follows: But Jesus yet answered nothing; so that Pilate marveled. He was unwilling to give an answer, lest He should clear Himself of the charge, and be acquitted by the Judge, and so the gain resulting from the Cross should be done away.

THEOPHYL. But Pilate wondered, because, though He was a teacher of the law, and eloquent, and able by His answer to destroy their accusations, He did not answer any thing, but rather bore their accusations courageously.

6. Now at that feast he released to them one prisoner, whomever they desired.

7. And there was one named Barabbas, which lay bound with them that had made insurrection with him, who had committed murder in the insurrection.

8. And the multitude crying aloud began to desire him to do as he had ever done to them.

9. But Pilate answered them, saying, Will you that I release to you the King of the Jews?

10. For he knew that the Chief Priests had delivered him for envy.

11. But the Chief Priests moved the people, that he should rather release Barabbas to them.

12. And Pilate answered and said again to them, What will you then that I shall do to him whom you call the King of the Jews?

13. And they cried out again, Crucify him.

14. Then Pilate said to them, Why, what evil has he done? And they cried out the more exceedingly, Crucify him.

15. And so Pilate, willing to content the people, released Barabbas to them, and delivered Jesus, when he had scourged him, to be crucified.

BEDE; Pilate furnished many opportunities of releasing Jesus, in the first place contrasting a robber with the Just One. Wherefore it is said, Now at that feast he released to them one prisoner, whomsoever they desired.

GLOSS. Which indeed he was accustomed to do, to obtain favor with the people, and above all, on the feast day, when the people of the whole province of the Jews flocked to Jerusalem. And that the wickedness of the Jews might appear the greater, the enormity of the sin of the robber, whom they preferred to Christ, is next described. Wherefore there follows: And there was one Barabbas, who lay bound with them that had made insurrection with him, who had committed murder in the insurrection. In which words their wickedness is shown both from the heinousness of his signal crime, in that he had committed murder, and from the way in which he did it, because he had in doing it raised a sedition and disturbed the city, and also because his crime was notorious, for he was bound with seditious persons.

It goes on: And the multitude, when it had come up, began to desire him to do as he had ever done to them.

AUG. No one can feel it a difficulty that Matthew is silent as to their asking some one to be released to them, which Mark here mentions, for it is a thing of no consequence that one should mention a thing which another leaves out. There follows: But Pilate answered them, saying, Will you that I release to you the King of the Jews?

For he knew that the Chief Priests had delivered him for envy. Some one may ask, which were the words of which Pilate made use, those which are related by Matthew, or those which Mark relates; for there seems to be a difference between, Whom will you that I release to you? Barabbas, or Jesus which is called Christ? as Matthew has it; and, Will you that I release to you the King of the Jews. as is here said. But since they gave to kings the name of Christs, he who said this man or that must have asked whether they wished the King of the Jews to be released to them, that is, Christ. It makes no difference to the sense that Mark has said nothing of Barabbas, wishing only to mention what belonged to the Lord, since by their answer he sufficiently showed whom they wished to have released to them.

For there follows, But the Chief Priests moved the people that he should rather release to them Barabbas.

BEDE; This demand which the Jews made with such toil to themselves still sticks to them. Because, when the choice was given to them they chose a robber instead of Christ, a murderer instead of the Savior, they deservedly lost their salvation and their life, and they subjected themselves to such a degree to robbery and sedition, that they lost their country and their kingdom which they preferred to Christ, and never regained their liberty, body or soul.

Then Pilate gives another opportunity of releasing the Savor, when there follows, And Pilate answered, and said again to them, What will you then that I should do to the King of the Jews?

AUG. It now is clear enough that Mark means by King of the Jews what Matthew means by the word Christ; for no kings but those of the Jews were called Christs. For in this place according to Matthew it is said, What then shall I do with Jesus which is called Christ? There follows, And they cried out again, Crucify him,

THEOPHYL. Now see the wickedness of the Jews, and the moderation of Pilate, though he too was worthy of condemnation for not resisting the people Fol they cried out, Crucify; he faintly tries to save Jesus from t their determined sentence, and again puts a question to them. Wherefore there follows, Then Pilate said to them, Why, what evil has he done? For he wished in this way to find an opportunity for releasing Christ, who was innocent.

BEDE; But the Jews giving loose to their madness do not answer the question of the judge. Wherefore it goes on, And they cried out the more exceedingly, Crucify him, that those words of the Prophet Jeremiah might be fulfilled, Mine heritage is to me as a lion in the forest, it cries out against me.

There follows, And so Pilate, willing to content the people, released Barabbas to them, and delivered Jesus, when he had scourged him, to be crucified.

THEOPHYL. He wished indeed to satisfy the people, that is, to do their will, not what was agreeable to justice and to God.

PSEUDO-JEROME; Here are two goats; one is the scape goat, that is, one loosed and sent out into the wilderness of hell with the sin of the people; the other is slain, as a lamb, for the sins of those who are forgiven. The Lord's portion is always slain; the devil's part, (for he is the master of those men, which is the meaning of Barabbas,) when freed, is cast headlong into hell.

BEDE; We must understand that Jesus was scourged by no other than Pilate himself. For John writes, Pilate took Jesus, and scourged him, which we must suppose that he did, that the Jews might be satisfied with His pains and insults, and cease from thirsting for His blood.

16. And the soldiers led him away into the hall, called Praetorium; and they call together the whole band.

17. And they clothed him with purple, and platted a crown of thorns, and put it about his head,

18. And began to salute him, Hail, King of the Jews!

19. And they smote him on the head with a reed, and did spit upon him, and bowing their knees worshipped him.

20. And when they had mocked him, they took off the purple from him, and put his own clothes on him.

THEOPHYL. The vainglory of soldiers, ever rejoicing in disorder and in insult, here displayed what properly belonged to them. Wherefore it is said, And the soldiers led him away into the hall called Praetorium, and they call together the whole band, that is, the whole company of the soldiers, and they clothed him with purple as a king.

BEDE; For since He had been called King of the Jews, and the scribes and priests had objected to Him as a crime that He usurped rule over the Jewish people, they in derision strip Him of His former garments, and put on Him a purple robe, which ancient kings used to wear.

AUG. But we must understand that the words of Matthew, they put on him a scarlet robe, Mark expresses by clothed him in purple; for that scarlet robe was used by them in derision for the royal purple, and there is a sort of red purple, very dike scarlet. It may also be that Mark mentions some purple which the robe had about it, though it was of a scarlet color.

BEDE; But instead of the diadem, they put on Him a crown of thorns, wherefore it goes on, And platted a crown of thorns, and put it about his head. And for a royal scepter they give Him a reed, as Matthew writes, and they bow before Him as a king, wherefore there follows, And began to salute him, Hail, King of the Jews!

And that the soldiers worshipped Him as one who falsely called Himself God, is clear from what is added: And bowing their knees, worshipped him, as though He pretended to be God.

PSEUDO-JEROME; His shame took away our shame; His bonds made us free; by the thorny crown of His head, we have obtained the crown of the kingdom; by His wounds we are healed.

AUG. It appears that Matthew and Mark here relate things which took place previously, not that they happened when Pilate had already delivered Him to be crucified. For John says that these things took place at Pilate's house; but that which follows, And when they had mocked him, they took off the purple from him, and put on him his own clothes, must be understood to have taken place last of all, when He was already being led to be crucified.

PSEUDO-JEROME; But in a mystic sense, Jesus was stripped of His clothes, that is, of the Jews, and is clothed in a purple robe, that is, in the Gentile church, which is gathered together out of the rocks. Again, putting it off in the end, as offending, He again is clothed with the Jewish people, for when the fullness of the Gentiles is come in, then shall all Israel be saved.

BEDE; Or else, by the purple robe, with which the Lord is clothed, is meant His flesh itself, which He gave up to suffering, and by the thorny crown which He carried is meant, the taking upon Him of our sins.

THEOPHYL. Let us also put on the purple and royal robe, because we must walk as kings treading on serpents and scorpions, and having sin under our feet. For we are called Christians, that is, anointed ones, just as kings were then called anointed. Let us also take upon ourselves the crown of thorns, that is, let us make haste to be crowned with a strict life, with self-denials and purity.

BEDE; But they smite the head of Christ, who deny that He is very God. And because men are wont to use a reed to write with, they, as it were, smite the head of Christ with a reed, who speak against His divinity, and endeavor to confirm their error by the authority of Holy Writ. They spit in His face, who spit from them by their accursed words the presence of His grace. There are some also in this day, who adore Him, with a sure faith, as very God, but by their perverse actions, despise His words as though they were fabulous, and think the promises of that word inferior to worldly allurements. But just as Caiaphas said, though he knew not what it meant, It is expedient for us that one man should die for the people, so also the soldiers do these things in ignorance.

20. - And led him out to crucify him.

21. And they compel one Simon a Cyrenian, who passed by, coming out of the country, the father of Alexander and Rufus, to bear his cross.

22. And they bring him to the place Golgotha, which is, being interpreted, The place of a skull.

23. And they gave him to drink wine mingled with myrrh: but he received it not.

24. And when they had crucified him, they parted his garments, casting lots upon them, what every man should take.

25. And it was the third hour, and they crucified him.

26. And the superscription of his accusation was written over, THE KING OF THE JEWS.

27. And with him they crucify two thieves; the one on his right hand, and the other on his left.

28. And the Scripture was fulfilled, which said, And he was numbered with the transgressors.

GLOSS. After the condemnation of Christ, and the insults heaped upon Him when He was condemned, the Evangelist proceeds to relate His crucifixion, saying, And led him out to crucify him.

PSEUDO-JEROME; Here Abel is brought out into the field by his brother, to be slain by him. Here Isaac comes forth with the wood, and Abraham with the ram caught in the thicket. Here also Joseph with the sheaf of which he dreamed, and the long robe steeped in blood. Here is Moses with the rod, and the serpent hanging on the wood. Here is the cluster of grapes, carried on a staff. Here is Elisha with the piece of wood sent to seek for the ax, which had sunk, and which swam to the wood; that is, mankind, which by the forbidden tree, fell down to hell, but by the wood of the cross of Christ, and by the baptism of water, swims to paradise. Here is Jonah out of the wood of the ship sent down into the sea and into the whale's belly for three days.

There follows: And they compel Simon a Cyrenian, who passed by, coming out of the country, the father of Alexander and

Rufus, to bear his cross.

THEOPHYL Now John says that He Himself bare His cross, for both took place; for He first bore the cross Himself, until some one passed, whom they compelled, and who then carried it. But he mentioned the name of his sons, to make it more credible and the affirmation stronger, for the man still lived to relate all that had happened about the cross.

PSEUDO-JEROME; Now since some men are known by the merits of their fathers, and some by those of their sons, this Simon, who was compelled to carry the cross, is made known by the merits of his sons, who were disciples. By this we are reminded, that in this life, parents are assisted by the wisdom and the merits of their children, wherefore the Jewish people is always held worthy of being remembered on account of the merits of the Patriarchs, Prophets, and Apostles. But this Simon who carries the cross, because he is compelled, is the man who labors for human praise. For men compel him to work, when the fear and love of God could not compel him.

BEDE; Or, since this Simon is not called Be a man of Jerusalem, but a Cyrenian, (for Cyrene is a city of Libya,) fitly is he taken to mean the nations of the Gentiles, which were once foreigners and strangers to the covenants, but now by obedience are heirs of God, and joint heirs with Christ. Whence also Simon is fitly interpreted 'obedient,' and Cyrene 'an heir.' But he is said to come from a country place, for a country place is called 'pagos' in Greek, wherefore those whom we see to be aliens from the city of God, we call pagans. Simon then coming out from the country carries the cross after Jesus, when the Gentile nations leaving pagan rites embrace obediently the footsteps of our Lord's Passion.

There follows: And they bring him to the place Golgotha, which is being interpreted, the place of Calvary. There are places without the city and the gate, in which the heads of condemned persons are cut off, and which receive the name of Calvary, that is, of the beheaded. But the Lord was crucified there, that where once was the field of the condemned, there the standards of martyrdom might be lifted up.

PSEUDO-JEROME; But the Jews relate, that in this spot of the mountain the ram was sacrificed for Isaac, and there Christ is made bald, that is, separated from His flesh, that is, from the carnal Jews. There follows: And they gave him to drink wine mingled with myrrh.

AUG. This we must understand to be what Matthew expresses by, mixed with gall; for he put gall for any thing bitter, and wine mingled with myrrh is most bitter; although there may have been both gall and myrrh to make the wine most bitter.

THEOPHYL Or, they may have brought different things, in order, some vinegar and gall, and others wine mixed with myrrh.

PSEUDO-JEROME; Or else, wine mingled with myrrh, that is, vinegar; by it the juice of the deadly apple is wiped away.

BEDE; Bitter the vine which bore the bitter wine, set before the Lord Jesus, that the Scripture might be fulfilled which said, They gave me gall to eat, and when I was thirsty, they gave me vinegar to drink.

AUG. That which follows, But he received it not, must mean, He received it not to drink, but only tasted it, as Matthew witnesses. And what the same Matthew relates, he would not drink, Mark expresses by, he received it not, but was silent as to His tasting it.

PSEUDO-JEROME; He also refused to take sin for which He suffered, wherefore it is said of Him, I then paid the things that I never took. There follows: And when they had crucified him, they parted his garments, casting lots upon them, what every man should take. In this place salvation is figured by the wood; the first wood was that of the tree of knowledge of good and evil; the second wood is one of unmixed good for us, and is the wood of life. The first hand stretched out to the wood caught hold of death; the second found again the life which had been lost. By this wood we are carried through a stormy sea to the land of the living, for by His cross Christ has taken away our torment, and by His death has killed our death.

With the form of a serpent He kills the serpent, for the serpent made out of the rod swallowed up the other serpents. But what means the shape itself of the cross, save the four quarters of the world; the East shines from the top, the North is on the right, the South on the left, the West is firmly fixed under the feet. Wherefore the Apostle says: That we may know what is the height, and breadth, and length, and depth. Birds, when they fly in the air, take the shape of a cross; a man swimming in the waters is borne up by the form of a cross. A ship is blown along by its yards, which are in the shape of the cross. The letter Tau is written as the sign of salvation and of the cross.

BEDE; Or else, in the transverse beam of the cross, where the hands are fixed, the joy of hope is set forth; for by the hands we understand good works, by its expansion the joy of him who does them, because sadness puts us in straits. By the height to which the head is joined, we understand the expectation of reward from the lofty righteousness of God; by the length, over which the whole body is stretched, patience, wherefore patient men are called long-suffering; by the depth, which is fixed in the ground, the hidden Sacrament itself. As long therefore as our bodies work here to the destruction of the body of sin, it is the time of the cross for us.

THEOPHYL. But their casting lots for His garments was also meant as an insult, as though they were dividing the clothes of a king; for they were coarse and of no great value. And John's Gospel shows this more clearly, for the soldiers, though they divided every thing else into four parts, according to their number, cast lots for the coat, which was without seam, woven form the top throughout.

PSEUDO-JEROME; Now the garments of the Lord are His commandments, by which His body, that is, the Church, is covered, which the soldiers of the Gentiles divide amongst themselves, that there may be four classes with one faith, the married, and the widowed, those who bear rule, and those who are separate. They cast lots for the undivided garment, which is peace and unity. It goes on: And it was the third hour, and they crucified him. Mark has introduced this truly and rightly, for at the sixth hour darkness overspread the earth, so that no one could move his head.

Catena Aurea: Commentary on the Gospel of St. Mark

AUG. If Jesus was given up to the Jews' to be crucified, when Pilate sat down at his tribunal about the sixth hour, as John relates, how could He be crucified at the third hour, as many persons have thought from not understanding the words of Mark? First then let us see at what hour He might have been crucified, then we shall see why Mark said that He was crucified at the third hour. It was about the sixth hour when He was given up to be crucified by Pilate sitting on his judgment seat, as has been said, for it was not yet fully the sixth hour, but about the sixth, that is, the fifth was over, and some of the sixth had begun, so that those things which are related of the crucifixion of our Lord took place after the finishing of the fifth, and at the commencement of the sixth, until, when the sixth was completed and He was hanging on the cross, the darkness which is spoken of took place.

Let us now consider, why Mark has said, It was the third hour. He had already said positively, And when they had crucified him, they parted his garments; as also the others declare, that when He was crucified His garments were divided. Now if Mark had wished to fix the time of what was done, it would have been enough to say, And it was the third hour why did He add, and they crucified him, unless it was that he wished to point to something which had gone before, and which if inquired into would be explained, since that same Scripture was to be read at a time, when it was known to the whole Church at what hour our Lord was crucified, by which means any error might be taken away, and any falsehood be refuted. But because he knew that the Lord was fixed to the cross not by the Jews but by the soldiers, as John very plainly shows, he wished to intimate that the Jews had crucified Him, since they cried out, Crucify Him, rather than those who executed the orders of their chief according to their duty. It is therefore implied, that it took place at the third hour when the Jews cried out, Crucify Him, and it is most truly shown that they crucified Him, when they so cried out. But in the attempt of Pilate to save the Lord, and the tumultuous opposition of the Jews, we understand that a space of two hours was consumed, and that the sixth hour had begun, before the end of which, those things occurred which are related to have taken place from the time when Pilate gave up the Lord, and the darkness overspread the earth. Now he who will apply himself to these things, without the hard-heartedness of impiety, will see that Mark has fitly placed it at the third hour, in the same place as the deed of the soldiers who were the executors of it is related. Therefore lest any one should transfer in his thoughts so great a crime from the Jews to the soldiers, he says it was as the third hour, and they crucified him, that the fault might rather by a careful inquirer be charged to them, who, as he would find, had at the third hour cried out for His crucifixion, whilst at the same time it would be seen that what was done by the soldiers was done at the sixth hour.

PSEUDO-AUG. Therefore he wishes to imply that it was the Jews who passed sentence, concerning the crucifixion of Christ at the third hour; for every condemned person is considered as dead, from the moment that sentence is passed upon him. Mark therefore showed that our Savior was not crucified by the sentence of the judge, because it is difficult to prove the innocence of a man so condemned.

AUG. Still there are not wanting persons who assert that the preparation, mentioned by John, Now it was the preparation about the sixth hour, was really the third hour of the day. For they say that on the day before the sabbath day, there was a preparation of the passover of the Jews, because on that sabbath, they began the unleavened bread; but however that the true passover, which is now celebrated on the day of our Lord's Passion, that is, the Christian not the Jewish passover, began to be prepared, or to have its parasceue, from that ninth hour of the night, when His death began to be prepared by the Jews; for parasceue means preparation. Between that hour therefore of the night and His crucifixion occurs the sixth hour of preparation, according to John, and the third hour of the day, according to Mark.

What Christian would not give in to this solution of the question, provided that we could find some circumstance, from which we might gather that this preparation of our Passover, that is, of the death of Christ, began at the ninth hour of the night,? For if we say that it began when our Lord was taken by the Jews, it was still early in the night, but if when our Lord was carried away to the house of the father in law of Caiaphas, where also He was heard by the chief priests, the cock had not crowed; but if when He was given up to Pilate, it is very plain that it was morning.

It remains therefore that we must understand the preparation of our Lord's death to have commenced when all the Chief Priests pronounced, He is guilty of death. For there is nothing absurd in supposing that that was the ninth hour of the night so that we may understand that Peter's denial is put out of its order after it really happened. It goes on: And the superscription of his accusation was written over, THE KING OF THE JEWS.

THEOPHYL. They wrote this superscription, as the reason why He was crucified, thus wishing to reprove His vainglory in making Himself a king, that so the passers by might not pity Him, but rather hate Him as a tyrant.

PSEUDO-JEROME; He wrote it in three languages, in Hebrew, Melech Jeudim; in Greek, in Latin, Rex confessorum. These three languages were consecrated to be the chief, in the superscription on the cross, that every tongue might record the treachery of the Jews.

BEDE; But this superscription on the cross shows, that they could not even in killing Him take away the kingdom over them from Him who was about to render to them according to their works. There follows: And with him they crucify two thieves, the one on his right hand, the other on his left.

THEOPHYL. They did this that men might have a bad opinion of Him, as though He also were a robber and a malefactor. But it was done by Providence to fulfill the Scriptures. There follows: And the Scripture was fulfilled which said, And he was numbered with the transgressors.

PSEUDO-JEROME; Truth was numbered with the wicked; He left one on His left hand, the other He takes on the right, as He will do at the last day. With a similar crime they are allotted different paths; one precedes Peter into Paradise, the other Judas into hell. A short confession won for him a long life, and a blasphemy which soon ended is punished with endless pain.

BEDE; Mystically, however, the thieves crucified with Christ signify those, who by their faith and confession of Christ undergo either the struggle of martyrdom, or some rules of a stricter discipline. But those who do these deeds for the sake of endless glory, are signified by the faith of the right hand robber; those again who do them for worldly praise copy the mind and the acts of the left hand robber.

THEOPHYL Or else; the two robbers were meant to point out the two people, that is, the Jews and the Gentiles, for both were evil, the Gentile as transgressing natural law, but the Jew by breaking the written law, which the Lord had delivered to them; but the Gentile was penitent, the Jew a blasphemer to the end. Between whom our Lord is crucified, for He is the corner stone, which binds us together.

29. And they that passed by railed on him, wagging their heads, and saying, Ah, you that destroys the temple, and builds it in three days,

30. Save yourself, and come down from the cross.

31. Likewise also the Chief Priests mocking said among themselves with the Scribes, He saved others; himself he cannot save.

32. Let Christ, the King of Israel descend now from the cross, that we may see and believe. And they that were crucified with him reviled him.

PSEUDO-JEROME; The foal of Judah has been tied to the vine,

and his clothes dyed in the blood of the grape, and the kids tear the vine, blaspheming Christ, and wagging their heads. Wherefore it is said: And they that passed by railed on him, wagging their heads, and saying, Ah, you that destroys the temple.

THEOPHYL. For the passers by blasphemed Christ, reproaching Him as a seducer. But the devil moved them to bid Him come down from the Cross; for he knew that salvation was being won by the Cross, therefore he again proceeded to tempt Christ, so that if He came down from the Cross, he might be certain that He is not truly the Son of God, and so the salvation, which is by the Cross, might be done away. But He being truly the Son of God, did not come down; for if He ought to have come down, He would not have ascended there at all; but since He saw that in this way salvation must be effected, He underwent the crucifixion, and many other sufferings, to the finishing of His work.

It goes on: Likewise also the Chief Priests mocking said among themselves with the Scribes, He saved others, himself he cannot save. They said this, to do away with His miracles, as though those which He had done were but the semblance of them, for by working miracles He saved many.

BEDE; Thus also they confess, though against their will, that He saved many. Therefore your words condemn you, for He who saved others could have saved Himself. It goes on: Let Christ the King of Israel descend now from the cross, that we may see and believe.

PSEUDO-JEROME; Afterwards they saw Him arise from the grave, though they would not believe that He could come down from the tree of the Cross. Where, O Jews, is your lack of faith? Your own selves I appeal to; your own selves I bring as judges. How much more wonderful is it that a dead man should arise, than that one yet living should choose to come down from the cross. you asked but small things, till greater should have come to pass; but your want of faith could not be healed by signs much greater than those for which you sought. Here all have gone out of the way, all are become abominable. Wherefore it goes on: And they that were crucified with him reviled.

AUG. How can this be, when according to Luke one only reviled Him, but was rebuked by the other who believed on God; unless we understand that Matthew and Mark, who touched but slightly on this place, put the plural for the singular number?

THEOPHYL. Or else, both at first reviled Him, then one recognizing Him as innocent, rebukes the other for blaspheming Him.

33. And when the sixth hour was come, there was darkness over the whole land until the ninth hour.

34. And at the ninth hour Jesus cried with a loud voice, saying, Eloi, Eloi, lame sabachthani? which is, being interpreted, My God, my God, why have you forsaken me?

35. And some of them that stood by, when they heard it, said, Behold, he calls Elias.

36. And one ran and filled a sponge full of vinegar, and put it on a reed, and gave him to drink, saying, Let alone; let us see whether Elias will come to take him down.

37. And Jesus cried with a loud voice, and gave up the ghost.

BEDE; This most glorious light took away its rays from the world, lest it should see the Lord hanging, and lest the blasphemers should have the benefit of its light. Wherefore it goes on: And when the sixth hour was come, there was darkness over the whole land until the ninth hour.

AUG. Luke added to this account the cause of the darkness, that is, the darkening of the sun.

THEOPHYL. If this had been the time for an eclipse, some one might have said that this that happened was natural, but it was the fourteenth moon, when no eclipse can take place. There follows: And at the ninth hour Jesus cried with a loud voice, saying, Eloi, Eloi, lama sabachthani.

PSEUDO-JEROME; At the ninth hour, the tenth piece of money which had been lost is found, by the overturning of the house.

BEDE; For when Adam sinned, it is also written that he heard the voice of the Lord, walking in paradise, in the cool after midday; and in that hour when the first Adam by sinning brought death into the world, in that same hour the second Adam by dying destroyed death. And we must observe, that our Lord was crucified, when the sun was going away from the center of the world; but at sunrise He celebrated the mysteries of His resurrection; because He died for our sins, but rose again for our justification. Nor need you wonder at the lowliness of His words, at the complaints as of one forsakes, when you look on the offense of the cross, knowing the form of a servant. For as hunger, and thirst, and fatigue were not things proper to the Divinity, but bodily affections; so His saying, Why have you forsaken me? was proper to a bodily voice, for the body is never naturally wont to wish to be separated from the life which is joined to it. For although our Savior Himself said this, He really showed the weakness of His body; He spoke therefore as man, bearing about with Him my feelings, for when placed in danger we fancy that we are deserted by God.

THEOPHYL. Or, He speaks this as man crucified by God for me, for we men have been forsaken by the Father, but He never has. For hear what He says; I am not alone, because the Father is with me. Though He may also have said this as being a Jew, according to the flesh, as though He had said, Why have you forsaken the Jewish people, so that they have crucified Your Son? For as we sometimes say, God has put on me, that is, my human nature, so here also we must understand you have forsaken me, to mean my nature, or the Jewish people.

It goes on: And some of them that stood by, when they heard it, said, Behold, he called Elias.

BEDE; These however I suppose were Roman soldiers who did not understand the peculiarity of the Hebrew tongue, but, from His calling Eloi, thought that Elias was called by Him. But if the Jews are understood to have said this, they must be supposed to do this, as accusing Him of folly in calling for the aid of Elias.

It goes on: And one ran and filled a sponge full of vinegar, and put it on a reed: and gave him to drink saying, let alone: let us see whether Elias will come to take him down. John shows more fully the reason why the vinegar was given to the Lord to drink, saying, that Jesus said, I thirst, that the Scriptures might be fulfilled. They however applied a sponge full of vinegar to His mouth.

PSEUDO-JEROME; Here he points out a similitude for the Jews; a sponge on a reed, weak, dry, fit for burning; they fill it with vinegar, that is, with wickedness and guile.

AUG. Matthew has not related, that the man who brought the sponge filled with vinegar, but that the others spoke about Elias; from whence we gather that both said it.

PSEUDO-JEROME; Though the flesh was weak, yet the heavenly voice, which said, Open me the gates of righteousness, waxed strong. Wherefore there follows: And Jesus cried with a loud voice, and gave up the ghost. We who are of the earth die with a very low voice, or with no voice at all; but He who descended from heaven breathed His last with a loud voice.

THEOPHYL. He who both rules over death and commands it dies with power, as its Lord. But what this voice was is declared by Luke: Father, into your hands I commend my spirit. For Christ would have us understand by this, that from that time the souls of the saints go up into the hands of God. For at first the souls of all were held in hell, till He came, who preached the opening of the prison to the captives.

38. And the veil of the temple was rent in two from the top to the bottom.

39. And when the centurion, which stood over against him, saw that he so cried out, and gave up the ghost, he said, Truly this man was the Son of God.

40. There were also women looking on afar off among whom was Mary Magdalene, and Mary the mother of James the less and of Joses, and Salome;

41. (Who also, when he was in Galilee, followed him, and ministered to him;) and many other women which came up with him to Jerusalem.

GLOSS. After the Evangelist has related the Passion and the death of Christ, he now goes on to mention those things which followed after the death of our Lord. Wherefore it is said: And the veil of the temple was rent in two from the top to the bottom.

PSEUDO-JEROME; The veil of the temple is rent, that is, the heaven is opened.

THEOPHYL. Again, God by the rending of the veil implied that the grace of the Holy Spirit goes away and is rent from the temple, so that the Holy of Holies might be seen by all; also that the temple will mourn amongst the Jews, when they shall deplore their calamities, and rend their clothes. This also is a figure of the living temple, that is, the body of Christ, in whose Passion His garment is torn, that is, His flesh. Again, it means another thing; for the flesh is the veil of our temple, that is, of our mind. But the power of the flesh is torn in the Passion of Christ, from the top to the bottom, that is, from Adam even down to the latest man; for also Adam was made whole by the Passion of Christ, and his flesh does not remain under the curse, nor does it deserve corruption, but we all are gifted with incorruption.

And when the centurion who stood, over against him saw. He who commands a hundred soldiers is called a centurion. But seeing that He died with such power as the Lord, he wondered and confessed.

BEDE; Now the cause of the centurion's wonder is clear, that seeing that the Lord died in that way, that is, sent forth His spirit, he said, Truly this man was the Son of God. For no one can send forth his own spirit, but He who is the Creator of souls.

AUG. This also he most of all wondered at, that after that voice which He sent forth as a figure of our sin, He immediately gave up His spirit. For the spirit of the Mediator showed that no penalty of sin could have had power to cause the death of His flesh; for it did not leave the flesh unwillingly, but as it willed, for it was joined to the Word of God in the unity of person.

PSEUDO-JEROME; But the last are now made the first. The Gentile people confesses. The blinded Jew denies, so that their error is worse than the first.

THEOPHYL. And so the order is inverted, for the Jew kills, and the Gentile confesses; the disciples fly, and the women remain. For there follows: There were also women looking on afar off, amongst whom was Mary Magdalene, and Mary the mother of James the less and of Joses, and Salome.

ORIGEN; But it seems to me, that here three women are chiefly named, by Matthew and Mark. Two indeed are set down by each Evangelist, Mary Magdalene, and Mary the mother of James; the third is called by Matthew, the mother of the sons of Zebedee, but by Mark she is called Salome.

BEDE; He means by James the Less, the son of Alphaeus, who was also called the brother of our Lord, because he was the son of Mary, our Lord's mother's sister, whom John mentions, saying, Now there stood by the cross of Jesus his mother and his mother's sister, Mary of Cleophas, and Mary Magdalene. And he seems to call her Mary of Cleophas, from her father or some relation. But he was called James the Less, to distinguish him from James the Great, that is, the son of Zebedee, who was called amongst the first of the Apostles by our Lord. Further, it was a Jewish custom, nor was it thought blamable after the manners of an ancient people, that women should furnish to teachers food and clothing out of their substance. Wherefore there follows: Who also when he was in Galilee followed him, and ministered to him. They ministered to the Lord of their substance, that He might reap their carnal things whose spiritual things they reaped, and that He might show forth a type for all masters, who ought to be content with food and clothing from their disciples. But let us see what companions He had with Him, for it goes on: And many other women which came up with him into Jerusalem.

PSEUDO-JEROME; As the female sex through the virgin Mary is not shut out from salvation, so it is not thrust away from the knowledge of the mystery of the cross, and of the resurrection, through the widow Mary Magdalene, and the ethers, who were mothers.

42. And now when the even was come, because it was the preparation, that is, the day before the sabbath,

43. Joseph of Arimathea, an honorable counselor, which also waited for the kingdom of God, came, and went in boldly to Pilate, and craved the body of Jesus.

44. And Pilate marveled if he were already dead: and calling to him the centurion, he asked him whether he had been any while dead.

45. And when he knew it of the centurion, he gave the body to Joseph.

46. And he bought fine linen, and took him down, and wrapped him in the linen, and laid him in a sepulcher which was hewn out of a rock, and rolled a stone to the door of the sepulcher.

47. And Mary Magdalene and Mary the mother of Joses beheld where he was laid.

GLOSS. After the passion and death of Christ, the Evangelist relates His burial, saying, And now when the even was come, because it was the preparation, that is, the day before the sabbath, Joseph of Arimathaea.

BEDE; What is called, parasceue in Greek, is in Latin praeparatio; by which name those Jews, who lived amongst Greeks, used to call the sixth day of the week, because on that day they used to prepare what was necessary for the rest of the sabbath day. Because then man was made on the sixth day, but on the seventh the Creator rested from all His work, fitly was our Savior crucified on the sixth day, and thus fulfilled the mystery of man's restoration. But on the sabbath, resting in the tomb, He was waiting for the event of the resurrection, which was to come on the eighth day. So we must also in this age of time be crucified to the world; but in the seventh day, that is, when a man has paid the debt to death, our bodies indeed must rest in the grave, but our souls after good works in hidden peace with God; till in the eighth period, even our bodies themselves, glorified in the resurrection, receive incorruption together with our souls.

But the man who buried the body of the Lord must needs by his righteous merits have been worthy, and by the nobility of worldly power able to perform this service. Therefore it is said, An honorable counselor, which also waited for the kingdom of God. He is called in Latin, decurio, because he is of the order of the curia, and served the office of a provincial magistracy; this officer was also called curialis, from his care of civic duties. Arimathaea is the same as Ramathain, the city of Elkanah and Samuel.

PSEUDO-JEROME; It is interpreted, taking down, of which was Joseph, who came to take down the body of Christ from the cross. There follows: Came and went in boldly to Pilate, and craved the body of Jesus.

THEOPHYL. He was bold with a praiseworthy boldness; for he did not consider within himself, I shall fall from my rich estate, and I shall be expelled by the Jews, if I beg for the body of Him, who was condemned as a blasphemer. It goes on: And Pilate marveled if he were already dead. For he thought that He should continue long alive upon the cross, as also the thieves used to live long, upon the instrument of their execution. It goes on: And calling to him the centurion, he asked him if he had been any while dead; that is, before the time when other executed persons usually died.

There follows: And when he knew it of the centurion, (that is, that He was dead,) he gave the body to Joseph.

BEDE; But it was not an obscure person, nor a man of mean rank, who could come to the governor and obtain the body. There follows: And he bought fine linen, and took him down, and wrapped him in the linen.

THEOPHYL. Burying the precious body preciously; for being a disciple of our Lord, he knew how greatly the Lord's body ought to be honored.

BEDE; By this however, according to a spiritual meaning, we may understand that the body of the Lord should not be wrapped in gold or gems, or silk, but in a clean linen cloth. Hence it became a custom in the Church that the sacrifice of the altar should not be celebrated in silk, or in a dyed cloth, but in linen produced from the earth just as the body of the Lord was wrapped in clean linen; as, we read in the Pontifical acts, it was ordered by the blessed Sylvester. Though it has also another meaning, that he who receives Jesus in a pure mind wraps Him in clean linen. There follows: And laid him in a sepulcher which was hewn out of a rock, and rolled a stone to the door of the sepulcher. It is said that the sepulcher of the Lord is a round cell, hewn out of the rock which was around it, so high, that a man standing upright could scarcely touch the roof with his outstretched hand; and it has an entrance to the east, to which the great stone was rolled, and placed upon it. In the northern part of it is the tomb itself, that is, the place where our Lord's body lay, made of the same rock, seven feet in length, raised three palms higher than the floor. It is not open from above, but on the south side, the whole of which is open, and through which the body was brought in. The color of the sepulcher and of the recess is said to be a mixed white and red.

PSEUDO-JEROME; By the burial of Christ we rise again, by His going down into hell we mount up into heaven; here is found the honey in the mouth of the dead lion.

THEOPHYL. Let us too imitate Joseph, taking to ourselves the body of Christ by Unity, and let us place it in a sepulcher, hewn out of the rock, that is, in a soul recollected, never forgetful of God; for this is a soul hewn out of the rock, that is, out of Christ, for He is our rock, who holds together our strength. We ought also to wrap Him in linen, that is, to receive Him in a pure body; for the linen is the body which is the clothing of the soul. We must, however, not throw open, but wrap Him up; for He is secret, closed and hidden.

There follows: And Mary Magadalene and Mary the mother of Joses beheld where he was laid.

BEDE; We read in Luke, that His acquaintances and the women who had followed Him stood afar off. When these then who were known to Jesus returned home after the burial of His body, the women alone, who were bound to Him with a closer love, after following the funeral, took care to see how He was laid, that they might be able at a fitting season to offer Him the sacrifice of their devotion. But on the day of the parasceue, that is, of the preparation, the holy women, that is, humble souls, do the same, when they burn with love for the Savior, and diligently follow the steps of His Passion in this life, where their future rest is to be prepared; and they weigh with a pious minuteness the order in which His passion was accomplished, if perchance they be able to imitate it.

PSEUDO-JEROME; These things also fit the Jewish people, which finally is believing, which is ennobled by faith to become the child of Abraham. It lays aside its despair, it waits for the kingdom of God, it goes in to the Christians, that it may be baptized; which is implied by the name of Pilate, which is interpreted, 'One who works with a hammer,' that is, he who subdues the iron nations, that he may rule them with a rod of iron. It seeks for the sacrifice, that is, the viaticum, which is given to penitents at their last end, and wraps it up in a heart clean and dead to sin; it makes it firm in the safeguard of faith, and shuts it up with the covering of hope, through works of charity; (for the end of the commandment is charity;) whilst the elect, who are the stars of the sea, are looking on from afar, for, if it be possible, the very elect shall be offended.

Mark 16

1. And when the sabbath was past, Mary Magdalene, and Mary the mother of James, and Salome, had bought sweet spices, that they might come and anoint him.

2. And very early in the morning the first day of the week, they came to the sepulcher at the rising of the sun.

3. And they said among themselves, Who shall roll us away the stone from the door of the sepulcher?

4. And when they looked, they saw that the stone was rolled away: for it was very great.

5. And entering into the sepulcher, they saw a young man sitting on the right side, clothed in a long white garment; and they were affrighted.

6. And he said to them, Be not affrighted: You seek Jesus of Nazareth, which was crucified: he is risen; he is not here: behold the place where they laid him.

7. But go your way, tell his disciples and Peter that he goes before you into Galilee: there shall you see him, as he said to you.

8. And they went out quickly, and fled from the sepulcher; for they trembled and were amazed: neither said they any thing to any man; for they were afraid.

PSEUDO-JEROME; After the sadness of the sabbath, a happy day dawns upon them, which holds the chief place amongst days, for in it the chief light shines forth, and the Lord rises in triumph. Wherefore it is said, And when the sabbath was past, Mary Magdalene, and Mary the mother of James and Salome, had bought sweet spices.

GLOSS. For these religious women after the burial of the Lord, as long as it was lawful to work, that is, up to sunset, prepared ointment, as Luke says. And because they could not finish their work from the shortness of the time, when the sabbath was over, that is, at sunset, as soon as the time for working came round again, they hastened to buy spices, as Mark says, that they might go in the morning to anoint the body of Jesus. Neither could they come to the sepulcher on the evening of the sabbath, for night prevented them.

Wherefore it goes on: And very early in the morning the first day of the week, they came to the sepulcher at the rising of the sun.

SEVER; The women in this place run abroad with womanly devotion, for they do not bring Him faith as though He were alive, but ointments as to one dead; and they prepare the service of their grief for Him as buried, not the joys of heavenly triumph for Him as risen.

THEOPHYL. For they do not understand the greatness and dignity of the wisdom of Christ. But they came according to the custom of the Jews to anoint the body of Christ, that it might remain sweat-smelling, and might not burst forth into moisture, for spices have the property of drying up, and absorb the moisture of the body, so that they keep the body from corruption.

GREG. But if we believe on Him who is dead, and are filled with the sweet smell of virtue, and seek the Lord with the fame of good works, we come to His sepulcher with spices. There follows: And very early in the morning the first day of the week, they came to the sepulcher at the rising of the sun.

AUG. What Luke expresses by very early in the morning, and John by early when it was yet dark, Mark must be understood to mean, when he says, very early in the morning, at the rising of the sun, that is, when the sky was growing bright in the east, as is usual in places near the rising sun; for this is the light which we call the dawning. Therefore there is no discrepancy with the report which says, while it was yet dark. For when the day is dawning, the remains of darkness lessen in proportion as the light grows brighter; and we must not take the words very early in the morning, at the rising of the surf, to mean that the sun himself was seen upon the earth, but as expressing the near approach of the sun into those parts, that is, when his rising begins to light up the sky.

PSEUDO-JEROME; By very early in the morning, he means what another Evangelist expresses by at the dawning. But the dawn is the time between the darkness of night, and the brightness of day, in which the salvation of man is coming forth with a happy closeness, to be declared in the Church, just as the sun, when he is rising and the light is near, sends before him the rosy dawn, that with prepared eyes she may bear to see the graciousness of his glorious brightness, when the time of our

Lord's resurrection has dawned; that then the whole Church, after the example of the women, may sing the praises of Christ, since He has quickened the race of man after the pattern of His resurrection, since He has given life, and has poured upon them the light of belief.

BEDE; As then the women show the great fervency of their love, by coming very early in the morning to the sepulcher, as the history relates, according to the mystical sense an example is given to us, that with a shining face, and shaking off the darkness of wickedness, we may be careful to offer the fragrance of good works and the sweetness of prayer to the Lord.

THEOPHYL. He says, On the first of the sabbaths, that is, on the first of the days of the week. For the days of the week are called sabbaths, and by the word 'una' is meant 'prima.'

BEDE; Or else, by this phrase is meant the first day from the day of sabbaths, or rests, which were kept on the sabbath. There follows: And they said among themselves, Who shall roll us away the stone from the door of the sepulcher?

SEVER. Your breast was darkened, your eyes shut, and therefore you did not before see the glory of the opened sepulcher. It goes on: And they looked, and saw that the stone was rolled away.

BEDE; Matthew shows clearly enough, that the stone was rolled away by an Angel. This rolling away of the stone means mystically the opening of the Christian sacraments, which were held under the veil of the letter of the law; for the law was written on stone. It goes on: For it was very great.

SEVER. Great indeed by its office rather than its size, for it can shut in and throw open the body of the Lord.

GREG. But the women who came with spices see the Angels; because those minds who come to the Lord with their virtues, through holy desires, see the heavenly citizens. Wherefore it goes on: And entering into the sepulcher, they saw a young man sitting on the right side, clothed in a long white garment; and they were affrighted.

THEOPHYL. Though Matthew says that the Angel was sitting on the stone, whilst Mark relates that the women entering into the sepulcher saw a young man sitting, yet we need not wonder, for they afterwards saw sitting within the sepulcher the same Angel as sat without on the stone.

AUG. Either let us suppose that Matthew was silent about that Angel, whom they saw on entering, whilst Mark said nothing of him, whom they saw outside sitting on the stone, so that they saw two and heard severally from two, the things which the Angels said concerning Jesus; or we must understand by entering into the sepulcher, their coming within some enclosure, by which it is probable that the place was surrounded a little space before the stone, by the cutting out of which the burial place had been made, so that they saw sitting on the right hand in that space him whom Matthew designates as sitting on the stone.

THEOPHYL. But some say the women mentioned by Matthew were different from those in Mark. But Mary Magdalene was with all parties, from her burning zeal and ardent love.

SEVER. The women, then, entered the sepulcher, that being buried with Christ, they might rise again for from the tomb with Christ. They see the young man, that is, they see the time of the Resurrection, for the Resurrection has no old age, and the period, in which man knows neither birth nor death, admits of no decay, and requires no increase. Wherefore what they saw was a young man, not an old man, nor an infant, but the age of joy.

BEDE; Now they saw a young man sitting on the right side, that is, on the south part of the place where the body was laid. For the body, which was lying on its back, and had its head to the west, must have had its right to the south.

GREG. But what is meant by the left hand, but this present life, and what by the right, but ever lasting life? Because then our Redeemer had already gone through the decay of this present life, fitly did the Angel, who had come to announce His everlasting life, sit on the right hand.

SEVER. Again, they saw a young man sitting on the right, because the Resurrection has nothing sinister in it. They also see him dressed in a long white robe; that robe is not from mortal fleece, but of living virtue, blazing with heavenly light, not of an earthly dye, as said the Prophet, You deck yourself with light as with a garment; and of the just it is said, Then shall the righteous shine forth as the sun.

GREG. Or else, he appeared covered with a white robe, because he announced the joys of our festivity, for the whiteness of the robe shows the splendor of our solemnity.

PSEUDO-JEROME; The white robe is also true joy, now that the enemy is driven away, the kingdom won, the King of Peace sought for and found and never let go by us. This young man then shows an image of the Resurrection to them who feared death. But their being frightened shows that eye has not seen, nor ear heard, neither have entered into the heart of man to conceive the things which God has prepared for them that love Him. There follows, And he said to them, Be not affrighted.

GREG. As though he had said, Let them fear, who love not the coming of the inhabitants of heaven; let them fear, who, weighed down with carnal desires, despair that they can ever attain to their company; but why should you fear, you who see your own fellow citizens.

PSEUDO-JEROME; For there is no fear in love. Why should they fear, who had found Him whom they sought?

GREG. But let us hear what the Angel adds; You seek Jesus of Nazareth. Jesus means the Savior, but at that time there may have been many a Jesus, not indeed really, but in name, therefore the place Nazareth is added, that it might be evident of what Jesus it was spoken. And immediately he subjoins the reason, Which was crucified.

THEOPHYL. For he does not blush at the Cross, for in it is the salvation of men, and the beginning of the Blessed.

PSEUDO-JEROME; But the bitter root of the Cross has disappeared. The flower of life has burst forth with its fruits, that is, He who lay in death has risen in glory. Wherefore he adds, He is risen; he is not here.

GREG. He is not here, is spoken of His carnal presence, for He was not absent from any place as to the presence of His majesty.

THEOPHYL. As if he had said, Do you wish to be certain of His resurrection, he adds, Behold the place where they laid him. This too was the reason why he had rolled away the stone, that he might show them the place.

PSEUDO-JEROME; But immortality is shown to mortals as due to thankfulness, that we may understand what we were, and that we may know what we are to be. There follows, But go your way tell his disciples and Peter that he goes before you into Galilee. The women are ordered to tell the Apostles, that as by a woman death was announced, so also might life rising again. But He says specially to Peter, because he had shown himself unworthy of being a disciple, since he had thrice denied his Master; but past sins cease to hurt us when they cease to be pleasing to us.

GREG. If again the Angel had not expressly named him who had denied his Master, he would not have dared to come amongst the disciples; he is therefore called by name, lest he should despair on account of his denial.

AUG. By saying, He will go before you into Galilee, there shall you see him, as he said to you, he seems to imply, that Jesus would not show Himself to His disciples after His resurrection except in Galilee, which showing, of Himself Mark himself has not mentioned. For that which He has related, Early the first day of the week he appeared to Mary Magdalene, and after that to two of them as they walked and went into the country, we know took place in Jerusalem, on the very day of the resurrection; then he comes to His last manifestation, which we know was on the Mount of Olives, not far from Jerusalem. Mark therefore never relates the fulfillment of that which was foretold by the Angel; but Matthew does not mention any place at all, where the disciples saw the Lord after He arose, except Galilee, according to the Angel's prophecy. But since it is not set down when this happened, whether first, before He was seen any where else, and since the very place where Matthew says that He went into Galilee to the mountain, does not explain the day, or the order of the narration, Matthew does not oppose the account of the others, but assists in explaining and receiving them. But nevertheless since the Lord was not first to show Himself there, but sent word that He was to be seen in Galilee, where He was seen subsequently, it makes every faithful Christian on the look out, to find out in what mysterious sense it may be understood.

GREG. For Galilee means 'a passing over'; for our Redeemer had already passed from His Passion to His resurrection, from death to life, and we shall have joy in seeing the glory of His resurrection, if only we pass over from vice to the heights of virtue. He then who is announced at the tomb, is shown in 'passing over,' because He who is first known in mortification of the flesh, is seen in this passing over of the soul.

PSEUDO-JEROME; This sentence is but short in the number of syllables, but the promise is vast in its greatness. Here is the fountain of our joy, and the source of everlasting life is prepared. Here all that are scattered are brought together, and the contrite hearts are healed. There, he says, you shall see Him, but not as you have seen Him.

AUG. It is also signified that the grace of Christ is about to pass over from the people of Israel to the Gentiles, by whom the Apostles would never have been received when they preached, if the Lord had not gone before them and prepared a way in their hearts; and this is what is meant by, He goes before you into Galilee, there shall you see him, that is, there shall you find His members.

There follows: And they went out quickly, and fled from the sepulcher, for they trembled and were amazed.

THEOPHYL. That is, they trembled because of the vision of Angels, and were amazed because of the resurrection.

SEVER. The Angel indeed sits on the sepulcher, the women fly from it; he, on account of his heavenly substance, is confident, they are troubled because of their earthly frame. He who cannot die, cannot fear the tomb, but the women both fear from what was then done, and still, as being mortals, fear the sepulcher as mortals are wont.

PSEUDO-JEROME; This also is spoken of the life to come, in which grief and groaning will flee away. For the women prefigure before the resurrection all that is to happen to them after the resurrection, namely, they flee away from death and fear. There follows, Neither said they any thing to any man, for they were afraid.

THEOPHYL. Either on account of the Jews, or else they said nothing because the fear of the vision prevented them.

AUG. We may however inquire how Mark can say this, when Matthew says, they departed quickly from the sepulcher with fear and great joy, and did run to bring his disciples word, unless we understand it to mean, that they did not dare to say a word to any of the Angels themselves, that is, to answer the words which they had spoken to them; or else to the guards whom they saw lying there; for that joy of which Matthew speaks is not inconsistent with the fear which Mark mentions. For we ought to have understood that both feelings were in their minds, even though Matthew had not mentioned the fear. But since he has also said that they came out with fear and great joy, he does not allow room for any question to be raised.

SEVER. It is said also in a marked manner, that they up said nothing to any one, because it is the part of women to hear, and not to speak, to learn, not to teach.

9. Now when Jesus was risen early the first day of the week, he appeared first to Mary Magdalene, out of whom he had cast seven devils.

10. And she went and told them that she had been with him, as they mourned and wept.

11. And they, when they had heard that he was alive, and had been seen of her, believed not.

12. After that he appeared in another form to two of them, as

they walked, and went into the country.

13. And they went and told it to the residue: neither believed they them.

AUG. Now we must consider how the Lord appeared after the resurrection. For Mark says, Now when Jesus was risen early the first day of the week, he appeared first to Mary Magdalene, out of whom he had cast seven devils.

BEDE; John tells us most fully how and when this appearance took place. But the Lord rose in the morning from the sepulcher in which He had been laid in the evening, that those words of the Psalm might be fulfilled, Heaviness may endure for a night, but joy comes in the morning.

THEOPHYL. Or else put a stop at, Now when Jesus was risen, and then read, early the first day of the week he appeared, &c.

GREG. For as Samson at midnight not only left Gaza, but also carried away the gates of it, so also our Redeemer rising, before the light, did not only come out free from hell, but destroyed also the very gates of hell. But Mark here testifies that seven devils were cast out of Mary; and what is meant by seven devils save all vices? for as by seven days is understood all time, so by the number seven a whole is fitly figured.

THEOPHYL. But Mary had seven devils, because she was filled with do all vices. Or else, by seven devils are meant seven spirits contrary to the seven virtues, as a spirit without fear, without wisdom, without understanding, and whatsoever else is opposed to the gifts of the Holy Ghost.

PSEUDO-JEROME; Again, He is shown to her, out of whom He had cast seven devils, because harlots and publicans shall go before the synagogue into the kingdom of heaven, as the thief reached it before the Apostles.

BEDE; In the beginning also woman brought man into sin, now she, who first tasted death, first sees the resurrection, lest she should have to bear the reproach of perpetual guilt amongst men; and she who had been the channel of guilt to man, now has become the first channel of grace. For it goes on: And she went and told them that had been with him as they mourned and wept.

PSEUDO-JEROME; They mourn and weep because they had not yet seen, but after a short time they shall receive a consolation. For blessed are they that weep now, for they shall be comforted.

BEDE; Fitly too is this woman, who was Be the first to announce the joy of our Lord's resurrection, said to have been cured of seven devils, lest any one worthily repenting of his sins should despair of pardon for what he had done, and that it might be shown that where sin abounded, grace did much more abound.

SEVER. Mary brings the news, not now as a woman, but in the person of the Church so that, as above woman was silent, here as the Church she might bring tidings and spear:. There follows, And they when they heard that he was alive and had been seen by her, believed not.

GREG. That the disciples were slow in believing our Lord's

resurrection was not so much a weakness of theirs as it our strength. For the resurrection itself through their doubts was manifested by many proofs; and whilst we read and acknowledge them, what do we but become firmer through their doubting? There follows, After this he appeared in another form to two of them as they walked and went to a farm house.

AUG. Luke relates the whole story respecting these two, one of whom was Cleophas, but Mark here touches but slightly upon it. That village of which Luke speaks may without absurdity be supposed to be what is here called a farm house, and indeed in some Greek manuscripts it is called the country. But by this name are understood not only villages, but also boroughs and country towns, because they are without the city, which is the head and mother of all the rest. That which Mark expresses by the Lord's appearance in another form, is what Luke means by saying that their eyes were holden that they could not know him. For something was upon their eyes, which was allowed to remain there, until the breaking of bread.

SEVER. But let no one suppose that Christ changed the form of His face by His resurrection, but the form is changed when of mortal it becomes immortal, so that this means that He gained a glorious countenance, not that He lost the substance of His countenance. But He was seen of two; because faith in the resurrection is to be preached and shown to two people, that is, the Gentiles and the Jews.

There follows, And they went and told it to the residue, neither believed they them. How are we to understand the words of Mark compared with the account of Luke, that they then said,

The Lord has risen indeed and has appeared to Simon, if we do not suppose that there were some there who would not believe?

THEOPHYL. For he does not say this of the eleven, but of some others, whom He calls the residue.

PSEUDO-JEROME; But in a mystic sense we may understand that faith here labors, leading the active life, but there it reigns secure in the contemplative vision. Here we see His face through a glass, there we shall see the truth face to face, wherefore He was shown to them as they were walking, that is, laboring, in another form. And when it was told, the disciples did not believe, because they saw, like Moses, that which was not enough for them, for he said, Show me yourself; forgetting his flesh, he prays in this life for that which w e hope for in the life to come.

14. Afterward he appeared to the eleven as they sat at meat, and upbraided them with their unbelief and hardness of heart, because they believed not them which had seen him after he was risen.

15. And he said to them, Go you into all the world, and preach the Gospel to every creature.

16. He that believes and is baptized shall be saved; but he that believed not shall be damned.

17. And these signs shall follow them that believe; In my name shall they cast out devils; they shall speak with new tongues;

18. They shall take up serpents; and if they drink any deadly

thing, it shall not hurt them; they shall lay hands on the sick, and they shall recover.

GLOSS. Mark, when about to finish his Gospel, relates the last appearance of our Lord to His disciples after His resurrection, saying, For the last time he appeared to the eleven as they sat at meat.

GREG. We should observe that Luke says in the Acts, As he was eating with them he commanded , that they should not depart from Jerusalem, and shortly afterwards, while they beheld he was taken up. For He ate, and then ascended, that by the act of eating, the truth of the flesh might be declared; wherefore it is also here said, that he appeared to them for the last time as they sat at meat.

PSEUDO-JEROME; But He appeared when all the eleven were together, that all might be witnesses, and relate to all men what they had seen and heard in common. It goes on: And upbraided them with their unbelief and hardness of heart, because they believed not them who had seen him after his resurrection.

AUG. But how was this done the last time? The last occasion on which the Apostles saw the Lord upon earth happened forty days after the resurrection; but would He then have upbraided them for not believing those who had seen Him risen, when they themselves had so often seen Him after His resurrection? It remains therefore that we should understand that Mark wished to say it in few words, and said for the last time, because it was the last time that He showed Himself that day, as night was coming on, when the disciples returned from the country into Jerusalem, and found, as Luke says, the eleven and those who were with them, speaking together concerning the resurrection of our Lord.

But there were some there who did not believe; when these then were sitting at meat, (as Mark says,) and were still speaking, (as Luke relates,) The Lord stood in the midst of them, and said to them, Peace be to you; as Luke and John say. The rebuke therefore which Mark here mentions, must have been amongst those words, which Luke and John say, that the Lord at that time spoke to the disciples. But another question is raised, how Mark says that He appeared when the eleven sat at meat, if the time was the first part of the night on the Lord's day, when John plainly says that Thomas was not with them, who, we believe, had gone out, before the Lord came in to them, after those two had returned from the village, and spoken with the eleven, as we find in Luke's Gospel.

But Luke in his relation leaves room for supposing that Thomas went out first, while they spoke these things, and that the Lord entered afterwards; Mark however from his saying, for the last time he appeared to the eleven as they sat at meat, forces us to believe that he was there, unless indeed, though one of them was absent he chose to call them the eleven, because the company of the Apostles was then called by this number, before Matthias was chosen into the place of Judas. Or if this be a harsh way of understanding it, let us understand that it means that after many appearances, He showed Himself for the last time, that is, on the fortieth clay, to the Apostles, as they sat at meat, and that since He was about to ascend from them, He rather wished on that day to reprove them for not having believed those who had seen Him risen before seeing Him themselves, because after His ascension even the Gentiles on their preaching were to believe a Gospel, which they had not seen.

And so the same Mark immediately after that rebuke says, And he said to them, Go you into all the world, and preach the Gospel to every creature. And lower down, He that believes not shall be condemned. Since then they were to preach this, were not they themselves to be first rebuked, because before they saw the Lord they had not believed those to who He had first appeared?

GREG. Another reason also why our Lord rebuked His disciples, when He left them as to His bodily presence, was, that the words which He spoke on leaving them might remain more deeply impressed, upon the hearts of His hearers.

PSEUDO-JEROME; But He rebukes their want of faith, that faith might take its place; He rebukes the hardness of their stony heart, that the fleshy heart, full of love, might take its place.

GREG. After rebuking the hardness of their hearts, let us hear the words of advice which He speaks. For it goes on: Go you into all the world, and preach the Gospel to every creature. Every man must be understood by every creature; for man partakes something of every creature; he has existence as have stones, life as trees, feeling as animals, understanding as have Angels. For the Gospel is preached to every creature, because he is taught by it, for whose sake all are created, whom all things are in some way like, and from whom therefore they are not alien. By the name of every creature also every nation of the Gentiles may be meant. For it had been said before, Go not into the way of the Gentiles. But now it is said, Preach the Gospel to every creature, so that the preaching of the Apostles which was thrust aside by Judea, might be an assistance to us, since Judea, had haughtily rejected it, thus witnessing to her own damnation.

THEOPHYL. Or else; to every creature, that is, whether believing or unbelieving. It goes on: He that believes and is baptized shall be saved. For it is not enough to believe, for he who believes and is not baptized, but is a catechumen, has not yet attained to perfect salvation.

GREG. But perhaps some one may say in himself, I have already believed, I shall be saved. He says what is true, if he keeps his faith by works; for that is a true faith, which does not contradict by its deeds what it says in words. There follows: But he that believes not shall be damned.

BEDE; What shall we say here about infants, who by reason of their age cannot yet believe; for as to older persons there is no question. In the Church then of our Savior children believe by others, as also they drew from others the sins which are remitted to them in baptism. It goes on: And these signs shall follow them that believe; In my name shall they cast out devils; they shall speak with new tongues; they shall take up serpents.

THEOPHYL. That is, they shall scatter before them serpents, whether intellectual or sensible, as it is said, you shall tread upon serpents and scorpions, which is understood spiritually. But it may also mean sensible serpents, as when Paul received no hurt from the viper. There follows: And if they drink any deadly thing, it shall not hurt them. We read of many such cases in history, for many persons have drank poison unhurt, by guarding themselves with the sign of Christ. It goes on: They shall lay hands on the sick, and they shall recover.

GREG. Are we then without faith because we cannot do these signs? Nay, but these things were necessary in the beginning of the Church, for the faith of believers was to be nourished by miracles, that it might increase. Thus we also, when we plant groves, pour water upon them, until we see that they have grown strong in the earth; but when once they have firmly fixed their roots, we leave off irrigating them. These signs and miracles have other things which we ought to consider more minutely.

For Holy Church does every day in spirit what then the Apostles did in body; for when her Priests by the grace of exorcism lay their hands on believers, and forbid the evil spirits to dwell in their minds, what do they, but cast out devils? And the faithful who have left earthly words, and whose tongues sound forth the Holy Mysteries, speak a new language; they who by their good warnings take away evil from the hearts of others, take up serpents; and when they are hearing words of pestilent persuasion, without being at all drawn aside to evil doing, they drink a deadly thing, but it will never hurt them; whenever they see their neighbors growing weak in good works, and by their good example strengthen their life, they lay their hands on the sick, that they may recover. And all these miracles are greater in proportion as they are spiritual, and by them souls and not bodies are raised.

19. So then after the Lord had spoken to them, he was received up into heaven, and sat on the right hand of God.

20. And they went forth, and preached every where, the Lord working with them, and confirming the word with signs following. Amen.

PSEUDO-JEROME; The Lord Jesus, who had descended from heaven to give liberty to our weak nature, Himself also ascended above the heavens; wherefore it is said, So then after the Lord had spoken to them, he was received up into heaven.

AUG. By which words He seems to show clearly enough that the foregoing discourse was the last that He spoke to them upon earth, though it does not appear to bind us down altogether to this opinion. For He does not say, After He had thus spoken to them, wherefore it admits of being understood not as if that was the last discourse, but that the words which are here used, After the Lord had spoken to them, he was received into heaven, might belong to all His other discourses. But since the arguments which we have used above make us rather suppose that this was the last time, therefore we ought to believe that after these words, together with those which are recorded in the Acts of the Apostles, our Lord ascended into heaven.

GREG. We have seen in the Old Testament that Elias was taken up into heaven. But the ethereal heaven is one thing, the aerial is another. The aerial heaven is nearer the earth, Elias then was raised into the aerial heaven, that he might be carried off suddenly into some secret region of the earth, there to live in great calmness of body and spirit, until he return at the end of the world, and pay the debt of death. We may also observe that Elias mounted up in a chariot, that by this they might understand that a mere man requires help from without. But our Redeemer, as we read, was not carried up by a chariot, not by angels, because He who had made all things was borne over all by His own power. We must also consider what Mark subjoins, And sat at the right hand of God, since Stephen says, I see the heavens opened, and the Son of Man standing at the right hand of God. Now sitting is the attitude of a judge, standing of one fighting or helping. Therefore Stephen, when toiling in the contest, saw Him standing whom he had for his helper; but Mark describes Him as sitting after His assumption into heaven, because after the glory of His assumption, He will in the end be seen as a judge.

AUG. Let us not therefore understand this sitting as though He were placed there in human limbs, as if the Father sat on the left, the Son on the right, but by the right hand itself we understand the power which He as man received from God, that He should come to judge, who first had come to be judged. For by sitting we express habitation, as we say of a person, he sat himself down in that country for many years; in this way then believe that Christ dwells at the right hand of God the Father. For or He is blessed and dwells in blessedness, which is called the right hand of the Father; for all is right hand there, since there is no misery.

It goes on: And they went forth and preached every where, the Lord working with them, and confirming the word with signs and wonders.

BEDE; Observe that in proportion as Mark began his history later, so he makes it reach in writing to more distant times, for he began from the commencement of the preaching of the Gospel by John, and he reaches in his narrative those times in which the

Apostles sowed the same word of the Gospel throughout the world.

GREG. But what should we consider in these words, if it be not that obedience follows the precept and signs follow the obedience? For the Lord had commanded them, Go into all the world preaching the Gospel, and, you shall be witnesses even to the ends of the earth.

AUG. But how was this preaching fulfilled by the Apostles, since there are many nations in which it has just begun, and others in which it has not yet begun to be fulfilled? Truly then this precept was not so laid upon the Apostles by our Lord, as though they alone to whom He then spoke were to fulfill so great a charge; in the same way as He says, Behold, I am with you always, even to the end of the world, apparently to them alone; but who does not understand that the promise is made to the Catholic Church, which though some are dying, others are born, shall be here to the end of the world?

THEOPHYL. But we must also know from this that words are confirmed by deeds as then in the Apostles works confirmed their words, for signs followed. Grant then, O Christ, that the good words which we speak may working confirmed by works and deeds, so that at the last, You working with us in word and in deed, we may be perfect, for Yours as is fitting is the glory both of word and deed. Amen.

Made in the USA
Lexington, KY
27 October 2014